The
State
of
Apartheid

The
State
of
Apartheid

edited by Wilmot G. James

Lynne Rienner Publishers • Boulder, Colorado

Published in the United States of America in 1987 by
Lynne Rienner Publishers, Inc.
948 North Street, Boulder, Colorado 80302

Library of Congress Cataloging-in-Publication Data

The State of apartheid.

  Bibliography: p.
  Includes index.
    1. Apartheid—South Africa.   2. South Africa—Race
relations.   3. South Africa—Politics and government—
1978–   .   I.   James, Wilmot Godfrey, 1953–
DT763.S773   1987   305.8'00968   86-17675
ISBN 0-931477-82-4 (lib. bdg.)

Printed and bound in the United States of America

The paper used in this publication meets the
requirements of the American National Standard
for Permanence of Paper for Printed Library   ∞
Materials, Z39.48-1984.

Contents

Preface

This book brings together current thinking on apartheid state structure and policies in the face of crisis, black resistance, and political breakdown. The book is based on four papers originally presented at a conference, "Economic Development and Racial Domination," that I organized at the University of the Western Cape, Bellville, South Africa, in October 1984, and on four other papers solicited from scholars working in the area of state and politics in South Africa. The book's coherence derives from its consideration of state institutions and the extent to which it takes seriously their policies.

The driving proposition of the book is that without an understanding of state dynamics, little sense can be made of the character of black resistance and of the political alternatives currently being shaped—among blacks—in the womb of a dying apartheid society. The state's overwhelming importance resides in the fact that it is both a terrain and an object of struggle. The literature on the state is very thin, and I hope this books fills some of the lacunae in the field.

I am grateful to the Southern African Research Program, Yale University, for a visiting fellowship I held in 1985, which essentially gave me the time to spend on this project. During the course of preparing the manuscript for publication, Pamela Baldwin, Marthe Muller, and Isabel Tang gave valuable assistance. Micheline Tusenius helped with the initial conceptualization of the book and edited the four conference papers for style. My thanks to them, and also to Larry Bowman of the University of Connecticut for his advice, and to Lynne Rienner of Lynne Rienner Publishers for her patience.

Wilmot G. James

Note on Terminology

South Africa is a terminological minefield. Racial categories, like the state, are both sources and objects of political conflict. This book is sensitive to the fact that South Africans—especially blacks—resent the formal racial designation thrust upon them by the government. The authors reject both the premise and purpose of formal racial designation, but they nevertheless are compelled to make distinctions among the various categories of black people in the subordinate population. Thus, coloreds—people of mixed descent, Indians—people of Asian descent, and Africans—people of central and southern African descent—are used to differentiate the subordinate population without endowing the categories with any inductive ethnic significance. Similarly, references are made to homelands, reserves, or Bantustans without implying that these are legitimate and credible phenomena for either the authors or the population of South Africa.

W.G.J.

The
State
of
Apartheid

1

WILMOT G. JAMES

The State of Apartheid: An Introduction

The conflict and violence in African townships are at the core of contemporary South African politics. As residential areas set aside for the exclusive occupation of the disenfranchised African majority, the townships have become arenas of contest regarding the limits of state power. Residents there repeatedly challenge the police and army and test their capacity to maintain order. More than fourteen hundred African civilians and approximately thirty-two policemen died as a result of this ongoing conflict between September 1985 and April 1986, and the daily tally of deaths goes on. The state of emergency declared in July 1985, whose intention was to pacify the African townships, failed to slow the conflict, despite or because of the brutalities inflicted on the township residents by the state's repressive forces. Indeed, after the state of emergency was lifted in March 1986, ostensibly because peace and normality had returned to the townships, the violence continued unabated.

The conflict in the townships is a lamentably dramatic illustration of the more general inability of the state to control the African majority. The police and army simply are incapable of maintaining order. The state of emergency, which provided an umbrella for the unrestrained use of state power, brought greater conflict, not peace and stability. But the mere fact that force is used to maintain order is testimony to a breakdown in governance. Those institutions designed to nourish conformity and obedience—that is, the new tricameral Parliament and the African community councils—met with widespread rejection by blacks; in the case of the community councils, this rejection largely dismantled them. Neither of these institutions succeeded in putting a mediating distance between the people and the police and army, and as a result recourse was taken to direct control and repression. In other areas of governance—for example, influx control—the state is incapable of

1

realizing basic regime goals and stands naked and vulnerable before a hostile and confident African population. This situation clearly signals a crisis in the hegemony of racial rule.

The causes of this crisis are complex and varied, but the crisis really erupted after the Botha regime began its reformist program of social, economic, and political change. P. W. Botha's National party (NP), which by the 1980s was a bourgeois white political party, incessantly declared that "apartheid is dead," that the South African economy and society ought to be "deracialized," and that racial discrimination is unjust and indefensible. The party pointed proudly to areas of life already in the process of being deracialized, such as sports and leisure, and celebrated its intention to do more in that direction. The reformist regime carefully introduced changes in the social order, for example, trade union rights, that were significant enough to unintentionally endow Africans with greater capacities to further resist apartheid, but sufficiently limited so as to ensure that whites retained control of the central levers of political power. The critical balance between reform and continued white control was hard and impossible to maintain, insofar as those little changes and minor adjustments to apartheid became cracks in the system. Deracialization and reform became problematic, and their consequences blew up in the faces of the reformers. Intending a more subtle and less coercive method of white rule, the reforms went haywire, did not accomplish their intended objectives, and resulted in a loss of control of the very process that was designed to ensure continued white dominance.

An entire range of state institutions and a compromised capitalist economy are embroiled in this crisis. The state's labor bureaucracies, in charge of influx control and pass laws—laws controlling the movement of Africans—watched as Africans evaded bureaucratic control and behaved as if the existence of the bureaucracies were ephemeral. The judicial system, in cahoots with the status quo, worried about the fact that it had little legitimate standing in the black community. The business citizenry felt that its relationship with apartheid threatened the survival of private property and private wealth and feared that it would be swept aside with apartheid as the crisis deepened. The responses of these institutions are instructive. The state promises to relieve the labor bureaucracies of their onerous task; the judicial system—notably the Supreme Court—seeks to distance itself from apartheid; and the business community forges a free-market ideology as a critique of apartheid and as a strategy for coopting middle-class blacks. Life under apartheid is no longer comfortable nor, as it were, safe.

Ultimately, the fabric of society is held together by the police and the army. Despite its evident enthusiasm, the police force is incapable of bringing township residents to heel. Out of weakness the police has called in the army, which now parades through the townships in force. But the army, too, by its own admission, cannot manage township control for a very long time. Involved in wars of destabilization in Angola and Mozambique—and to a lesser extent in Lesotho and Zimbabwe—the army, the most powerful and sophisticated of its kind in Africa, plays a dangerously extended role in southern African politics. It destabilizes bordering countries, still occupies Namibia, fights a counterinsurgency war against African National Congress (ANC) guerrillas, and now puts the lid on townships. It cannot hope to keep the lid on. Never before in the history of the South African state have its institutions been so beleaguered and vulnerable, stretched beyond the limits of their capacities to rule and control.

This book explores the three central themes of the contemporary South African state—reform, deracialization, and the breakdown of governance.

In Chapter 2, Craig Charney gives an account of the changing class foundations of the ruling National party and explains the origins and persistence of the fissures that plague it. He argues that the National party is a weak institution, incapable of holding together the coalitions of apartheid, and that it is drifting toward a surrender to the democratic opposition.

Wilmot G. James and André du Pisanie (Chapter 3) examine the contradictions of the National party's new constitution. They claim that instead of taking race out of politics, the constitution reinforces racial and ethnic boundaries. They also argue that rather than prolonging white rule, the constitution in effect contributed to the creation of a revolutionary situation. Indeed, things began to fall apart immediately after the constitution's introduction.

In Chapter 4, Stanley B. Greenberg inquires into the dynamics of state reconstruction. He examines the deracialization ideology, shows how state collaborative institutions have broken down, and wonders aloud about the unreality of reform and deracialization. He claims that the deracialization project is an impossible—and deceptive—attempt to breathe fresh life into racial rule at a time when other social processes (for example, markets and resistance) continually undermine it.

Simon Bekker and Richard Humphreys outline the dilemmas and contradictions of the labor bureaucracies and the policy of influx control in Chapter 5. With careful and detailed documentation, they argue that influx control is ambiguous, confused, and ultimately ineffective. Attempts at modifying and tinkering with the system weaken it and pave the way for its abolition.

In Chapter 6, Hugh Corder explores a much neglected part of the state in the literature—the Supreme Court. By argument and case examination, he puzzles over the legitimacy of the Supreme Court and suggests how deeply compromised the court is. He shows how the Supreme Court is attempting to reconstruct its relation to apartheid and how partial and ultimately ineffective this reconstruction might be.

William Munro (Chapter 7) investigates the evolution of state policy toward sports. He examines how international sanctions affect domestic sports policy and how tortuously policymakers seek to deracialize it without threatening white interests. His is a good example of the full implications of deracialization.

Annette Seegers, in Chapter 8, writes one of the first concise histories of South Africa's military apparatus. She elaborates the multifaceted role of the military and explains the limitations under which it functions. By her account, the military presents itself as a neutral force, but its partiality to white rule is transparent to blacks, who regard it presently as an occupation force in the townships.

In Chapter 9, Heribert Adam and Kogila Moodley survey South Africa's regional foreign policy. They argue that South Africa is successfully recolonizing the region by destabilization, economic penetration, and diplomatic treaties. They also contend that the recolonization of the region erodes the expectation of liberation by external means and forces blacks to focus more realistically on internal political change.

CRAIG CHARNEY

2

The National Party, 1982–1985: A Class Alliance in Crisis

The apartheid state is the creation of the National party (NP), although, of course, racial segregation predates the party. From 1948, when the NP came to power, until the early 1970s, the party remained in firm control of segregation policy in pursuit of separate development, or apartheid. By the 1980s, however, the NP was split, control of policy became weak, and the ideology and practice of apartheid approached incoherence. A unified Afrikaner community, the traditional support base of the NP, no longer existed.

In this chapter, Craig Charney begins his account of the NP in the 1970s, takes us through the 1982 split in the party, and brings the narrative to the present crisis. His central theme is realignment in the face of crisis: how the party's social base has changed, and the support for and limits to reformist alternatives that are the consequences of that change. The heart of the chapter's argument is that the NP has become the party of the Afrikaner bourgeoisie, which shares an interest in economic liberalization with English-speaking and foreign capitalists but fears political liberalization because of its continuing dependence upon state patronage and power. As a result, the NP still clings to the racially exclusive state, but painfully tries to mollify racial rule through a reform that is neither fast enough nor comprehensive enough to satisfy black demands. Crisis and stalemate are the result, not only for the state but for the economy as well. As the crisis grinds on, the options open to the NP for a settlement are diminishing rapidly.

W. G. J.

At a certain point in their historical lives, social classes become detached from their traditional parties. In other words, the traditional parties in that particular organisational form, with the particular men who constitute,

represent, and lead them, are no longer recognised by their class (or fraction of a class) as its expression. . . . These situations of conflict between
"represented and representatives" reverberate out from the terrain of the
parties (the party organisations properly speaking, the parliamentary-
electoral field, newspaper organisation) throughout the State or-
ganism. . . . In every country, the process is different, although the content
is the same. And the content is the crisis of the ruling class's hegemony.

Antonio Gramsci[1]

The challenges to state and capital that engulfed South Africa in the 1980s
brutally put the ruling National party (NP) to the test—and the party failed.
The NP had evolved into a party dominated by the Afrikaner bourgeoisie;
the NP restructured the use of African labor, sought to broaden the base of
the regime, and provoked the 1982 breakaway of the far right. Yet the party
refused to abandon the fundamentals of apartheid or to set up democratic
institutions that might avert revolution.

The NP's behavior is rooted in the ever-deepening crises of accumulation and hegemony, which drove a wedge between the classes and the
categories that had been allied behind the NP. Its efforts to resolve these
crises to capital's satisfaction alienated the deeply conservative allied and
supporting classes of whites. But the NP's incapacity to accommodate the
growing black-nationalist and working-class movements became apparent
during the popular struggles of 1984 and 1985 and led most English-
speaking and foreign capitalists to turn their backs on the Nationalists as
well. The National party itself was divided at every level about how to re-
spond. Abandoned by their allies, unable to replace them, their own followers confused and demoralized, by late 1985 the Nationalist leadership appeared paralyzed and isolated from the ensemble of social forces within the
country.

In consequence, the Nationalists faced a dilemma created by their own
policies and social base. While all sections of the bourgeoisie demanded a
degree of economic liberalization, Afrikaner capital remained too dependent
upon state power and patronage to easily accept genuine power sharing or
majority rule. Furthermore, although a bourgeois democracy required a ruling party capable of posing as the representative of the "national" interest,
electoral competition obliged the NP to present itself as the party of Afrikaner (and white) sectional interests. The NP was thus torn between the
need to ensure preferential access to the state on a racial basis and the need
to advance to a nonracial South African nationalism under capitalist leadership in order to prevent the state's overthrow.

This analysis highlights the centrality of white partisan and class struggles.
In the short term, their resolution will determine the strategic environment

in which the national democratic and socialist movements must operate. In the longer run, the response of state leadership to the impasse generated by the traditional mode of political regulation in South Africa will prove important for the outcome of the struggle for South Africa. To justify these claims, this chapter examines the class character of the National party split, the struggles that followed, and the intensification of the NP's internal contradictions during the 1984–1985 crisis. In conclusion, the rapidly narrowing options remaining for the leaders of the apartheid regime are investigated.

The Party Split

The motive force in the realignment of the white parties was, as Dan O'Meara put it, "the emergence of a class of aggressive, self-confident Afrikaner capitalists, whose interests went beyond those of the narrow class alliance out of which they emerged."[2] The embryonic Afrikaner capitalist class was closely linked to the National party from its establishment in 1912. William A. Hofmeyr, first chairman of Sanlam, which would become the largest Afrikaner finance house, was also the Cape NP's first organizing secretary, while Federale Volksbeleggings' (an Afrikaner investment bank) first board was dominated by Cape NP and Sanlam men. In the north, members of the Nationalist vanguard, the Afrikaner Broederbond secret society, were the driving force behind fledgling businesses. The founding board of Volkskas Bank—soon to be the other financial pole of Afrikanerdom—contained seven prominent Broeders, while the directors of Rembrandt—now the largest nonfinancial Afrikaner firm—included the Bond's secretary and two future NP cabinet ministers. The NP took power in 1948 as a coalition dominated by the Afrikaner petite bourgeoisie, a handful of Afrikaner finance capitalists, and the Cape agricultural bourgeoisie, drawing votes from farmers, lower state officials, and the Afrikaans-speaking majority of the white working class.[3]

Once in office, the Nationalists established the racially exclusive regime of accumulation called apartheid.[4] The low-wage system for black workers was extended to secondary industry, while demands for the "white goods" it produced were supplied by the growing white middle class.[5] Rigorously racist ideology was proclaimed as the justification for the low-wage system, and complete racial exclusion also became the basis of the political regime. Black opposition was crushed; the major political movements—the African National Congress (ANC) and the Pan-African Congress (PAC)—were banned, and the trade unions were driven into dormancy.

The Nationalists also fostered an Afrikaner state capitalism, filling the expanding parastatals with supporters, while using state patronage to promote private Afrikaans business. In the words of Piet Meyer, former Broederbond chairman, the NP government created the "sympathetic political climate necessary" for Afrikaner business success.[6] The control of state industries gave the Afrikaner bourgeoisie a sizable base of accumulation. For example, if South African Transport Services (SATS) were capitalized in market terms, it would be worth substantially more than Anglo-American, the largest private firm.[7] Likewise, shifts of state contracts helped Volkskas Bank to multiply its deposits fivefold during the first decade of NP rule, while General Mining's first major coal contract came from the state steel firm, Iron and Steel Corporation (Iscor). In the 1960s and 1970s, the New Industries Committee oversaw a self-sufficiency drive and ensured that Afrikaner firms got a share of high-technology industries, while foreign firms were keen for joint ventures with Afrikaner firms because of the latter's political connections.[8] Meanwhile, farm price and credit policies encouraged the development of a highly capitalized agricultural bourgeoisie. The Afrikaner-controlled enterprises that emerged displayed certain structural vulnerabilities. They tended to be smaller than English firms in their sectors, were bunched in the less profitable lines, and were more dependent upon the state.

Nevertheless, the size and scope of Afrikaner enterprises were impressive, and the growth of the Afrikaner business class helped transform the social composition of Afrikanerdom. Afrikaner control of private industry rose from 10 percent to 21 percent between 1948 and 1975, while, including the parastatals, Afrikaner control of industrial output rose to 45 percent. In the wake of the rise of the Afrikaner bourgeoisie, the proportion of Afrikaners in the professions doubled. The percentage of Afrikaners in white-collar jobs increased from 28 percent in 1948 to 65 percent in 1975, while numbers of farmers and blue-collar workers fell sharply.[9] Increasingly, the views of the new Afrikaner middle class converged with those of affluent English-speakers on economic and social questions.[10]

Growing tension prevailed from the 1960s on between the largely middle-class sophisticates favoring relaxation of racial restrictions (*verligte,* or enlightened, Afrikaners) and those opposed (the *verkramptes,* or narrow-minded). By the late 1970s, the new balance of class forces within Afrikanerdom, along with the growing challenges to the status quo from blacks, had created divisions cutting clean across the old ethnic blocs. Striking evidence of this emerged in a survey of Johannesburg-area whites taken just before the National party split. They were asked about the integration of private schools, state schools, and public transport and whether coloreds should be accepted in the "white group" (see Table 2.1). In both language groups, the middle-class "A" and "B" groups reacted relatively favorably to integration and the working-class "C" and "D" groups unfavorably. The percentages in favor of integration were almost as high among Afrikaners as among English-speakers in the higher managerial/professional "A" group. The differences between "A" and "D" (lower supervisory, clerical, artisans, and unskilled

TABLE 2.1 Socioeconomic Status and Ideology Among Johannesburg-area Whites, 1982

	English				Afrikaners				All
	A	B	C	D	A	B	C	D	
	%	%	%	%	%	%	%	%	%
Should private schools be integrated?									
Yes	76	62	48	28	73	38	15	8	44
No	12	22	30	32	20	42	72	77	36
Should government schools be integrated?									
Yes	38	41	32	22	30	19	10	6	28
No	32	41	50	42	60	68	81	86	53
Should public transport be integrated?									
Yes	62	52	44	33	67	31	21	12	41
No	20	27	37	44	25	48	68	82	42
Should coloureds be considered part of the white group?									
Yes	57	41	37	25	40	35	10	13	33
No	13	31	39	40	27	36	75	78	42

Source: Star Retail Data Library survey, April 1982.
Note: Category A represented higher professional and managerial personnel, category B included intermediate professional, managerial, and supervisory workers, and categories C and D included lower supervisory, clerical, artisan, and unskilled workers. The sample size was approximately three thousand.

workers) within each ethnic group were almost always larger than the differences between English and Afrikaners of the same economic status. The changes this evolution produced in the National party were profound, as a leading Nationalist recognized: "Now, the NP has become bourgeois itself, espousing middle class values and finding bridges across language and racial barriers."[11] The election of Cape NP leader P. W. Botha as prime minister in 1978 confirmed the ascendancy of politicians close to the Afrikaner bourgeoisie at the summit of the party.[12]

Despite hesitations and deliberate ambiguity, Botha's government defined a new strategy to meet the crises confronting the state after the Soweto uprisings of 1976; his government developed verligte ideas and policies first broached or initiated under his predecessor, John Vorster.[13] These policies—restructuring the position of the African working class and courting allies among the colored and Indian minorities—addressed the labor needs of the bourgeoisie and the dangers posed by the resurgence of African working-class political and guerrilla struggles under the aegis of trade unions, community and student groups, and the ANC. As a party of the bourgeoisie, the NP developed an ideology presenting its class interests as "general interests," while still trying to retain the image of an Afrikaner ethnic party. However, the party's new line was increasingly incompatible with the NP's traditional alliance of Afrikaners of all classes bound by rigid racism and exclusive access to the state.

The overarching theme in NP ideology in the Botha era became the pursuit of economic growth. Overtly racist themes, already deemphasized under Vorster, were abandoned. Instead of the Verwoerdian dictum, "better poor and white than rich and mixed," accumulation was presented as in everyone's interest. Whites could continue to enjoy their privileges, while growth would offer higher living standards to blacks. As Hermann Giliomee put it, "In the Botha Administration . . . a strong tendency has developed . . . to present the whites as a modernising elite and to portray economic growth, training, job creation, food production, and above all political stability, which is seen as making all these things possible, as sufficient justification for National Party rule."[14] Such crude arguments for policies that suit capital were presented more subtly in the stress on technical rationality and "scientific" policy-making that took the place of the populist rhetoric and ideology of earlier times. This technocratic theme, borrowed directly from the NP's liberal capitalist opponents of the 1950s and 1960s, was exemplified by the commissions loosed on South Africa's social problems, representing the state, capital, and *verligte,* or liberal, academics.[15] The best known were the Wiehahn Commission on labor relations, the Riekert Report on the pass laws, and the de Lange Committee on education.

The third stress of the NP's new approach was survival—"adapt or die," as Botha put it. The threat posed by the reappearance of the ANC was developed into a war psychosis, which was far greater than that justified by the military situation in the late 1970s and early 1980s, to build support for the government's "total strategy." (This term, taken from the defense white paper of 1977, connoted the mobilization of all South Africa's resources against revolution.) One official admitted privately, "There is a threat as perceived by government, but the concept of this threat is used for other reasons than the real threat: to bring people together whom government thinks should be together."[16] The appeal was not just aimed at whites, but also at coloreds and Indians who feared majority rule. Finally, there was a stress on replacing explicitly racial discrimination with economic or other forms of discrimination. Jan Lombard, a leading *verligte* ideologue, declared that "if . . . the maintenance of order requires discriminatory provisions in our legal system, these provisions must be defined in terms of other characteristics [than race]."[17] Along with this went the promotion of economic stratification among blacks in order to win allies and acquiescence. For less well-off whites, the threat to their status was evident.

The NP's major substantive policy changes occurred regarding labor and were designed to meet the needs of a capitalist class worried by an underskilled and angry African work force. The Botha government's reversals are well known: obeying the Wiehahn Commission's calls to abolish statutory job reservation, to open apprenticeships to Africans, and to register black trade unions; accepting Riekert's call for greater mobility for urban Africans with Section 10 rights; committing itself to education of equal quality for all races in response to the de Lange Report; and offering large tax concessions for in-service training of blacks. Deeds lagged behind words, but the intent was clear: to close the skills gap and increase demand for skilled labor by incorporating an organized urban African working class into the labor aristocracy. However, the renegotiation of the labor process with the black work force could hardly fail to anger white workers whose wages were already falling behind inflation. It represented the reversal of the NP's old view that economic integration would inevitably lead to political integration.

Almost as striking were the overt changes in the NP's attitude toward capital. Botha spelled out his stand on the role of "free enterprise" at the 1979 Carlton Center Conference, where he brought together the country's business elite. "We have our differences," he argued, "but we are creating reciprocal channels to plan national strategy in South Africa as a team." Contrast this to the attitude of Vorster: "In my time, I also talked to all the leading English businessmen; but I never involved them in planning and decision-making."[18]

There were also reductions in petty apartheid, in line with the NP's commitment to the elimination of so-called unnecessary and hurtful discrimination, such as the opening of many theaters, cinemas, hotels, and restaurants to blacks. Although these changes only benefited a few blacks, they still represented a departure from policy in force until the 1970s, when the NP tried to make it impossible for South Africans of different races to meet other than as masters and servants in the workplace. The new line is both a gesture to the black petite bourgeoisie and a crack in apartheid's front of racial privilege. Finally, Botha abandoned the Verwoerdian shibboleth of dividing power between the races and accepted a circumscribed notion of power sharing between white, colored, and Indian. Indeed, in terms of the 1983 constitution, the very party that disfranchised coloreds and Indians granted each group a chamber of Parliament alongside the white one. However, to many Nationalists, accepting coloreds and Indians in Parliament threatened white control of the state, on which their vital interests depended. More specific anxieties were felt by civil servants about black competition and by working-class whites about the levelling down of state services.

Botha's policies consequently intensified the class conflicts in the NP's base. Three months after he took office, white miners struck to defend racial job reservation, while their former allies in the Nationalist government sided with management. During the year that followed, the prime minister's endorsement of labor law liberalization and reformist speeches provoked by-election swings to the far right of up to 40 percent in traditional NP farming and mining seats. In the white general election of 1981, support for the Herstigte Nasionale party (HNP) and other far-right groups increased almost six-fold to 15 percent of the vote.[19] It was the last straw when the new constitutional scheme came before the NP caucus on 23 February 1982. A group of twenty-three Members of Parliament (MPs) stormed out, including Transvaal leader Andries Treurnicht; fifteen left the NP to establish a new Conservative party (CP) in March. Within weeks one-fourth of the Transvaal NP district and branch committee members—often the most committed—defected, shattering many constituency organizations.[20] What many thought impossible had happened—the National party had split from top to bottom.

Struggles After The Split

The split triggered conflicts among Afrikaners on a scale unknown since the 1940s, thereby initiating intense party-political struggles and convulsing almost every social institution in Afrikanerdom. The clashes were motivated both by specific sectional interests and by fears of the loss or dilution of white control of the state. The far right clung to the old policies and alliances, accusing the NP of deviating from the heritage of Hendrik Verwoerd, the major architect of orthodox apartheid. The Nationalists claimed to take the next step on his path, even as they reached out to English-speakers of similar social class. By early 1984, the Nationalists appeared to be reclaiming control of the situation.

Support for the National party among white South Africans had slipped gradually after Botha took office, but following the split support fell sharply. The NP vote dropped from 52 percent in an August 1981 survey to 43 percent in a survey taken just after the split in April 1982 (see Table 2.2). The same survey showed the new CP and the HNP together polling 22 percent, a dramatic increase from the far right's 1977 and 1981 showings, with the lion's share going to the Conservatives. The results stood out in even sharper relief in survey figures on Afrikaners alone, which showed NP support dropping from 82 percent in October 1976 to 56 percent in October 1982.[21] In Transvaal province, the poll found, Nationalists had been reduced to a minority of Afrikaners. (The split also increased the reliance of the Nationalists on their English-speaking supporters. They now provided one of every four Nationalist votes, against one in seven in 1974.) By-elections in Afrikaans working-class and farming seats revealed swings to the right ranging from 10 percent to 27 percent after the split. Together the CP and HNP outpolled the NP in three traditional Nationalist provincial council seats, thereby serving notice that few NP seats could still be counted "safe."

The split forced the NP to make substantial changes in its methods of

TABLE 2.2 Partisan Support Among White South Africans, 1981–1985 (in percentage)[a]

	National Party	Progressive Federal Party	New Republic Party	Conservative Party	Herstigte Nasionale Party	No Response
Aug 1981	52	22	7	2[b]	8	9
Jan 1982	48	21	7	2[b]	6	16
Apr 1982	43	22	6	20[b]	2	8
Oct 1982	44	18	6	16	3	14
Mar 1983	49	20	6	13	2	10
May 1983	50	18	6	12	3	11
Jul 1983	51	19	5	12	3	11
Feb 1984	54	17	6	11	2	10
Jul 1984	56	17	5	10	2	11
Oct 1984	51	19	4	11	2	12
Feb 1985	52	18	3	13	2	13
Apr 1985	47	19	3	13	2	15

Sources: Rapport, 2 May 1982 and 12 May 1985.

[a] From a random sampling of approximately three thousand whites.

[b] For August 1981, support is shown for National Conservative party, which later joined the Conservative party. For April 1982, Conservative party and National Conservative party support is combined, although the formal merger had not yet occurred.

organization and fundraising. Traditionally, it had worked largely through enthusiastic volunteer organization in close contact with friends and neighbors at the base. With the loss of party cadres in the split—and continuing defections thereafter—many constituency organizations (particularly in the Transvaal) were hobbled at the very moment in which they had to face the most serious electoral challenge in more than thirty years. The NP's response was to move away from personal contact and part-time workers and hire more full-time organizers, computerize record keeping, and run a campaign of advertisements and public meetings to try winning over wavering voters.[22]

A *Rapport* survey found that the NP counteroffensive restored the party's support to its 1981 level by May 1983. However, the results of the "Battle of the Bergs" that month suggested otherwise.[23] Andries Treurnicht, the CP leader, resigned and won back his Waterberg seat on a 27 percent swing, while manpower minister S. P. Botha (who had offered to fight his own seat if Treurnicht contested his) nearly lost his Soutspansberg constituency to a CP challenger. Equally significant were the results of the November 1983 Middleburg by-election, where the right wing again gained a majority. Nevertheless, the two-thirds yes vote in the constitutional referendum of November 1983 represented a triumph for Botha and hinted at the shift back to the NP in polls. But the results also pointed to consolidation of far-right support. Prereferendum surveys suggested that roughly 20 percent of the electorate regarded the proposal as too liberal; these were voters probably lost for good by the NP. To win, Botha had to rely on more English-speaking support than any previous NP leader: A rough estimate suggests English-speakers formed about one-third of his majority, furthering Nationalist inroads into the English-speaking electorate.

These electoral and poll results were not just the consequences of overtly political struggles; they reflected the results of profound conflicts within Afrikaner social institutions and groups. These conflicts often took on regional forms that can be traced to provincial variations in class alignments within the national patterns. The unpredictable shifts of initiative reflected the skill and will of the contestants in maneuvering on the terrain established by the broader configuration of social forces.

The split provoked a clash between leading Afrikaner business interests and a *verkrampte* minority clinging to old ties; the split also led to new overtures from the NP toward the English-speaking bourgeoisie. The dominant Afrikaans business group, the Sanlam empire, a pillar of Botha's Cape NP, controlled the leading Afrikaans press group, Nasionale Pers. Most of the Transvaal Afrikaans bourgeoisie that emerged in the 1960s and 1970s (often tied to Sanlam's Federale Volksbeleggings investment arm) were also behind the *verligtes*. In the parastatal corporations and the civil service, the Botha era saw the appointment of a new generation of *verligte* managers at the top echelons.

However, in the Transvaal, the Volkskas bank and the Perskor newspaper group grew up dependent on Broederbond links to civil servants, farmers, and white workers. Conservatives on the boards of Volkskas and Perskor attempted a rear guard action against the Botha line. Perskor managing director Marius Jooste threatened to bring his papers behind the CP. Jooste's death and the success of Nasionale's *verligte* newspaper, *Beeld* (Mirror), among the young, affluent Transvaal Afrikaners led instead to the closure of Perskor's morning papers in Johannesburg and Pretoria.[24] Likewise, Volkskas struck up an alliance of convenience with *verligte* Anton Rupert's Rembrandt Group to challenge Sanlam's control of General Mining, the second largest mining house. Their bid was easily repulsed, however, and soon the press reported that the Sanlam-dominated Afrikaanse Handelsinstituut (Afrikaans Commercial Institute, or AHI) was urging Afrikaner businesses to shift their accounts from Volkskas to Sanlam's Trust Bank.

Following the split, the NP needed R 3 to R 5 million for its counteroffensive, which compelled it to launch an unprecedented drive for funds among English businessmen as well as among Afrikaners. Traditional Nationalist funding sources were wholly inadequate for expenditures of this scale. The Cape NP's subscriptions covered only operating costs, while the Transvaal party, with no equivalent, was even more reliant upon large donations. The "beat Treurnicht" campaign made significant inroads, particularly among New Republic party supporters. Counting Afrikaner contributions as well, by 1983 the National party probably could claim almost as much financial support from business as could the Progressive Federal party (PFP), the white official opposition, which was closely identified with English-speaking capitalists.[25] Most business leaders of both language groups also supported the new constitution at the 1983 referendum as "a step in the right direction," and many English-speaking capitalists (as well as Afrikaners) contributed to the Vote Yes campaign. Capital enthusiastically endorsed the Nkomati and Lusaka peace accords signed with Mozambique and Angola in March 1984.[26] At that point, Botha's goal of uniting the bourgeoisie as a whole under his leadership appeared within sight.

On the other hand, struggles wracked the Broederbond—the interlocking directorate of Afrikaner organizations—as Botha's policies threatened its allies and offended its members. Carel Boshoff, who succeeded *verligte* Gerrit Viljoen in 1981 as chairman of the secret society, was identified in press reports as a Conservative party supporter. Further evidence of right-wing resistance came in reports of the Bond's reversal of its 1972 decision to expel members belonging to the HNP and of intense infighting about the NP's constitutional proposals.[27] The Federation of Afrikaans Cultural Societies (FAK), the Broeder front dominating Afrikaner cultural and organizational life, was also in Conservative hands, and the Afrikaans Student Bond (ASB), dominated by the Bond's Ruiterwag youth wing, replaced a *verligte* president with a Conservative in 1982. However, the Nationalist press riposted—in an unheard-of lifting of the veil around the Bond—with reports on Boshoff's opposition to the constitutional plan, thereby forcing his resignation as chairman in mid-1983.[28] He was replaced by a government supporter, J. P. de Lange. Taking the Bond in hand, the NP then forced through an endorsement of its reform scheme, leading to Boshoff's resignation from the Bond's Executive Council.

The Nationalists' reassertion of control of the Broederbond left them strategically placed to recapture the network of groups that radiate out from the Bond. They ousted most far-right representatives from the FAK executive at its 1984 congress.[29] *Verligtes* also emerged victorious after a court battle for the leadership of the Ruiterwag (the Youth Brigade of the National party), itself an extraordinary phenomenon for a secret society.[30] The right wingers subsequently lost control of the ASB as well. However, the politicization of these institutions caused grave tensions within them. In these circumstances, they were hardly capable of playing the opinion-leading role on behalf of the NP in Afrikaner communities that the united network of Broeder-related institutions had fulfilled in the past.

The threat that the loss of such notables posed can be seen in the fillip the Dutch Reformed Churches gave the far right. The unashamedly proapartheid 1982 synod of the Nederduits Gereformeerde Kerk (the Dutch Reformed Church, or NGK) gave Treurnicht a warm ovation, while the Nederduitsch

Hervormde Kerk (the Dutch Reformed Church, or NHK) was publicly accused of opposing the NP by a Nationalist MP.[31] Surveys suggest the dissenting *dominees* (clergy) were helping sway their flocks against the NP. Among NHK members, the NP and the far right were level pegging at 40 percent, while in the Gereformeerde ("Dopper") Kerk (the Reformed Church, or GK), another small, conservative sect, the right led the NP 45 percent to 37 percent. The dominant NGK was split provincially, with 31 percent of its Transvaal members opting for the CP or HNP, against 15 percent in the other provinces. Irrespective of denomination, Afrikaners who went to church at least twice monthly were almost twice as likely to support the far right as those who did not.[32]

The right also made inroads in the civil service. The bureaucrats who ran or gained from apartheid were chary of reforms that threatened their functions or promotion prospects.[33] They also were angered by the precipitate decline in real public sector pay after the beginnings of salary equalization, a fall averaging 23 percent in central government and 12 percent in the provinces between 1974 and 1979.[34] Bureaucratic foot-dragging on the implementation of reformist policies was notorious. One *verligte* minister compared trying to put his policies into effect with "trying to drive a car with the handbrake on." The discipline of government patronage seems to have kept most voting in line, but the CP's respectable 20 percent showing in the 1983 by-election in Waterkloof, where many state employees live, indicated the wavering loyalty of an overwhelmingly Afrikaner civil service.

As in the 1930s, the country's farmers—also mostly Afrikaners—have tended to divide according to scale of enterprise (large versus small farms) and market (domestic versus export).[35] The Botha government's agricultural policy was seen as favoring the large farmer over the small, industry over farming, and Cape and Natal exporters over Transvaal and Free State food producers. The government's relaxation of labor and racial policies was regarded as threatening black labor supplies and the whole labor-repressive system on which small farmers, particularly, depend. There was a big swing to the right, mostly to the CP, among farmers in the Transvaal, Northern Free State, and Northeast Cape. In those regions live the maize farmers, who depend heavily on government decisions on the price of inputs and produce. They partly blamed low official producer prices and protection for fertilizer and machinery makers for their growing debts. They were also hit by the 1982–1983 drought, and those near homelands (mostly in the Transvaal) feared losing their land through the implementation of consolidation.[36] Beef producers in these parts also cried out for drought relief and alleged that corrupt allocation of slaughter permits had hurt the small farmer. The preferential treatment accorded rural members of the Broederbond by state- and Nationalist-controlled organizations also irked many farmers.

In 1980, the South African Maize Producers Institute (an HNP-leaning body representing the more numerous small farmers) merged with the South African Maize Specialists Organisation (Samso) representing large-scale producers, to create the National Maize Producers Organisation (Nampo), which has since stood out as the voice of the right. The extensive cooperative network also became a force of opposition to the NP in many areas. For instance, although the Central Western Transvaal Coop had traditionally supported the NP in local elections, in 1982 it ran its own candidate against the unofficial NP candidate, who finished fourth. The NP grip on rural clientele networks was slipping while farmers' discontent was spilling over into country towns and smaller cities.

By contrast, the NP's strongest agricultural support was among the agricultural bourgeoisie and the export-oriented farmers of the Cape, Natal, and Southern Free State. They are the base of the South African Agricultural Union (SAAU), the pro-NP voice of the big farmers establishment. Cape wine farmers in particular received exceptionally favorable treatment under Botha. The government endorsed their creation of a marketing monopoly over the objections of its own Monopolies Commission and set up an inquiry into possible protection against imports.[37] Nationalists among northern farmers tended to be old, strongly identified *bloednatte* (blood Nats, or members of the NP), ex-members of Samso, which represented mostly large farmers or people with Broederbond ties.

The right wing also stirred up a storm in working-class Afrikaner constituencies after the split. This was hardly surprising, considering that between 1974 and 1984 minimum wage rates for artisans fell by 26 percent in real terms, while those for unskilled black laborers went up 26 percent. Government plans for black job advancement also stimulated strong hostility among working-class whites.[38] Feelings ran particularly high among mine workers and others whose positions were protected by legal or de facto job reservation. As a result, the far right outpolled the NP in by-elections in Carletonville and Germiston district. The CP drew in most of the dissidents. The HNP appeared to revert to its pre-1981 role as a poor white protest party, with fully 68 percent of its shrinking support from the less than R 13,000 a year group.[39] A right-wing offensive was also under way, albeit slowly, on the trade union front, where Arrie Paulus's Mine Workers Union sought to extend its scope of organization with the aim of uniting all white wage earners in a single union. Although the NP retained 44 percent of white working-class voters in 1982, this appeared due to the support of English-speaking workers, who moved to the NP after the collapse of the United party. However, because most English-speaking South African wage earners had no party identification, they, too, were potential rightists.[40]

If these struggles seemed to have a Transvaal versus Cape or town versus country character, it is largely because of the geographic location of economic groups. Thus, the domestic-market maize and meat producers are in the Transvaal and the adjacent portions of the Free State and Cape, and most of the industries employing white workers cluster around the Pretoria-Witwatersrand-Vereeniging triangle. All these groups had grievances against the government. The Cape, Natal, and Southern Free State house wine, sugar, and wool exporters, along with Afrikanerdom's leading financial combine, Sanlam, had been beneficiaries of official policy. The rural-urban split reflected in part the dependence of the rural petite bourgeoisie on local farmers and the greater dependence of their urban counterparts on industrial capital. More broadly, these distinctions were based upon historic differences in class alignments between the southern and northern provinces. In the Cape, agricultural and finance capital had dominated, while in the Transvaal and Free State the party linked together workers, small farmers, civil servants, and fledgling capitalists. The National party broke along the same regional lines of cleavage as those that divided Afrikaners in the 1930s, with most of the newer, dynamic elements drawn to the *verligtes,* while the far right tried to use its fixed positions in the institutions to reconstitute the old alliance.

Yet despite certain signs of the persistent vigor of the far right, by the middle of 1984 the drift of events looked favorable for the NP. It had scored an important victory in the constitutional referendum, and the colored and Indian elections that would permit its implementation were approaching. The major Afrikaner institutions appeared to be falling into line. The Nkomati and Lusaka accords and Botha's subsequent European tour raised hopes of stabilizing the security position vis-à-vis Mozambique and Angola and breaking out of South Africa's diplomatic isolation. Finally, four years had passed without a major outbreak of internal disorder. In consequence, Botha's prestige stood at a high level, and polls placed NP support at 56 percent, which was well above even the 1981 mark. The NP leadership was able to feel that things were going its way.

The Tide Turns

The Nationalist's moment of triumph proved short-lived. The profound worsening of the political and economic situation in the second half of 1984 reopened the cracks in the Nationalist alliance. As government bogged down in strategy conflicts, the Nationalist party organization appeared to be weakening and the party's base itself breaking up. The party's very success in reasserting control of Afrikaner institutions proved to have been a Pyrrhic victory. The intensification of black community, worker, and military resistance polarized the white population around choices to the right or left of those open to the NP.

The upsurge of opposition at home and aggression abroad cost the NP government the initiative it had tried to regain. The colored and Indian electoral boycotts in August 1984 and the simultaneous protests against rent increases in African townships marked the turning of the tide. These campaigns were organized under the banner of the United Democratic Front (UDF), a coalition of several hundred antiapartheid groups that the state called a front for the ANC. UDF affiliates made use of the opportunity for action occasioned by the government's post-1976 and post-1980 reforms. The mobilization they achieved discredited the government's new political dispensation (the tricameral Parliament and the financially independent African municipalities). The state's repressive response fed a succession of riots, mass strikes, and school and consumer boycotts, thereby weakening business confidence and deepening cyclical recession into depression.

Beyond the borders, South Africa's continued destabilization of Angola and Mozambique turned the Nkomati and Lusaka accords into dead letters. This permitted stepped-up guerrilla attacks by the ANC and the South West African People's Organization and alienated Western allies hoping for a Namibian settlement. Botha himself admitted his government's loss of control of the situation before the House of Assembly in April 1985.

> Any analysis of the menaces which weigh on the security of the country is at present determined by the radical escalation of a revolutionary climate. Politicisation and mobilisation, processes in which the UDF has played an important role and which are occurring in an unfavourable economic context, have attained such proportions that the risks of a generalisation of violence across the country have considerably increased.[41]

The government's response to the crisis was incoherent, reflecting shifts in the balance of forces within its evermore divided ranks. At first the "hawks" seemed in command. Thus, after house-to-house township searches by police and army provoked the October 1984 Transvaal General Strike, hardliners in the cabinet advocating detention of the strike leaders prevailed over their opponents.[42] But by the beginning of the 1985 parliamentary session, the *verligtes* were on the offensive. Botha (who was the newly elected executive state president in accordance with the terms of the new constitution) said he would talk to the ANC and release its imprisoned leader, Nelson Mandela, if they renounced violence. Botha's remarks were accompanied by declarations from Nationalist ministers and MPs that the reform agenda was open-ended. (The extreme *verligte* Wynand Malan even told Parliament that apartheid could be considered "structural violence."[43]) Several much-criticized discriminatory laws were repealed, including those banning interracial sex, mixed marriages, and multiracial political parties. *Verligtes* also pressed for the ouster of law and order minister Louis le Grange, who had outdone his well-earned reputation for brutality and insensitivity in handling the township disorders.

However, from midyear on, the pendulum was swinging back, as *ver-*

ligte rhetoric failed to calm the townships while it alienated white voters. In July, the hardliners convinced Botha to declare a state of emergency throughout much of the country, detain hundreds of opponents, and ban the Congress of South African Students, the black pupils' organization. *Verligte* foreign minister Pik Botha, in what might have been an attempt to force the government's hand, promised foreign diplomats an announcement of major reforms in Botha's 15 August speech before the Natal NP Congress. However, Botha was unable to push the proposed federal scheme through the cabinet after "moderate" ministers (Gerrit Viljoen and F. W. de Klerk) cast their lot with hardliners urging no changes in grand apartheid.[44]

The infighting within the NP leadership continued as the end of 1985 approached. A *verligte* revolt got under way after Botha's 15 August speech (in which he promised power sharing with all communities), with demands for his head audible in Nationalist circles. Pressure groups favoring reformist policies formed within the Nationalist Parliamentary Caucus and among party leaders in Pretoria, Johannesburg, and Cape Town. Breaking with the party line, Wynand Malan declared that the distance between the ANC and the government had to be bridged.[45] In November, *verligtes* sent secret feelers for peace talks to the ANC leadership in Lusaka, Zambia, amid a flurry of press reports of Mandela's imminent release.[46] However, the "doves"—including Pik Botha and Free State leader Kobie Coetsee—again lost out in the cabinet. The state president, along with le Grange and Defense Minister Magnus Malan, expressed repeatedly and publicly his opposition to negotiations with the nationalist movement.[47] Simultaneously, South Africa launched a death squad and an economic blockade aimed at driving ANC members out of neighboring Lesotho.

In his parliamentary program speech on 31 January 1986, Botha struck a more conciliatory note, perhaps reflecting a new cabinet equilibrium. He finally accepted the Riekert Commission's 1979 proposal to eliminate passes as the basis of influx control, relying instead on controlling access to jobs and housing. He also agreed to other measures reformers had urged since 1976, including freehold title in African townships and "gray areas" for black business in white city centers. He hinted that he might soon free Nelson Mandela and proposed a statutory council that would permit Africans to join in constitutional negotiations. However, he must have known that the proposed council's structure—in which homeland leaders and other government-nominated Africans would join official appointees of other races—would be unacceptable to every component of the popular opposition movement. His rhetoric was more liberal than ever before; a declaration that "apartheid is outmoded" was followed by newspaper ads promising power sharing with Africans. In reality, Botha was once more buying time with socioeconomic concessions and political repression, while again proposing puppet multiracial bodies and liberal gestures to disguise his failure to give ground on political power. The goal was an "internal settlement" excluding the people's movement, rather than one including it.

At lower levels of the party, the unhappy combination of unsuccessful repression and reformist rhetoric drove out members and sapped the vitality of the organization. The fragility of party structures was highlighted in early 1985 when hints that the government might negotiate with the ANC provoked the largest exodus from the NP since the 1982 split. Thousands of former members joined the CP.[48] In the Transvaal, the number of NP branches also declined, a sign that the party's traditional organizational base was withering.

The party's new reliance on professional organization and mass media proved to be a poor substitute for more personalized campaigning. The NP no longer had close touch with sentiment in the constituencies, as in the past when frequent information meetings were held.[49] The new system of block-by-block organization in urban constituencies appeared unable to close the gap. Television and newspaper advertisements were also unable to keep the NP's traditional identifiers, accustomed to a more personalized style of politics, with the party. The estrangement between leaders and led also was furthered by the decline in the role of party congresses. (Previously, they permitted representatives of the base to debate all new policies, but Botha decided in 1982 that congresses could only consider broad principles.)

Within the white electorate as a whole, opinion surveys revealed that NP support melted away as the crisis heated up. Nationalist support declined from a high of 56 percent in the halcyon days of July 1984 to 47 percent nine months later (see Table 2.2). The share of the vote going to the right-wing parties rose from 12 percent in July 1984 to 15 percent in April 1985. However, those expressing no opinion increased from 9 percent to 15 percent of the white electorate during the same period, a sign that whites were losing their identification with the National party.[50]

Once again, by-elections revealed a larger erosion of the Nationalist vote than that reported by the polls. In December 1984, there was a 22 percent swing to the far right in the East Rand mining seat of Primrose and smaller swings in two Cape constituencies (including P. W. Botha's former seat). The CP came within an ace of winning the rural Free State seat of Harrismith in May 1985, a seat the right had not even contested in 1981. The worst news for the NP came in the by-elections of 31 October 1985. The HNP won its first election victory ever in Sasolburg, an industrial town in the unrest-stricken Vaal triangle, on a 15 percent swing. Three other contested seats were also previously strong Nationalist constituencies, yet the average swing from the NP to the right for the five by-elections that day was 24 percent. Nationalist majorities were slashed to highly marginal levels in three of the four seats the party won. Estimates based on these trends suggested that there was a strong likelihood that the NP would lose its majority in the white chamber of Parliament if a general election were held.[51]

The decline in NP support was the product of the disintegration of the alliance of classes and occupational categories won over by Botha or traditionally behind his party. Local and foreign capitalists took their distances from the government, thereby leaving the links between the power bloc and the men directing the state in an increasingly tenuous position. Struggles also intensified within Afrikaner cultural, intellectual, and professional spheres, breakaways occurring to the right and splintering to the left. Occupational groups that had already been excluded from the alliance stiffened their opposition, while many former supporters wavered. Protest meetings of Afrikaners opposed to government policy—rare in the previous four decades—became regular occurrences. Rather than drawing together under pressure, the bloc of supporters the NP leadership had worked to unite appeared to be cracking up.

The most striking development was the draining away of business support. By late 1984, as the fires of revolt spread and the prospect of regional peace faded, enthusiasm for the ruling party vanished among South African capitalists. Instead, ever more vocal criticism of official policy was voiced by representatives of business, including Afrikaner business. A series of joint public declarations urging the liberalization of race policies, unprecedented in strength and frequency, was made by the leading organizations of the capitalist class—the AHI joining with the FCI (Federated Chamber of Industry), the Chamber of Mines, and Assocom.[52] The chiefs of important monopolies, including those of Sanlam and Rembrandt as well as those of Anglo-American or Barlow Rand, were also increasingly outspoken.[53] (The Volkskas group, nonetheless, was conspicuously absent from the chorus.)

Equally troubling for government were signs that the confidence of foreign investors (and governments) was slipping. The motivations were obvious. Average returns on foreign investments in South Africa had slid from 20 percent in 1980 to 5 percent in 1985, while doubt was growing about the future of private enterprise in the country and its continued membership in the Western camp.[54] Between September 1984 and September 1985, eighteen U.S. firms pulled out or reduced holdings, including major companies such as Ford. Jitters spread among firms of other nationalities as well, thereby helping to produce a massive capital flight and the fall of the rand. (These, in turn, worsened both recession and inflation.) The multinationals who remained began intervening in domestic politics with a new overtness, lobbying publicly and privately for the scrapping of racial laws in hopes of protecting their own long-run interests.[55]

Meanwhile, within the petit-bourgeois bulwark of Afrikaner communal institutions, *verligte* gains from the 1983–1984 counteroffensive were substantially eroded by a series of splits on the right and individual drifts to the left. The *verkramptes* regrouped after their defeats, creating a network of counterinstitutions for cultural affairs, as they had already done on the party-political terrain. Conservative party sentiment in the Broederbond was strong; an English language newspaper put it at 50 percent in 1983.[56] After the *verligte* Nationalists reestablished control, right wingers began to quit. In 1984, they established a secret society of their own called Toekomsgesprek, with aims and organizational practices similar to those of the Bond.[57] To counterbalance the FAK, a new cultural body called the Volkswag was set up in an enthusiastic Pretoria mass meeting the same year. Led by ousted Broederbond chairman Boshoff, the group could claim 12,000 members (against 27,000 for the FAK) by the time of its first congress in November.[58] Likewise, young conservatives also broke away from the Ruiterwag in early 1985, with 1,000 of the group's 4,500 members expected to join the rebel association.[59] In July 1985, *verkramptes* turned back a *verligte* challenge to their control of the Voortrekkers, the Afrikaans Boy Scouts, and the ubiquitous Boshoff narrowly won reelection.[60]

The divisions within the NP and the Broederbond were again reproduced within the Afrikaans churches. The NHK remained defiant toward the government.[61] The GK was torn between relatively *verlig* trends among its clergy (and at its Potchefstroom University theological school) and the conservatism of its rural Transvaal membership. It made a few *verligte* gestures at its 1985 synod but referred most controversial issues back to committee.[62] On the other hand, the NGK synod in the Western Cape, the bastion of *verligtheid* (enlightenment, reform-mindedness), led the way toward abandoning the notion that apartheid was biblically ordained.[63] A few NGK theologians went further; sixteen at Stellenbosch University signed a "confession of guilt" regarding their church's role in apartheid.[64]

The erosion of the NP position on the left was indeed greatest among Afrikaner intellectuals, although the erosion remained a molecular process of individual defections and intraparty debates rather than one of mass breakaways from the fold. The *verligte* academics and students who had backed (and often helped formulate) Botha's reformist initiatives were aghast at his ineffectual response to the crisis; liberal ideology and constitutional notions made great advances among them.[65] Dissidence was most vocal at Stellenbosch in the Western Cape. In September 1985, the Students Representatives Council there announced that it intended to go to Lusaka for talks with the ANC (although the government refused passports for the trip).

Signs of disaffection appeared elsewhere as well. For example, a call for the abolition of the pass laws came from the 1985 congress of the ASB, to which Stellenbosch is not affiliated.[66] The fortress of the far right remained the University of Pretoria, always closely tied to the conservative Transvaal Broederbond network. The *broedertwis* (fraternal struggle) thus fractured Afrikaner institutions and sharply reduced their capacity for mobilization precisely when grounds for discontent among the election-deciding categories of whites they had helped to organize were more sharply felt.

Both corporate interests and ideology continued to push civil servants toward the far right. As the economic situation worsened, public sector pay was frozen in September 1984, despite an annual inflation rate of nearly 20 percent. Austerity measures in 1985 included reductions in annual bonuses and the elimination of most merit pay awards. These moves provoked a series of angry meetings among SATS workers and mutterings of strikes from normally docile white functionaries.[67] Moreover, the opening of more civil service posts to coloreds and Indians and the possibility of similar concessions to Africans were alarming.

Among farmers, the swing to the right threatened to become an avalanche. This already troubled sector was hammered by a combination of drought, high interest rates, and government pricing decisions. Farm income in 1983 was down 42 percent from 1982, and 1982 had been a bad year.[68] By 1985, total farm debt soared towards R 1 billion, and half the country's farmers were reported to be close to bankruptcy.[69] The flashpoint was reached in April 1985 when the Agriculture Ministry refused to grant an increase in the maize producer price after decades of regular yearly rises.[70] The government showed itself more preoccupied with the burning townships (whose staple is maize) and with livestock raisers using maize feed than with the interests of rural supporters who had been faithful since 1948.

Maize men were furious. Although the price stayed fixed at R 240 a ton, production costs averaged R 277. The eight Nampo members of the Maize Board resigned in protest, and an angry Klerksdorp meeting of 4,000 decided to withhold maize deliveries.[71] Although the government rode out the boycott, the political cost was high. However, the government was kinder to Natal farmers, setting the price of sugar, the province's main product, at almost three times the world price.[72] Nonetheless, there were rumblings of disaffection there, too; more than fifteen'hundred farmers staged a protest meeting in early 1985.[73] The rural discontent translated into more by-election swings against the NP. Even in 1983 the right-wing parties had majorities in Parys and Middleburg. Despite the NP recovery in 1984, the CP won Fanie Botha's seat when his involvement in a scandal provoked a second Soutspansberg by-election. The October 1985 results were even more disturbing for Nationalists. The CP slashed the NP majority by two-thirds in the Free State maize seat of Bethlehem, while the vote in Vryheid (rural Natal) also revealed significant gains by the far right.

White wage earners also continued to defect from the NP, worried by wage trends, labor policy, and—for the first time since the 1930s—unemployment. Most artisan rates gazetted in 1985 were again down in real terms from the preceding year's, and white miners were in much the same position.[74] As the economic depression hit home, white joblessness tripled to an estimated one hundred thousand (5 percent).[75] Although the drive for a single white union bogged down in legal red tape, the all-white South African Confederation of Labor moved close to the right-wing parties. Conservative trade unionists also urged their members to join the Volkswag cultural front.[76] For their part, the right-wing parties used worker discontent to pry voters from their NP ties. Sasolburg HNP candidate Louis Stofberg explained his approach on the eve of his by-election victory: "The appeal for reform does not strike emotional cords in the Afrikaner. . . . You must tell him, in the midst of inflation and the falling value of the rand, how much money the government is spending on black education and development, and he will go crazy."[77] The consequences were seen at the polls. Besides the setbacks for the NP in Primrose and Sasolburg, the NP also lost votes to the far right in working-class seats in Parow (Western Cape) and Springs (East Rand).

Although the unraveling of the NP's social fabric was serious, the government's problems became acute after capital's recession-deepening collapse of confidence following Botha's 15 August fiasco. The first red light had been Chase Manhattan Bank's refusal to renew South African loans in July 1985.[78] After the state president ruled out major reforms in Durban, overseas banks and companies rushed for the exits. Foreign banks refused en masse to roll over South African loans and thus cut the country off from capital inflows essential for renewed growth. Within weeks a number of multinationals had also announced plans to pull out, including three of eight automakers (Peugeot, Renault, and Alfa Romeo). In the wake of the loans freeze, even conservative governments overseas made it clear that they viewed Botha's regime as a liability.

For the English-speaking bourgeoisie, already fearful of the future and hesitant to invest, the loan moratorium was the last straw. In the aftermath of Botha's 15 August speech, the advice to the state president from the *Financial Mail,* representative of much English business opinion, was categorical: "Leave now."[79] The major representative bodies of English-speaking business, the FCI and Assocom, issued a joint statement with the National African Chamber of Commerce urging the lifting of the state of emergency, the release of Nelson Mandela, and negotiations with the ANC. Two weeks after the debt freeze, English capital placed a stunning vote of no confidence in the Nationalist government, when leading English-speaking monopolists flew to Lusaka to meet the ANC leadership. Signs of disarray were evident among Afrikaner capitalists unhappy with official policy yet abstaining from joining in the initiatives of their English-speaking colleagues. With the appearance of these wide breaches in the unity of the dominant classes and of the government, what had begun on the white political scene as a crisis for the National party had become an open crisis of regime. As the end of 1985 approached, Fritz Leutweiler, South Africa's negotiator in debt rescheduling talks, was perfectly explicit about the danger, warning, "Time is running out for South Africa."[80]

The Nationalist Dilemma

Since the upsurge of resistance at the start of the present phase of the crisis, P. W. Botha has seemed in his public statements to be squirming in the grip of his own contradictions. For example, in a January 1985 television address, he refused black demands for one person, one vote and insisted upon white political control ("the non-abdication of whites").[81] Yet in April, before an African religious meeting, he offered a mea culpa: "In the past we have not really talked to each other. Let us come together and do so. . . . In the past we have not really listened to each other. Let us begin to listen to each other. We must jointly strive to solve our problems."[82]

Botha remained deaf to the demands of the popular movement in an October interview, however, and once again rejected "a state where the white minority is overwhelmed without structures to protect its birthright."[83] In November, however, he made a declaration that almost sounded as if it came from a representative of the UDF: "The government is committed to the principle of a united South Africa, of the same citizenship and of political rights for all, in the framework of structures chosen by South Africans themselves."[84] Commenting on a series of confusing statements by government spokesmen, the *Financial Mail* concluded, "What government really means when it talks of 'open-ended agendas' and non-prescriptive negotiation is that anything goes—within the parameters of Nationalist policy."[85]

Nevertheless, the fashionable tendency to consider white party politics irrelevant is erroneous and dangerously misleading. In this view, "total strategy" (the defense of the white regime on all fronts) serves as a *deus ex machina* linking military, political, and business leaders in an alliance, under the generals' control, that decides the major lines of policy.[86] This position ignores the clear evidence of major divergences among these different groups despite their shared desire to preserve capitalism and avert revolution. The military and political leaders have clashed regarding questions such as the Namibia settlement and the conduct of the destabilization policy.[87] Likewise, Afrikaner *verligtes* and English-speaking liberals have had much more trouble finding each other than the total strategy analysis implies. The Afrikaner bourgeoisie and intellectuals close to it have been far more timid and vague than English or foreign capitalists regarding political concessions to blacks, despite calls for social and economic changes. The AHI pointedly failed to join in the appeal by Assocom and the FCI for talks with the ANC, and Rembrandt chairman Anton Rupert publicly opposed the liberation of Nelson Mandela.[88] These differences at top levels of the military, business, and the state apparatus permit the political leadership to arbitrate among them and exercise its relative autonomy.

Furthermore, white political parties certainly do not behave as if party politics were the charade adherents of the total strategy theory believe. Total

strategy is entirely dependent upon continued Nationalist rule because electoral victory by the far right would abrogate the NP-military alliance.
Nationalists have shown their awareness of this by back pedalling on reform
after by-election setbacks. Likewise, the PFP continues to speak and behave
as if its differences with the NP were important, differences that concern the
immediate response to the crisis and the ultimate constitutional settlement.
The NP may be headed for the dustbin of history, but it does not make policy
based on that assumption. The party is trying to reach a constitutional (if undemocratic) solution through constitutional means, a strategy that requires
the NP to try keeping some sort of political base intact within some kind of
legalistic framework.

Contradictory pronouncements by Nationalist leaders reflect the fact
that they are capable neither of reconstituting the old grouping of dominant
and allied classes, nor of forging a new historical bloc capable of a national-
popular appeal to oppressed and exploited blacks. Fundamentally, the political crisis represents a crisis in the party-political representation of class
forces. The separation between state and civil society is very far advanced.
The hegemonic apparatus that kept the dominated classes in thrall is col-
lapsing. The supporting and allied classes of whites organized by the NP
have been peeling away, and the most powerful segments of the bourgeoisie
have despaired of the Nationalists. The NP's perpetual temporizing and its
continual talk of power sharing (which is rendered meaningless by inac-
tion) have cost the party its traditional electorate without attracting new support. The verbal gyrations of Botha and his colleagues constitute increasingly desperate attempts to reconcile the contradictory demands of their
former allies. But the conditions for the resolution of the legitimacy crisis
appear increasingly incompatible with those for the NP's continued participation in state power on a constitutional basis.

The NP's failure to democratize the state is related to its character as the
party representing and organically linked to the Afrikaner bourgeoisie. The
political interests of the Afrikaans-speaking section of the bourgeoisie remain opposed to those of English-speaking capitalists, even though both
share an interest in the efficient employment of black labor. Accumulation
by Afrikaners is still largely dependent upon the state and its influence. Afrikaner managers in the public sector obviously owe their position to
Nationalist power. Even much of Afrikaans private business, structurally
often the weak relation of its English competitors, remains dependent upon
state patronage, protection, or nonintervention. In the case of Afrikaner finance capital, Volkskas still has many state accounts, while Sanlam would
lose a lot of insurance business if state medical and pensions schemes were
established. Nor should the importance of state orders for Afrikaner industrial undertakings be minimized. The agricultural bourgeoisie relies on government pricing, input, and credit policies as well as on subsidies. (An esti-

mated 20 percent of farm income comes directly from the state[89]). Admitting the black petite bourgeoisie to the power bloc would pit the Afrikaans-speaking bourgeoisie against a power competitor for state largesse. As Sam Nolutshungu has pointed out, "A significant sharing of state power with blacks . . . would directly threaten not only the position of the (white) petite bourgeoisie but also of the bureaucratic bourgeoisie itself."[90]

The deracialization of the state would also endanger the largely Afrikaner occupational categories constituting what is left of the supporting classes of the NP. It would directly menace the jobs and living standards of whites in state and parastatal organizations who make up nearly half of economically active Afrikaners and probably a majority of the NP's remaining supporters. Even informal legal equality for Africans would overstretch the state's capacity to meet their needs while maintaining current white standards in the provision of services and amenities. Enormous expenditures would be required to equalize state services. All this—along with the prejudices cultivated for decades to rationalize the status quo—helps explain why as recently as September 1985 a majority of Afrikaners said in a survey that they were still "happy" with apartheid.[91]

Consequently, the NP approach to political reform consists of establishing a multiracial franchise and administration while stripping representative institutions of power. In practice, this approach translates into the establishment of an autonomous executive capable of enforcing its will without a parliamentary majority. Thus, under the 1983 constitution, the executive state president is elected by a white majority electoral college. The NP will be able to elect all the white members as long as it remains the largest single party in the white chamber, even if it loses its majority. In such circumstances the president would be able to play off the three racial chambers of Parliament and the multiracial President's Council (where his appointees form a majority) to ensure that his will becomes law.[92] The abolition of provincial councils, announced in 1985, is another step in the same direction.[93] They will be replaced with government-appointed executive committees, which also may be multiracial in composition. This strategy toward political regulation explains constitutional development minister Chris Heunis's remark, "Remember, at best we can have a limited democracy in this country."[94]

The confederal or federal schemes of government that have been broached by Botha and others offer scant hopes of moving beyond the limits of NP policy. Such proposals call for the devolution of politically sensitive service and collective consumption functions (education and housing, for example) to the local or regional level.[95] The more affluent white areas could thus afford services substantially superior to those in poor black areas. The Regional Services Councils (RSCs) already being set up to control "nonpolitical" functions (sewerage, electricity, and so on) will remain under effective white control. Representation on these councils will be attributed to racial local authorities according to taxes paid within each, ensuring the vast majority of seats for highly rated, industrialized white areas on these unrepresentative local oligarchies.

The state and central government schemes that have been suggested hardly appear more democratic or more capable of responding to black aspirations. Racial gerrymandering could make possible the establishment of a number of nearly all-white or all-black states, while electoral systems could be arranged to protect white power in mixed states. Indirect election of state executives would produce results no more equitable than those for the RSCs. The major alternative under consideration, the Buthelezi Commission plan for Natal, would guarantee whites half the seats in the state legislature and places in the executive as well as veto rights on all decisions.[96] The proposal repeatedly floated for a central federal chamber or upper house based upon delegates sent by such state governments would merely create at least one more tier of government unresponsive to the majority. Even if a second house were established upon the basis of universal suffrage, the assignment of blocking power to the upper house and the narrow competences that would be left to Parliament by devolution would leave the house impotent to alter the distribution of wealth and services. The blueprints under discussion seem reminiscent of the Imperial German constitution, in which powerless central representative institutions were combined with a conservatively run federal state (Prussia) controlling most of the wealth and land.[97]

Schemes for the privatization of parts or functions of the state also do not appear to offer the Nationalists a way out. It has been suggested that selling off state industries would reduce the regulatory power of the state (for example, its control of jobs, salaries, and investment). The state's selloff of the Sasol oil-from-coal firm is cited as an example. Similarly, full or partial privatization of state services would permit their unequal provision to whites and blacks on a market-related basis. The object would be a state sufficiently weak to be safely deracialized.[98] Up to now, proposals for large-scale privatization have been bogged down by government fear of losing control of privatized entities or services.[99] If accepted, however, these proposals could prove too clever by half. Privatization extensive enough to protect the interests of most of the white population would leave a stunted state incapable of responding to the class demands of the black petite bourgeoisie, let alone those of workers.

In short, the NP government appears unable to resolve the crises of state legitimacy and capitalist hegemony by constitutional means. It may continue to muddle through for a time, swinging between bouts of repression and reformist initiatives. By early 1986, there were signs that economic conditions were easing as gold rose and oil fell. The government hoped to win a respite by rescheduling external debt payments, reflating the economy, and implementing the reforms Botha outlined in his 31 January speech. In the short-to-medium term, however, the government appears likely to confront a series of serious problems. First, the confidence of capitalists at home and abroad has been gravely impaired. Although foreign bankers may not wish to write off loans already outstanding, little investment can be expected from overseas (or local) firms until the regime has crushed or coopted enough of the opposition to reestablish stability. Second, unless the government enlarges its political base beyond the white electorate, the NP will eventually have to go to the polls in a white election in which it may lose its preeminence among white parties and thus lose control of the state.[100] Finally, the popular movement appears to have reached a point where it cannot be destroyed by normal political means.[101] The combination of politicized followers, national leaders, and a sizable body of cadres dispersed in the trade union, student, community, and underground politicomilitary organizations means that the movement will be capable of maintaining and increasing its activity until the government seriously attempts to satisfy the movement's demands. Thus, the NP may be obliged to admit it cannot master the situation, perhaps sooner than many expect given the way the growth of the resistance movement to date has outstripped all expectations. If the NP cannot close the gap between the state and the people, then only two choices remain.[102]

The first would be the abandonment of constitutionalism and party politics and the complete autonomization of the state from civil society. The state would make a tabula rasa of opposition on the left, Chilean-style, while cracking the whip to keep right-wing whites in line. This would enable the authorities to push through the deracialization of the state and the economy without having to concede to workers' and democrats' demands. The racial "democracy" of the National party would give way to nonracial dictatorship in the hopes of eventually restoring conditions permitting capital accumulation and investor confidence. The economic counterpart of this authoritarian approach is already openly advocated by certain major Afrikaner capitalists who urge the establishment of a siege economy. However, such a crackdown would be a very dangerous strategy for the authorities. It would risk resistance on both right and left that could hasten rather than postpone the overthrow of the state (including possible mutinies in the Citizen Force, a strike of public servants, bureaucratic opposition, and general strikes or insurrections in the townships). Given the degree of world attention to which South Africa is subject, there also would be a serious possibility of international sanctions.

The second possibility—toward which the government appears to be drifting—is a surrender to the democratic opposition after negotiations or a violent uprising. This option—attempting to make the state conform more closely to the contours of civil society—implies deracializing the state via effective universal suffrage and submerging the National party within a broader bourgeois alliance. Although both the politicians who control the state and the Afrikaner capitalists who profit from it have hesitated before this option, they could be compelled to take the plunge. At some point, the loss of the advantages of exclusive state power must be outweighed by the dangers to the survival of the regime and capital in the retention of the racially exclusive state. Yet genuine political liberalization (including the unbanning of the ANC and the Communist party), let alone the acceptance of one person, one vote, would open real possibilities of movement beyond bourgeois democracy to socialism by constitutional or revolutionary means.[103]

At the time of this writing (January 1986), these possibilities were beginning to appear on the horizon, although they still seemed some way off. The nationalist and working-class movements had not yet scored a decisive advantage, but political, economic, and military pressures on the NP government were mounting. Nevertheless, although the seventy-four-year-old ruling party seemed to be approaching the end of the road, the way ahead remained uncertain. The situation resembled that described by Gramsci when he wrote:

> If the ruling class has lost its consensus, i.e. is no longer "leading" but only "dominant", exercising coercive force alone, this means precisely that the great masses have become detached from their traditional ideologies, and no longer believe as previously. The crisis consists precisely in the fact that the old is dying and the new cannot be born; in this interregnum a great variety of morbid symptoms appear.[104]

Notes

The author wishes to thank *Rapport* and *The Star* for access to unpublished survey data.

1. Antonio Gramsci, *Selections from the Prison Notebooks* (New York: International Publishers, 1971), 210.

2. Dan O'Meara, "Muldergate and the Politics of Afrikaner Nationalism," *Work in Progress* 24 (1982):10.

3. Dan O'Meara, *Volkskapitalisme (People's Capitalism)* (Cambridge: Cambridge University Press, 1982).

4. Exclusive regimes of accumulation are typical of peripheral industrialization at the stage of consumer durables production. See Pierre Salama, "Vers un nouveau modèle d'accumulation?" ("Toward a New Model of Accumulation?"), *Critiques de l'economie politique (Critique of Political Economy)* 16/17 (1974):42–89; and Pierre Salama and Gilberto Mathias, *L'etat surdéveloppé* (The Overdeveloped State) (Paris: Maspero/La Decouverte, 1983).

5. What is particular in the South African case is the racially exclusive basis of the regime of accumulation. See Harold Wolpe, "Capitalism and Cheap Labour-Power in South Africa," *Economy and Society* 1 (1972):425.

6. O'Meara, *Volkskapitalisme,* 158.

7. *Financial Mail,* 29 March 1985.

8. Craig Charney, "The Wooing of Big Business," *Management* (October 1982):24.

9. Hermann Giliomee and Heribert Adam, *Ethnic Power Mobilized: Can South Africa Change?* (London: Yale University Press, 1979), 169, 170–171.

10. Stanley Greenberg, *Race and State in Capitalist Development: Comparative Perspectives* (New Haven, Conn.: Yale University Press, 1980), 190.

11. Personal interview. A survey taken just after the split found that 30 percent of NP supporters earned more than R 22,000 annually, 32 percent earned between R 13,000 and R 22,000, and only 38 percent numbered among the "little men" (less than R 13,000) who had brought the party to power. "Mark-en-Meningopnames" ("Market and Attitude Polls"), *Rapport Poll* (April 1982).

12. O'Meara, "Muldergate"; and Giliomee, *Ethnic Power Mobilized.*

13. See, among others, Glenn Moss, "Total Strategy," *Work in Progress* 11 (1981):1; John Saul and Steven Gelb, *The Crisis in South Africa* (New York: Monthly Review Press, 1982); and South African Review Service (SARS), *South African Review I* (Johannesburg: Ravan Press, 1983).

14. Hermann Giliomee, *The Parting of the Ways* (Cape Town: David Philip, 1983), 150.

15. Craig Charney, "A Political Weapon in the Struggle over Apartheid," *Times Higher Education Supplement* (May 1982).

16. On this point generally, see Giliomee, *Ethnic Power Mobilized,* Chapter 5. The quote comes from a personal interview with a high official.

17. Cited in Deborah Posel, "State Ideology and Legitimation: The Contemporary South African Case" (Paper delivered at the Conference on South Africa and the Comparative Study of Class, Race, and Nationalism, New York, 1982).

18. Giliomee, *The Parting of the Ways,* 37.

19. Craig Charney, "Towards Rupture or Stasis? An Analysis of the 1981 South African General Election," *African Affairs* 81 (1982):528.

20. Personal interview with a Nationalist MP.

21. Theodore Hanf et al., *South Africa: The Prospects of Peaceful Change* (London: Rex Collings, 1981); "Mark-en-Meningsopnames."

22. Charney, "The Wooing of Big Business," 25.

23. Past surveys have consistently underrated support for the right-wing parties, particularly the HNP. Part of the reason for this underrating seems to be that these parties, without media support, can mobilize their potential supporters only with election-time propaganda barrages. Much the same phenomenon was noted with the British Liberal party prior to the formation of the alliance. See David Butler et al., *The British General Election 1974* (London: Macmillan, 1975). Another problem is the "lie factor": Afrikaner voters are often unwilling to admit they intend to vote against the NP, from embarrassment or for fear of victimization. In 1981, mid-campaign surveys by *The Star* and the *Sunday Times* both put the HNP vote at half or less of the election-day total. This suggests that by-election results are a better gauge of the right's strength than are survey findings.

24. Perskor had already been hard hit soon after Botha took office, when Nasionale Pers won a tender for half its lucrative telephone directory printing business.

25. Charney, "The Wooing of Big Business"; and *Sunday Times,* 27 June 1982, *Sunday Express,* 15 August 1982, and *Die Afrikaner,* 17 October 1982.

26. Robert Davies, *South African Strategy Towards Mozambique in the Post-Nkomati Period* (Uppsala: Scandinavian Institute of African Studies, 1985), 35–51.

27. *Die Afrikaner,* 17 November 1982 and 1 December 1982.

28. *Rapport,* 3 July 1983.

29. *The Star,* 3 January 1985.

30. Ibid.

31. *Sunday Tribune,* 1 August 1982. The NHK is the only church in the world that excludes blacks from membership.

32. "Mark-en-Meningsopnames," *Rapport Poll* (July 1982). This is not because Conservatives are more observant. The survey showed that they do not go to church more often than Nationalists.

33. See Giliomee, *Ethnic Power Mobilized,* 221–232; and Merle Lipton, "White Labour, the White Bureaucracy, and Their Growing Conflict with Capital," *Optima* 28, nos. 2/3 (1980):184–201.

34. Jan Lombard and Jan Stadler, *Focus on Key Economic Issues: Income Distribution* 31 (November 1982):4.

35. For a discussion of the split of the 1930s, see O'Meara, *Volkskapitalisme,* chapters 2 and 3. The discussion that follows on the politics of white farmers in the 1980s is largely based upon an interview with Beaumont Schoeman, former editor of the HNP newspaper, *Die Afrikaner.*

36. Riaan de Villiers, "Apocalypse on the Platteland," *Frontline* (March 1983):14; and *Financial Mail,* 4 February 1983.

37. *Rand Daily Mail,* 26 March 1983. Some twelve Cape Nationalist MPs are wine farmers, and four are directors of the KWV Cooperative, a dominant force in the new marketing monopoly. Anton Rupert's Rembrandt group, the major spirits producer, has historically been the second-strongest business influence upon the Cape NP (after Sanlam).

38. *Sunday Times* (Business Times), 31 March 1985; and *Natal Mercury,* 13 March 1985.

39. "Mark-en-Meningsopnames," *Rapport Poll* (November 1982).

40. Charney, "Towards Rupture or Stasis?" 542.

41. South African Embassy (France), *Perspectives sudafricaines* (South African Perspectives), 29 April 1985 (author's translation).

42. *Sunday Express,* 18 November 1984.

43. *The Star,* 18 February 1985.

44. *Financial Mail,* 23 August 1985; *Le Monde,* 1 November 1985; and *The Star,* 11 February 1985.

45. *Financial Mail,* 23 August 1985, 6 September 1985, and 13 September 1985; and *The Star,* 16 September 1985.

46. *New African* (January 1986); *The Economist,* 30 November 1985; and *The Observer,* 8 November 1985.

47. *The Economist,* 10 January 1986.

48. *The Star,* 11 February 1985 and 18 February 1985.

49. *Sunday Star,* 24 February 1985.

50. The surveys also underlined two other phenomena of note. One was the continuing shrinkage of the New Republic party, as its component class elements broke apart in search of parties better suited to their interests. The other was that, thanks largely to working-class English support, the NP was almost level pegging the PFP among English-speaking voters (37 percent versus 39 percent). See *Rapport,* 10 March 1985. Together, these figures represent the definitive refutation of the myth that most white English-speakers are liberal.

51. *The Star,* 29 April 1985.

52. White commercial capital—large and small—was under particularly intense pressure, as it was hard hit by black consumer boycotts during 1985. In Port Elizabeth, the boycott had led to business-community talks that resulted in the release of political detainees and the withdrawal of troops from the townships. Elsewhere on the Platteland, the boycotts forced even small-town Afrikaner traders to call for government reforms. See *The Observer,* 6 October 1985; and *Liberation,* 14 August 1985 and 24 December 1985.

53. *Financial Mail,* 6 September 1985; and *The Star,* 30 September 1985.

54. *Business Week,* 23 September 1985. Assets and profits repatriated by U.S. firms from South Africa totaled $493 million during 1984, according to the same source. It added that almost every U.S. firm in South Africa had a contingency plan for disinvestment.

55. *Liberation,* 28 November 1985.

56. South African Institute of Race Relations (SAIRR), *Annual Survey of Race Relations* (Johannesburg: SAIRR, 1983), 24. According to the same source, even the progovernment *Die Burger* estimated support for the new constitution in the Bond at no more than 60 percent.

57. *Rapport,* 26 May 1985.

58. *The Star,* 29 July 1985 and 19 November 1985.

59. *The Star,* 24 February 1985.

60. SAIRR, *Annual Survey,* 7.

61. *The Star,* 12 November 1984.

62. *The Star,* 4 February 1985.

63. SAIRR, *Annual Survey,* 629.

64. Eastern Cape presbytery chairman Ben Kotze went so far as to call on the NGK to identify itself with "the victims of the system." See *The Star,* 16 September 1985.

65. *Financial Mail,* 1 November 1985.

66. *The Star,* 22 July 1985.

67. *Rand Daily Mail,* 7 March 1985; *City Press,* 31 March 1985; and *The Star,* 2 August 1985.

68. *Sunday Times,* 17 June 1984.

69. *The Star,* 27 May 1985.

70. *Rapport,* 28 April 1985.

71. *Rapport,* 5 May 1985. Insult was added to injury when President Botha brushed aside the demands of a Nampo delegation, then told them, "Write that down! You must tell the *boere* [farmers] what happened here."

72. *Rapport,* 5 May 1985.

73. *The Star,* 27 May 1985.
74. *Sunday Times,* 31 March 1985.
75. *Rapport,* 19 May 1985.
76. *Financial Mail,* 26 April 1985.
77. *The Guardian,* 30 October 1985.
78. *New York Times,* 16 September 1985.
79. *Financial Mail,* 6 September 1985.
80. *Journal de Geneve,* 28 November 1985.
81. *The Star,* 18 February 1985.
82. *Rapport,* 14 April 1985.
83. *The Times,* 21 October 1985.
84. Agence France Presse, 14 November 1985.
85. *Financial Mail,* 23 August 1985.
86. For example, Robert Davies and Dan O'Meara, "La Stratégie totale en Afrique australe" ("Total Strategy in South Africa"), *Politique africaine* (African Politics) 19 (September 1985):7–28.
87. Zaki Laidi, "La politique regionale sudafricaine," ("Regional Politics in Southern Africa") *Les temps modernes* (forthcoming).
88. *Financial Mail,* 6 September 1985. Because talking to the ANC implied having something to talk about, the business community's advocacy more or less implied the eventual acceptance of a nonracial state, the unbanning of prohibited political movements, and a universal franchise. This, in turn, is why such suggestions were anathema to Botha and most of his supporters.
89. *The Star,* 10 June 1985.
90. Sam Nolutshungu, *Changing South Africa: Political Considerations* (Manchester: Manchester University Press, 1982), 106. Similar conclusions were reached twenty years ago in Stanley Trapido, "Political Institutions and Social Structures in the Republic of South Africa," *American Political Science Review* 57 (1963):75–76.
91. *The Star,* 9 September 1985. Also see *Rapport,* 19 May 1985, which found a 52 percent majority of Afrikaners against *any* opening of white residential areas to blacks (even on a selective and limited basis). An overwhelming 82 percent remained against the complete elimination of residential apartheid, even if it were gradually phased out.
92. For more detail see Craig Charney, "Cooption and Control in the New South African Constitution," *Review of African Political Economy,* no. 29 (1984):29.
93. *Financial Mail,* 10 May 1985. The immediate loser will be the NRP, which lost the Natal Provincial Assembly, the only remaining white representative forum not in the hands of the NP. As Alf Stadler has pointed out, the move will also wipe out the provincial electoral competitions that have largely structured provincial class alliances underlying the white South African party system.
94. *Rapport,* 21 April 1985.
95. See the lengthy analysis of such proposals by William Cobbett et al., "Regionalism, Federalism, and the Reconstruction of the South African State," *South African Labour Bulletin* 10, no. 5 (April 1985):87–116.
96. *Financial Mail,* 9 August 1985. For a devastating critique of such schemes, see Part I of Nolutshungu, *Changing South Africa.*
97. Reference was made to the "Bismarck option" in a speech by Willie

Breytenbach of the Ministry of Constitutional Development. For more detail on the Bismarckian constitution, see Arthur Rosenberg, *Imperial Germany* (Oxford: Oxford University Press, 1970).

98. The best-known advocate of such an approach was Jan Lombard, who is followed by other University of Pretoria economists. The de Lange Committee report on education followed much the same line, calling for the expansion of state-aided, fee-paying private schools.

99. *Financial Mail,* 29 March 1985.

100. The government used the 1983 constitution act to prolong the white Parliament elected in 1981 until 1989, by making its length coterminous with that of the colored and Indian chambers elected in 1984. It is doubtful, however, that this gambit can be used again.

101. Gramsci, *Selections from the Prison Notebooks,* 152–154.

102. A third possibility, sometimes suggested, would be a partition of South Africa between blacks and whites. Such is the goal of the Orange Workers' Union, and public reference to such an eventuality has been made by Gerrit Viljoen (*The Star,* 17 December 1984). However, such schemes are pure fantasy. It is difficult to imagine black or international acceptance for such a scheme, without which it would be unworkable. Furthermore, it is difficult to see how whites accustomed to affluence would accept menial jobs as janitors or farm laborers doing work now performed by blacks. Proponents of partition schemes propose a high-technology utopia where poor whites would not exist, but they remain mum on where the massive funding required to realize such schemes would come from.

103. See Archie Mafeje, "Soweto and Its Aftermath," *Review of African Political Economy,* no. 11 (1977); and David Lewis, "Le capital, les syndicats, et la lutte de liberation nationale" ("Capital, Unions, and the Struggle for National Liberation") *Les temps modernes* (forthcoming).

104. Gramsci, *Selections from the Prison Notebooks,* 275–276.

3

WILMOT G. JAMES
ANDRÉ DU PISANIE

End of a "New Deal": Contradictions of Constitutional Reform

The National party's major reformist initiative is the new constitution of 1984, which granted coloreds and Indians, two numerical minorities in the population, the right to vote. Their representatives sit in segregated chambers of Parliament, and their social life is still hemmed in by segregation in schooling, residence, and so on. Wilmot G. James and André du Pisanie try to make sense of this peculiarly South African absurdity, where citizenship rights for minorities change nothing at all. They argue that the tricameral Parliament and its enabling legislation reproduce rather than adulterate racial and ethnic boundaries—their professed intention—and their true purpose is to entrench and protect the group rights of whites.

An account also is given of the constitutional place of Africans in the polity. The authors claim that homelands are impossible solutions to the problem of African citizenship and that the most recent attempt at creating autonomous township government has failed. As a result, no mediating institutions of governance exist between Africans and the state, and consequently the latter resorts to direct force and repression. Thus, constitutional change—for coloreds and Indians on the national level and Africans on the local level—has the consequence of weakening white rule and creating a revolutionary situation. Thus, the state has to start afresh with collaborative initiatives, but it lacks the capacity to genuinely coopt blacks in the creation of a new racial order.

W. G. J.

In January 1985, South Africa's new tricameral Parliament assembled for the first time in the city of Cape Town, the legislative capitol of the nation. The Parliament, created by constitutional legislation passed the previous year, consisted of three chambers, one each for whites, coloreds, and Indians. Africans, the nation's majority, were conspicuous by their absence from the new arrangement. The objective of the new constitution and Parliament was to coopt coloreds and Indians—as "junior partners" of apartheid—and to maintain the constitutional rightlessness of Africans on the national level. As a quid pro quo, Africans received the Black Local Authorities Act, which augmented the powers of representative government on a local township level. From the government's point of view, this "new deal" was major testimony to its reformist intentions.

The success of the new constitutional regime depended on the participation of coloreds and Indians in the tricameral Parliament and on African participation in community councils, the instrument of township self-governance. Neither objective was realized. Colored and Indian participation in the elections held for the tricameral Parliament was marginal. As for African participation, the Africans not only boycotted community council elections but essentially dismantled the councils that were nevertheless constituted. By 1986, the conflict regarding community councils and governance in African townships had overwhelmed politics and reduced the tricameral Parliament to a relatively meaningless sideshow in the broader struggle for state power. Instead of introducing a more stable form of white rule, the "new deal" produced, in effect, a revolutionary situation.

The contradictions of the "new deal" are therefore of central importance in a more thorough understanding of contemporary South African politics and of the conflict and violence prevailing therein. This chapter seeks to situate the struggle against apartheid in a political economy of constitutional change by arguing that the new deal contributes to the weakening of the capacity of the state to govern the African majority.

Minority Cooptation

Colored and Indian South Africans are numerical minorities in the population, making up 9 percent and 3 percent respectively of a nation of approximately 32 million.[1] The 1984 constitution extends parliamentary representation to these minorities and thereby enlarges the population base of the new electorate to 28 percent of the nation—whites make up 16 percent of the population. However, whites, coloreds, and Indians do not form part of a single electorate, but are three separate electorates, sending their own respective representatives to three separate chambers of Parliament—that is, the House of Assembly (whites), the House of Representatives (coloreds), and the House of Delegates (Indians). The House of Assembly dominates Parliament, having the largest share of representation—178 seats to the 78 and 45 seats for coloreds and Indians respectively—and effective veto power over the other houses. The National party (NP), the majority party in the House of Assembly, essentially controls Parliament.

The major reason for this arrangement is that an integrated white, colored, and Indian electorate would weaken the National party majority in Parliament because most coloreds and Indians would vote for the parliamentary opposition.[2] As architect of the new constitution, the National party did not want to take any chances on this score. An integrated electorate would enhance the power of the parliamentary opposition and might compel the National party to form a coalition with the liberal Progressive Federal party (PFP), the largest parliamentary opposition party. From this would follow all sorts of evils—from the National party's point of view—such as desegregation and majority rule. To integrate was to possibly lose power, and, consequently, preference was given for a Parliament segregated by race. Thus, coloreds and Indians were granted the right to vote but denied the opportunity of displacing the National party and changing any of the major laws underwriting racial segregation.

A majority of coloreds and Indians reject racial separation and are particularly opposed to the segregation of schools and neighborhoods.[3] Under the new constitution, the segregation of schools and neighborhoods is entrenched. There was therefore little point to participating in elections held under the auspices of such a restrictive arrangement. The whole affair amounted to apartheid under a new name—as the United Democratic Front (UDF) pointed out to colored and Indian voters—and the constitution failed to address the central dilemma of politics: African citizenship rights. Launched on 20 August 1983 to combat the new deal, the UDF, a front representing hundreds of locally based opposition groups, campaigned against the elections and was joined by the National Forum (NF)—a black consciousness mouthpiece—and more locally based organizations. Their campaigns as well as more general political apathy and indifference resulted in an 80 percent stay-away from the polls in August 1984.[4] Of all the eligible voters, only 20 percent of coloreds and Indians cast ballots. In cities, where most of the coloreds and Indians live, the polls registered an average of 10 percent ballots cast.

Those who cast ballots were persuaded by the conviction—sold to the electorate by the participating parties and by government spokespersons—that cooptation had its own rewards and that greater resources would be made available to the participants and their supporters. In the Cape, where the majority of coloreds live, most of the ballots were cast by rural folk and those who were part of the patronage system run by the Labour party, the colored party ultimately victorious in the elections. A similar pattern prevailed in Natal, where the majority of Indians live. Of those who voted, the majority were supporters of the Solidarity and the National Peoples parties, two of the Indian parties who campaigned in favor of the new constitution.

One year later, support for the parties participating in the tricameral Parliament remained marginal. Asked during the first quarter of 1986 who they would vote for in an open electoral competition, 11 percent of the colored respondents (in a total sample of 1,731) favored the Labour party. The Solidarity party and National Peoples party received 5.2 percent and 6.7 percent from Indian respondents respectively.[5] Indian and colored sympathies were elsewhere. The Progressive Federal party, a predominantly white liberal party in favor of a peaceful transition to majority rule—with a mechanism of minority rights protection—was favored by coloreds and Indians to the tune of 31 percent and 20.5 percent respectively. Next favored was the UDF with 12 percent and 18.2 percent respectively. The rest of their preferences were for smaller parties. That they are predisposed toward the PFP is interesting and probably reflects the continuing ambivalence of coloreds and Indians toward an outright support for black majority rule. For our purposes here, the point is that there was a large-scale rejection of the tricameral Parliament and of the parties who participate in it. The very people who were to benefit from the new arrangement refused to participate in it and undermined the regime's cooptative goals.

Ethnic Boundaries

The segregation of parliamentary representation by ethnic criteria is just and proper, government spokespersons claim, because whites, coloreds, and Indians are separate and distinct ethnic groups. This is obviously a matter of debate. From an ethnological point of view, there are as many ethnic differences between these groups as there are within them, not to mention ethnic similarities. For example, a majority of coloreds share with Afrikaners a language—Afrikaans. Ethnic differentiation is therefore a political device designed to serve a purpose other than accurate ethnic designation—that is, to legitimate the group rights of whites and their privileged access to the better neighborhoods, schools, and public amenities.

Once arbitrary definitions of ethnic boundaries are nevertheless institutionalized in a body as important as Parliament, they become very real and develop their own dynamic, and competition for state resources becomes an ethnic struggle. The colored and Indian houses want more resources—lots more—and they are agreed that the white house has far too much. For example, the white house has control of much higher per capita spending on (white) pensions and education than do the colored and Indian houses. Because they are compelled to compete against whites as formally constituted ethnic representatives of formally constituted ethnic groups, the boundaries between the groups are more firmly drawn and of greater consequence than was previously the case.

Ethnic competition for state resources means different things for the parties in Parliament. For the colored and Indian parties, a lack of sufficient returns for their participation and collaboration means that their legitimacy, already precarious since they declared their willingness to enter Parliament in 1983, will be further undermined. For purposes of legitimation, they need major concessions from the government in order to improve their standing. They have received minor concessions—for example, the repeal of the so-called sex laws, which barred interracial sex and marriage; but this is an issue that does not affect the balance of power between the competing groups at all. With regard to the more major issues of segregation, such as residential and educational segregation, no concessions have been forthcoming.

The dominant white National party has a different set of political concerns. The extreme right wing of the electorate has grown from a political force commanding 3 percent of the white vote in 1977 to 22 percent in 1982.[6] Much of the increase in right-wing support is due to the fact that white standards of living have declined during the last decade. Too many concessions to coloreds and Indians, and especially concessions on group areas and education, would enhance white support for right-wing parties. The National party, concerned about the growth of right-wing support, would resist granting concessions to coloreds and Indians at the expense of whites. Although competition for resources need not be zero sum, the fact that there is competition between ethnically based parties means that ethnic boundaries are reinforced and reproduced. Thus, instead of taking race and ethnicity out of politics, the tricameral Parliament functions in such a way as to entrench and reproduce ethnic and racial boundaries.

Group Rights

A central distinction made in the constitution and embodied in the functioning of the tricameral Parliament is that of "own affairs" and "general affairs." Own affairs are those matters pertaining to a particular ethnic group's interests—for example, housing, education, social welfare, and so on. General affairs, such as security and foreign policy, are matters of relevance to all ethnic groups. No one ethnic group can ostensibly intervene in the "own affairs" of another group, and therefore, for example, the Indian house has no power over the distribution of pensions funds to whites or coloreds. The same is true for all matters defined as "own affairs."

Two matters are of crucial importance in this regard. One is residential segregation, governed by the Group Areas Act of 1950. Historically, the implementation of this legislation resulted in the dislocation of colored and Indian communities (District Six in Cape Town, where thousands of people were removed to distant colored townships is the most notorious case), shunted out of so-called white areas, and herded into "colored" and "Indian" areas, often at considerable financial loss.[7] Their houses were sold to whites at below-market rates, and many of their businesses were forcibly closed down. The memory of this dispossession is deeply inscribed in the collective consciousness, especially among those who lost their property and businesses. The continuation of group areas under the new system brings no relief to that memory, nor does it provide opportunities for a growth in propertied wealth for those middle-class coloreds and Indians who seek it.

The other issue of central importance is segregated education, which is defined as an "own affair." The individual houses control their respective education systems. Segregated schools, colored and Indian teachers have long argued, are inferior schools. Making up the bulk of the professional middle class, these teachers want a desegregated school system administered by a single department of education and supported by nondiscriminatory state spending. Their schools are overcrowded, lacking in resources, and badly administered. They face continued school boycotts and cannot cope with the situation without some relief. The students are tired of inferior schooling and confront teachers and school principals with demands they can do nothing about. Neither can the colored minister of education and culture, Carter Ebrahim, who, stuck with an "own affair," is incapable of desegregating the education system.[8]

By maintaining a segregated system of education, which the "own affair" system invariably does, the crisis cannot be resolved and is consequently deepened. Indeed, unable to persuade pupils to return to their schools during the boycotts of 1985, the colored minister closed down the schools and threatened to relieve "troublemaking" teachers of their duties. The police in the Western Cape area used harsh, repressive measures to (barely) keep the colored education system going. In a number of significant cases, the police kept guard over those students who decided to write their final exams. If anything is an illustration of the incapacity of government to realize regime objectives, it is this. Unable to obtain the cooperation of high school (and even elementary) students, the government uses force of the most blatant kind to keep a deeply troubled school system going.

Group areas and segregated education retain what is central to apartheid—that group rights preside over individual rights and ethnic boundaries over free association. As a result, colored and Indian support for the tricameral Parliament is marginal and as long as it remains in place will remain marginal. Thus, the central objective of the tricameral Parliament, which is to coopt coloreds and Indians on the side of whites against the African majority, has not succeeded.

The African Majority

Since the founding of the Union of South Africa in 1910, Africans have never had the constitutional right to vote, with the exception of their qualified voting rights in the Cape. From 1910 to 1936, Africans of some wealth and property were allowed to vote in the Cape, although they could not stand as candidates for Parliament. The 1936 Natives Representation Act took that right away and replaced it with the Natives' Representative Council, a body with advisory but no legislative powers. The act also introduced a segregated system of indirect representation where four whites represented all African interests in Parliament.

The National party abolished these. The Natives' Representative Council was abrogated in 1951, a mere formality because it had not been in session since 1946, when its members walked out in the face of government intransigence on the issues raised by the 1946 African mine workers' strike.[9] Indirect African representation went the same way in 1960 when the last of the four white representatives of African interests left Parliament. By the 1960s, therefore, Africans had no participation of any sort in Parliament.

As an alternative, the National party embraced the idea that the African reserves, territories scattered throughout South Africa's countryside and encompassing 13 percent of the land, should be seen and made to be seen as the natural homelands of Africans. Here Africans could exercise their voting rights and enjoy civil liberties denied them in South Africa. They could form self-government and, as the plan unfolded, become independent states. Under a disingenuously progressive concept of self-determination, homelands settled the constitutional place of Africans in the polity.

There were two problems with the concept and practice of homelands. First, South Africa could not do without African labor, and as a consequence, a substantial part of the African population remained outside of the homelands. Second, the homelands were very poor in resources and could not even minimally satisfy the material demands of their citizens. Thus, more and more homelands residents were pushed into major metropolitan areas. By the 1970s, these problems were acute, and the demands of Africans for inclusion in the central Parliament had intensified. As if to rebuff these demands, the new constitution and the tricameral Parliament simply reinforced African exclusion.

Homelands

The concept of homelands for Africans has been a central pillar of apartheid. Essentially, the practice of homelands is a system of divide and rule where Africans are divided into ten or so ethnic groups—Xhosa, Tswana, Sotho, Zulu, Swazi, and so on—and in these designated ethnic terms are allocated citizenship rights to be exercised in their respective homelands. African claims on state resources have had to be processed through the segregated ethnic channels of various homeland governments. This has essentially two implications. First, African claims on entitlements and resources have been institutionally transferred from central government to homeland governments with the result that when Africans have made claims on central government, those claims have been repressed. Second, because the homelands are ethnically segregated, African claims have become institutionally fragmented. Thus, homelands have attempted to serve the two cardinal requirements of divide and rule—fragmentation and displacement of African claims on state entitlements and resources.

The formation of homelands, however, has failed to make adequate constitutional provision for Africans. The poverty of the homelands has propelled Africans to cities; market processes have ensured that many Africans remain in urban-industrial areas, and, despite the application of influx control, the result is that at least half of the African population resides in areas outside the homelands.[10] The idea that homelands could accommodate the greater majority of Africans is pure political fantasy. Which is not to say that successive governments did not attempt to make the reality fit the fantasy. The Surplus Peoples' Project estimates that about 2.5 million Africans have been moved, mostly coerced, from "white" areas—"black spots" as they are called—to the homelands.[11] Indeed, from a social engineering point of view, removals have been quite successful. Charles Simkins, a University of Cape Town demographer, notes that despite urbanization, homeland populations have remained constant and that probably as many people have moved into homelands as have left them. Resettlement and influx control have succeeded in keeping constant the proportion of Africans in urban-industrial areas to about 50 percent of the African population between 1950 and 1970.[12] Population growth within city boundaries as opposed to the larger metropolitan areas has increased, although by how much the population census has been unable to accurately ascertain.

But the reality could never approach the fantasy. African presence in cities meant that African claims and grievances were directed at central government, not at the homeland governments with whom they had little or no affiliation. For example, African worker demands for trade union rights in the 1970s, the education demands of students during the Soweto uprising in 1976, and the more recent demands emanating from the townships were all directed at central government. The processes that made for a permanent and substantial African presence in cities have been powerful countervailing forces to the formation of homelands and, as a consequence, have undermined the goals of divide and rule.

Because the government abolished all forms of African representation in Parliament, there are no institutions available to central government that can process African claims outside of the homeland structures. Sam Nolut-shungu has argued that this is the central structural dilemma of the racial state.[13] He contends that by virtue of the fact that the state has systematically expelled Africans from central institutions of representation, there are no institutions nor concepts by which African claims can be processed orderly outside of homeland governments.[14] The only means available to government in its response to African claims are repressive ones.

Homelands, therefore, have not succeeded in accommodating African claims for constitutional rights. They are, as Stanley Greenberg has argued, implausible solutions to the dilemma of African citizenship.[15] At the time of the new constitution's introduction, the exclusion of Africans was still legitimized on the basis of homelands. But the argument wore thin very quickly. In 1983, the government appointed a committee to investigate the position of urban Africans in nonhomeland South Africa; this was virtually an admission that the issue was problematic. By 1985, government spokespersons refrained from making too much of the homelands and abandoned them as final solutions to the dilemma of African citizenship. In 1986, that abandonment went a step further, as P. W. Botha restored in principle South African citizenship to all Africans.[16] Africans were invited to serve on the central government's National Statutory Council to discuss an agenda by which Africans could participate in national politics.

This is not to say that homelands are to be dismantled. On the contrary. They remain, and one homeland—KwaNdebele—is taking independence, bringing the number of independent homelands to six. But homelands are not conceived as grand ideological solutions to the problem of African citizenship; they now are simply part of an inherited political landscape and have no constitutional importance beyond that. Ideologically, homelands are deemphasized and no longer form a central part of the government's political rhetoric, but they nevertheless continue to follow the political logic of their creation.

Having deemphasized the importance of homelands, the government also seeks to reconstruct the place of homelands in the political economy. Regional development policies, introduced in 1981, include homelands as areas in need of "development." Homelands—independent and dependent—are not excluded from the priorities of the entire country, and the potential exists, as some authors are arguing, for their reintegration into existing or new regional political boundaries of a unitary but federated state.[17] The government stops short of articulating a federal vision, but present regional policies are not incompatible with such an idea. Indeed, federal policies are the only way in which the government can reincorporate homelands without dismantling their political and power structures, which the homeland policies created in the first place.

On the level of national politics, the homelands did not manage to effectively serve regime goals. African claims to citizenship and voting rights persisted outside of homelands, but no place was made for these rights in the tricameral Parliament. As a quid pro quo for their exclusion, Africans were granted voting rights on a local level, but these were the cause of the unending township disorders that have overwhelmed national politics since September 1985.

Township Governance

The Black Local Authorities Act of 1983 augmented the powers of local township councils, which are elective governing bodies introduced for Africans in the late 1970s. One of the three Koornhof bills, the only one to pass into legislation, the act acknowledged in principle that Africans in cities ought to run their own townships with minimum interference from central government.[18] The councils were to collect their own taxes and rents, run the infamous beer halls, and take care of essential services and public amenities. The community councils, as they became known, were central institutions of self-government on a local level.

The councils were introduced in the late 1970s primarily because direct white control of townships was politically too explosive. During the Soweto uprising of 1976 and the subsequent sporadic unrest during the following years, state property and administration buildings were targets of arson, and white officials felt increasingly ill at ease and unsafe in the areas. It would be better, the government argued, to have Africans staff the state administrative apparatus, so as to create some political distance between the African population and the state. In effect, community councils were intended to be a form of indirect rule whereby the white state controlled African townships through African intermediaries.

Thus, African townships received their own town councils, with duly elected African mayors as well. At first, the government attached the towns to homelands—that is to say, African townships could become city-states outside of but politically affiliated with homelands. The idea was not terribly plausible and disappeared soon after it was mooted. What remained was an intention simply to create African community councils with as much local autonomy as possible, much like the colored and Indian management committees introduced in the 1970s and the white municipalities in place since the early twentieth century. If successful, racial self-government would prevail in all South Africa's towns and cities.

To make this scheme work, the government had to find African candidates willing to serve as community councillors; it also had to hold run-off elections with a reasonable voting turnout. During the first round of elections in the early 1980s, government found candidates willing to serve on the councils and a barely willing electorate. A new round of elections, held under the auspices of the Black Local Authorities Act of 1983, reconstituted the councils, with some reelected and new councillors serving. The UDF campaigned against these elections as well as those held for the tricameral Parliament. Pamphleteering and house-to-house campaigns were undertaken by the UDF with the intention of persuading Africans not to participate in institutions of their own oppression.

A combination of political apathy and deliberate absenteeism resulted in an 80 percent stay-away from the polls, 90 percent in Soweto.[19] On average then, 20 percent of the African electorate cast ballots, and on this basis, community councils were constituted under the 1983 act. They were short-lived, however, and became the central targets of African hostility and violence during 1985. Councillors were seen as stooges, sellouts, and collaborators and partly as a result were physically assaulted, killed, or compelled to resign. Of the thirty-eight councils that had maximum autonomy, only two were left by the time the state of emergency was declared in July 1985. Of the total fifty-two community councils, a few were functioning by May 1986. Thus, these institutions of indirect rule were routed from the townships.

With no visible means of governance in townships and faced with a seemingly unending spiral of violence, the state sent in the police to deal with protest and resistance. Despite its evident enthusiasm, the police did not perform very well. In a number of significant cases, the police provoked African riots and then violently repressed them.[20] But police tactics did not restrain the violence and in some instances simply made it worse. In the Transvaal, the army was called in to help, and its units swept through the townships in house-to-house searches. Indemnified by the state of emergency, the army had unfettered powers to search, arrest, and in some cases kill African civilians. Africans came face to face with the unmediated and repressive powers of the state.

Direct control of a hostile African population has its limits. The presence of the army in townships is an indication to Africans not of state power, but of its vulnerability. Army spokespersons feel that army units are incapable of direct rule in all the townships for an extended period of time. In addition to the army's destabilizing duties in Southern Africa, counterinsurgency activities against African National Congress (ANC) guerrillas, and its continued occupation of Namibia, extended township control would drain the army's resources and personnel and contribute to a weakening of the army's capacity to maintain the ultimate security of the white state. The army hierarchy, ironically, has an interest in a political solution to township violence, but the government is incapable of offering any. All of the previous attempts—from homelands to community councils—have not succeeded in their objectives, that is, to introduce lasting institutions of African governance.

Conclusion

One of the many secrets to apartheid's longevity is the regime's ability to control the subordinate majority—African, colored, and Indian—through indirect means. The most recent attempts on the part of the regime to create such indirect collaborative institutions have broken down to the extent that blacks directly confront the repressive organs of the state and maintain a situation of ungovernability and crisis. Can the state forge new institutions of collaboration, or will it have to rely on direct repressive measures to maintain racial rule?

Fresh attempts at creating new collaborative institutions will have to contend with a set of African demands that are more pervasively radical. The maximum demands are for a one-person, one-vote, majority-rule system, the minimum demand for some sort of power sharing. The latter obviously is the material of collaboration. Any lasting form of collaboration would have to, at a minimum, involve power sharing, but this, too, has its special problems.

Power sharing with Africans by way of representative parliamentary institutions raises the question of political arithmetic. There are seven Africans to three whites, coloreds, and Indians combined, and six Africans to every one white. To grant Africans representation in Parliament—even in a separate chamber of Parliament—means that whites will be outnumbered and lose their majority position in Parliament. This holds even if the homeland populations are excluded from parliamentary representation—whites would be outnumbered, more or less, by three to one. From the point of view of white interests, African parliamentary representation is an undesirable—from the right wing's point of view, impossible—choice *unless* Parliament itself is emasculated of all meaningful power. Under the present tricameral constitution, the Parliament's capacity to formulate policy is already much reduced and that of the executive and its supportive institutions—notably the State Security Council (SSC)—much increased.

Thus, African representation in an impotent Parliament and real power sharing on an executive level are formulas by which the National party could grant Africans franchise rights without handing over power to the extraparliamentary opposition and without the automatic desegregation of society. The obvious candidate for an executive power-sharing model is Chief Gatsha Buthelezi, head of the KwaZulu homeland—and if the power-sharing exercise in Natal comes to fruition, there as well—and in charge of the Inkatha political machine.[21] Between Buthelezi, Inkatha, and the National party deals could be made—a little desegregation here, the retention of segregation there, a concession here, none there—and all under the watchful eye of both Buthelezi and Botha—or whoever succeeds him—and, under circumstances where both the left and extreme right are kept under tight control. Although it would be folly to second-guess those energetic state constitutional planners who wish to realize an effective collaboration, power sharing along these lines must rank a firm favorite.

But, like Rhodesia's Muzorewa, power sharing is a vulnerable alternative to majority rule. Both the left and the extreme right would reject it and refuse to participate in its institutions. The left—here we mean the UDF, NF, and the ANC—would be a powerful, if not overwhelming, countervailing force. It would control the townships and be entrenched in the institutions of civil society, constituting a hegemonic political and cultural force capable of overturning the state at its weakest moment in history, when it seeks to share power. The right would threaten civil war, especially if power sharing also meant the sharing of civil service jobs and parity in state spending between white and black. Indeed, a coalition between Buthelezi and Botha might well be a revolutionary invitation to the left and a counterrevolutionary invitation to the right.

Notes

1. South African Institute of Race Relations (SAIRR), *Annual Survey of Race Relations* (Johannesburg: SAIRR, 1985), 99–100.
2. Institute for Black Research (IBR), *Choices of Disenfranchised South Africans 1986* (Durban: IBR, 1986), 9.
3. See SAIRR, *Annual Survey of Race Relations* (Johannesburg: SAIRR, 1983), 81–85.
4. *Cape Times,* 30 August 1984.
5. IBR, *Choices of Disenfranchised,* 9, 11.
6. Craig Charney, "Restructuring White Politics," in South African Review Service (SARS), *South African Review I* (Johannesburg: Ravan Press, 1982), 142.
7. See John Western, *Outcast Cape Town* (Minneapolis: University of Minnesota Press, 1982); and Heribert Adam and Kogila Moodley, *South Africa After Apartheid* (Los Angeles: University of California Press, 1986).
8. *Cape Times,* 6 January 1986.
9. Dan O'Meara, "The 1946 African Mineworkers Strike and the Political Economy of South Africa," *Journal of Commonwealth and Comparative Politics* 13, no. 2 (1976):146–173.
10. Charles Simkins, *The Past, Present and Future Distribution of the Black Population of South Africa* (Cape Town: Southern African Labour and Development Research Unit, 1984).
11. Laureen Platzky and Cheryl Walker, eds., *Surplus Peoples Project,* 5 vols. (Cape Town: SPP, 1984); see abridged version, Laureen Platzky and Cheryl Walker, eds., *The Surplus People: Forced Removals in South Africa* (Johannesburg: Ravan Press, 1985).
12. Simkins, *The Past, Present and Future Distribution,* 120.
13. Sam Nolutshungu, *Changing South Africa: Political Considerations* (Man-

chester: Manchester University Press, 1983), 6–20.

14. Ibid., 102–110.

15. Stanley Greenberg, *Race and State in Capitalist Development: Comparative Perspectives* (New Haven, Conn.: Yale University Press, 1980).

16. *Financial Mail,* 26 April 1986.

17. William Cobbett et al., "Regionalism, Federalism, and the Reconstitution of the South African State," *South African Labour Bulletin* 10, no. 5 (April 1985):87–116.

18. Heather Hughes and Jeremy Grest, "The Local State," in SARS, *South African Review I,* 122–124.

19. Graham Howe, "Cycles of Civil Unrest 1976/84," *Indicator 3* (Winter 1985).

20. Parliamentary opposition members often accuse the police of provoking township violence by maintaining a provocative presence there. See D. Kannemeyer, *Commission Appointed to Inquire into the Incident Which Occurred on 21st March 1985 at Uitenhage* (Pretoria: Government Printers, RP74/1985).

21. Inkatha is a Zulu ethnic organization with a claimed membership of more than one million.

STANLEY B. GREENBERG

Resistance and Hegemony in South Africa

The racial state is by definition partial to whites. Historically, it has inter-vened in capital, property, and labor markets in favor of whites and against the interests of blacks. Thus, blacks do not accept the state as theirs, not only because they lack participatory rights but also because the state prevents blacks from pursuing valued private goals, including the accumulation of wealth. Stanley B. Greenberg puzzles over the recent attempt of the state to get out of the market and the private lives of Africans. The state, he writes, celebrates the "death of apartheid," but Africans bury each other. Home-lands are no longer solutions, declares the South African Broadcasting Cor-poration (SABC), but another homeland takes independence. The state em-braces free enterprise, but blacks are still not allowed to freely buy property or make money. The state lauds new township governments, but Africans find their jurisdiction and power too circumscribed. In other words, the at-tempt to deconstruct apartheid and reconstruct a new racial order is a disin-genuous and desperate ideological attempt to legitimate the illegitimate, to get Africans to freely consent to universal values without putting in place institutions with universal legitimacy. The state remains trapped in institu-tions partial to white interests. It cannot successfully undo itself. But the at-tempt to do so makes possible more black resistance and protest, the undo-ing of apartheid.

W. G. J.

From Boycott to State of Emergency:
South Africa in the Mid-1980s

South Africa has never previously experienced so extended and violent an expression of the disaffection festering in its African townships as it has in the mid-1980s. In the eighteen months preceding the state of emergency, scattered student boycotts became more general and gave way to protests and marches by adults, to stone throwing and blockades, to bus boycotts and general strikes. Local officials and the police, white and black, could not contain the unrest; army units also were deployed and moved from township to township, but they, too, failed to bring quiet. The state of emergency announced in July 1985 was an expression of state power, but also of state impotence and vulnerability. The state confronted, and could barely quell, the gathering chorus of African voices that rejected the schools, the new township governments and administration boards, the new constitutional order, white officials and police, and, above all, local and national African collaborators.

The unrest began in early 1984 in Atteridgeville, a township near Pretoria, where African students stubbornly resisted government efforts to cajole and coerce them to return to class. Their example spread to other townships where school boycotts and disparate demands seemed now a growing and endemic feature of township life, a persistent gnawing at state authority. When the new African town councils in the Vaal triangle, southeast of Johannesburg, sought to raise rents, township resistance escalated to a new level of intensity and articulation. In September 1984, residents attacked and burned the rent and administration board offices in Sebokeng and destroyed public buildings, shops, and banks in the other Vaal triangle townships, including Sharpeville, Bophelong, Bolpatong, and Evaton. The unrest quickly engulfed the African councillors who had joined the government's latest attempt to establish legitimate authority in the African areas. Three councillors, including two deputy mayors, were killed, and the mayors were forced to flee the townships, their burned-out houses behind them. These attacks quickly spread to the Witwatersrand, where protestors bombed the mayors' homes in Soweto, Dobsonville, Katlehong, Leandra, and Vosloorus. At the end of October, the government set in motion Operation Palmiet, a combined army and police operation to encircle and penetrate Sebokeng. The minister of law and order declared that the army intended to quell the unrest and "to show that the state can be in authority of the situation, that it has the machinery to be in command of a particular situation."

The direct military intervention further politicized and influenced the African resistance. A coalition of African organizations, including the major African trade union federations, called for a two-day general strike; they demanded, among other things, an end to the army and police presence in the townships, the release of detainees, the resignation of town councillors, and the freezing of rents. By various estimates, the strikes were extraordinarily successful, producing a 50 to 66 percent stay-away in Soweto, a yet higher figure in the East Rand, and an 85 to 90 percent participation rate in the Vaal triangle. The school boycotts gained new impetus with the strikes, rising to 400,000 participants in November. In response, the government detained the strike organizers as well as the heads of the Federation of South Africa Trade Unions and the Council of Unions of South Africa.

By new year 1985, the resistance had spread with a vengeance to townships across the country, particularly to the eastern Cape. There, the strikes spread even to small towns like Cradock, where students carried on year-long boycotts of the schools and where residents boycotted the official institutions of black administration. Near the larger cities, protests, police and military action, massive funerals, and further military involvement seemed to offer the prospect of only escalating violence. In March 1985, at Langa township near Uitenhage, the police, on the twenty-fifth anniversary of the 1960 Sharpeville massacre, killed nineteen Africans, which produced a wave of rage and disorder. In April alone, there were more than fifteen hundred "reported incidents of unrest" across the country, more than half in the eastern Cape. In Duduza township near Johannesburg, protests brought the schools to a standstill, the abandonment of the town council, and the expulsion of the black police.

When the government declared the state of emergency on 13 July 1985, officials formally acknowledged the scope of the black resistance. There were three hundred fifty thousand African township residents in the Vaal triangle who had not paid rent since the September unrest; 155 townships had ultimately been caught up in the spreading unrest, and at least three hundred homes of town councillors and African policemen were damaged by protest actions; 12 town councillors were killed, and 240 town councillors had resigned their positions; an unknown number of black police had to be housed in white areas. Between two hundred fifty thousand and six hundred fifty thousand students were boycotting classes at any given time during the previous year. Three thousand Africans were arrested before the state of emergency and at least eight thousand during it, while the principal leaders of the umbrella-type protest organizations were put on trial for treason; during the course of the unrest (at the time of this writing), more than sixteen hundred Africans had been killed.[1]

Although the state of emergency was formally ended on 7 March 1986, there was little evidence that the government had regained control of the townships. The daily death toll continued to rise through 1986 as new waves of protest and violence enveloped Alexandra township where town councillors resigned under community pressure and Crossroads where collaborative and younger elements fought for control. The government was forced to reimpose military "control" and seek new powers of detention without trial. On May Day 1986, the independent trade unions and protest organizations declared a general strike, joined by 1.5 million workers, that effectively stopped work in the eastern Cape, Natal, the Witwatersrand, and even in the gold mines.

Urban Disorder and the Legitimacy Problem

The present wave of unrest underscores three aspects of the legitimacy problem in South Africa. First, the state stands visibly dominant over society and markets; it stands, consequently, unmediated before a disaffected African citizenry. Second, for all its resources and military strength, the state faces severe, perhaps growing, limits on its capacity to realize regime goals in the whole area of urban black administration and governance. Third, growing dependence by the state on coercive methods and direct rule, the state's continuing loss of control of African townships, and African domination of the political agenda have caused white leaders to become even more preoccupied with fashioning some kind of legitimacy.

Urban Africans—those with established "rights" of residence and work, the supposed "privileged" strata in the government-fashioned labor market, and the object of any proposed legitimacy project—have through their actions in this period exposed the fragility of state institutions and reforms. The Black Local Authorities Act of 1983 was after all a centerpiece in the reform initiative. On the one hand, it showed urban Africans (as opposed to those in the Bantustans) that there was a participatory role for them at the local level, a quid pro quo for colored and Indian incorporation into the national institutions; on the other hand, it offered the prospect that the administration boards, as instruments of the central state, would become local "development" boards, and housing, tax and fee collections, and influx control would be managed by Africans themselves.

In the mid-1980s, urban Africans scorned that initiative and overture, leaving the state without any alternative to the police and army cordons and the white-run administration boards. Just as coloreds and Indians largely boycotted the August 1984 elections for the subordinate colored and Indian parliamentary chambers (more than 80 percent failed to cast ballots), urban Africans turned away from the state's effort to shift attention to local African institutions. Almost 80 percent of township residents nationally and 90 percent of those in Soweto declined to participate. The assassination and resignation of town councillors have left the fledgling system of local governance and collaboration in shambles. Although thirty-eight town councils had been granted maximum "autonomy," only two or three were still functioning when the state of emergency was declared in 1985. In many areas, government officials acknowledge, the African local authorities have become "disestablished" and their functions transferred back by necessity to the white officialdom (Advisor, Constitutional Development).[2]

This halting attempt to devolve administration to local African collaborators has furthered the breakdown of state administration in African areas. Local African officialdom has proved completely ineffectual in controlling squatting and illegal lodging. African areas are kept "fairly clean" only when the "whites are still controlling it" (DL: West Rand). The collection of rents and fees, critical to the financing of local governance, has broken down. In the hostels, where white officials retain control, relatively orderly administration remains, but elsewhere, rent payments have fallen seriously into arrears, and the local accounts have shown growing deficits (AB: West Rand). One official, never particularly sympathetic to local African participation, states boldly that "the white's African allies can't cope. . . . You can't squeeze the tomato before it is ripe" (DL: Central Transvaal).

African local officials, most likely with white official connivance, are visibly corrupt. The African councils have allocated housing and sites to Africans who would cooperate with the new administration, particularly those in the employ of the councils. Bribes and special preferences for friends have replaced the "bureaucratic queuing principles" that historically governed housing allocation (AB: East Rand; West Rand). When a government commission finally investigated the precipitating violence in the Vaal triangle, it, too, could not avoid the spreading corruption and incompetence. African councillors, the report found, had divided the lucrative liquor outlets among themselves; they handled rent increases "overhastily, unwisely, clumsily and insensitively."[3]

Government initiatives, like the establishment of African local authorities and the policy for "orderly urbanization," are increasingly subject to the limits imposed by a politicized African majority. Unrelenting unrest has made officials, who traditionally are confident about their control of events, "very, very, very sensitive to taking any action that could make things worse." It is no longer possible, if squatter communities grow up, "to send in 20 trucks and move the people. This is a sensitive time" (DL: West Rand). On the East Rand, Africans always moved closer to industry by squatting on nearby farms. "In the past, we picked them up and forced them back to the homeland," one official observes, but now, that option is not readily available. The people "have risen up and forced the government to reorient the policy" (AB: East Rand; also Deputy Secretary, Constitutional Development). In Cape Town, "the sheer reality of the situation," the massive uncontrolled influx of Africans, has brought control efforts to a standstill. "The concept illegal has no meaning any more." The forces compelling the government to action no longer originate within the state.

The breakdown of state control of the townships and the resort to repressive methods have occasioned a renewed determination to find some formula that will satisfy urban Africans and that will support collaboration on a broader scale. Few officials or business leaders now seem willing to live with the military presence or direct administration of the African areas as a long-term solution.

Officials, even those most wedded to the traditional order, have come to recognize the deligitimating consequences of direct state administration of the African majority. The administration boards were responsible for development but also, on an agency basis, for influx control, urbanization, resettlement, and uncontrolled squatting. Because of that contradiction, the administration boards "got a little smell. . . . We are most unpopular with some groups" (DL: Central Transvaal). Other officials are less qualified about the "smell": "The boards must go. They are an abortion. They have been the oppressor, seen to be executing repressive laws while, at the same time, trying to develop the community" (AB: Western Cape). Upper level officials recognize that the state must "go soft," that the "control thing" must become "much less visible" (Advisor, Constitutional Development).

The business community has reacted to the growing African unrest by seeking first to limit direct state controls of Africans, and, second, by assuring Africans that they have a guaranteed future within a unitary South Africa. After the military intervention in the Vaal triangle and the successful general strike in November 1984, the major business associations issued a joint appeal to the government warning that state action endangered peaceful relations between employers and workers in the private realm.

The business community, rather than confronting the government on issue after issue, has sought to reinforce trends evident within the state, particularly on urbanization and citizenship. Various associations, including the Urban Foundation and the Federated Chamber of Industries (FCI), as well as major industrial groups have applauded government "rethinking" about the value and permanence of urbanization.[4] They have called on the government to develop, relax, soften, or abolish the pass laws, to allow informal squatter areas to develop, to abolish development boards, and to incorporate blacks into nonracial local and regional bodies.[5] They urged the President's Council to resist pressures from "some quarters" to use the unrest to justify "a security clampdown and the repatriation of unemployed workers to rural areas."[6]

More broadly, business has sought, in response to the disorder, an affirmation of the unity and the broad identity of the state. At the most basic level, business leaders have called on the government for a clear, reassuring statement on citizenship. "It needs to be spelt out," the *Financial Mail* declared, "that government accepts the principle of equal citizenship for all South Africans in the borders of the old Union of South Africa."[7] The Association of

Chambers of Commerce (Assocom) has posed even more fundamental questions. What common principles or norms will allow blacks and whites to develop mutual loyalties within a common state? Assocom has offered an "agenda for negotiation" that centers on the elimination of racism and the fostering of principles such as personal freedom, freedom of property, and personal culpability; the organization also has argued for the creation of a federal-state structure.[8]

The business community has looked to the government for a dramatic initiative, one that would convince the outside world and the African majority that developments were heading assuredly toward a solution based on universal principles. The international debt crisis, in particular, created a special urgency, for it "brought home the total interrelationship of politics and economics" (Prominent Business Association). However, the state president, faced with the crisis and even after a high-level meeting with the U.S. secretary of state, failed to offer such dramatic gestures. After the Rubicon speech (in which Botha declared that the government was willing to share power with blacks), a major business leader recalls, "that night I got totally drunk, because I knew exactly what would happen . . . a total disaster" (Prominent Business Association). Within the association, member firms began demanding some government initiative to resolve the crisis.

At the outset of 1986, the FCI called upon the government to bring order and to set a clear course: "There is at present more discontent inside the country, not to mention internationally, than ever before in our history." The government requires a "realistic and visible programme" to restore "credibility and confidence."[9]

The state president suggested before the new tricameral Parliament that established principles defining the position of Africans be reexamined. In particular, he suggested that the citizenship question needed to be investigated further and that urban African communities might achieve some form of constitutional status in the future.[10] With the townships in flames and town councillors on the run, it was a modest statement but a suggestion nonetheless that the government would need to explore other ways of calming and incorporating the African working class communities.

As the violence escalated, so did the rhetoric of the government affirming the need to come to terms with the settled Africans. Indeed, the minister for constitutional development affirmed that incorporation of Africans into the constitutional system was the "highest political priority."[11] The South African Broadcasting Corporation (SABC)—the mouthpiece for official policy—adopted this rearranged priority for the new year 1985 and promoted it incessantly as the disorders spread. SABC editorial broadcasts looked back on the turmoil of 1984 and observed that "it has been the year in which the question of achieving full rights for Blacks living in the urban areas has moved to the top of the political agenda, where it is clearly going to remain for some time to come."[12] The government, it declared, "will be required to move purposely on the position of Blacks outside the national states, the most intractable and urgent political problem with which the country is faced."[13]

Specifically, the SABC stated that urban blacks are "permanent inhabitants of this country" and that they would have to be accommodated outside the Bantustans and as part of some national political institutions: "Clearly, constitutional structures over and above those provided by the national states [Bantustans] had to be devised to give appropriate expression to the principle of community security and self determination."[14] When the government reiterated its willingness to negotiate the citizenship question, the SABC was moved to a bold declaration on a unified national identity.

> [The] incongruity of the approach has become intolerable. It is simply not possible to justify, logically or humanely, a policy that would strip of his citizenship a person who has always lived in this country and always will live here, as will his children and their children. To do so at all is merely a legal fiction, one that is so much at odds with economic and social realities that it can never find expression in a workable constitutional system.[15]

The state president at the outset of 1986 sought to dramatize the government's commitment to a new and decisive direction. In addition to reaffirming specific policy initiatives such as a "single citizenship," freehold property rights, and the eventual end to influx control, the state president sought to identify the state with universal principles. A government advertisement, published in newspapers across South Africa, declared:

> We are committed to equal opportunity for all. Equal treatment. And equal justice. . . .
> I said that no South African will be excluded from full political rights. That they should participate both in Government and the future of this country through their elected leaders. This is now reality.

The advertisement concluded with an appeal from the state president: "From my heart I ask you to share in the future. To share in the new South Africa."[16] Later, a government commission investigating the 1984 unrest at Sebokeng and elsewhere in the Vaal triangle would discover (what most others took for granted) that "perhaps we have alienated more of these people than we realize." The state president, in this new mood of understanding, took his case directly to Africans via state TV channels reserved for an African audience: "Nobody should underestimate the Government's sincere determination to succeed with negotiation to find peaceful solutions to South Africa's problems."[17]

There is an incongruity to the present period in South Africa. On the one hand, repression on a large scale and the defense of archaic racial structures continues unabated. On the other hand, the dissolution of racial structures, including the whole system of township administration, and calls for unity and incorporation escalate. But just such incongruities inform this analysis. Attempts to manage the emergent African working class and urban population have produced perplexing results that challenge the order of control. In the process, the state has been drawn both to coercive methods and, paradoxically, and perhaps necessarily, to methods that seek to broaden support for the political and economic orders.

The Quest for a Legitimacy Formula

State efforts to broaden support for government policy have centered on the interpenetration of state and markets in South Africa.[18] Officials have tried to articulate the relationship between race and developing capitalist relations and how that relationship has come to compromise both the state and the economy. Government strategy has been to give greater scope to the private realm through deregulation in selected areas and through a greater ideological deference to markets and entrepreneurs. Government leaders have sought to depoliticize society and diminish the potential for conflict by substituting technocratic and process issues for grand theories and societal goals and by fragmenting and localizing political functions and authority. They have sought to reduce the burdens and exposure of state institutions by limiting their direct coercive role and by delegating control functions to private actors and cooperative local blacks. Thus, these strategies have laid the groundwork for a fragmented order in which broader participation, even "one person, one vote," might be possible without compromising the white's ultimate control of the economy and polity.

"Apartheid Is Dead"

The South African government has gone to great lengths, particularly in the present period, to pronounce the "death" of apartheid. That project is no doubt important for the white electorate, as it reduces the likelihood that voters will turn to even more right-wing political parties (such as the Conservatives or the Herstigte Nasionale Party) proposing a return to traditional racial practice. Proclaiming apartheid's demise aids South Africa as it seeks to avoid isolation and to align itself with the West. But the burial of apartheid is also a principal ideological precondition for any legitimating project in the African community. First, it removes the shroud of illegitimacy hanging over the South African state and broadens the regime's social base and capacity for collaboration. Second, by removing grand social designs such as apartheid from the political discourse, the questions that need to be settled by politics diminish. Finally, and most importantly, apartheid's death removes from ideological debates the specific form of racial domination that encouraged a superordinate role for the state.

During 1985, as the turmoil spread across South Africa, the state radio proceeded to pull apart and deny the basic elements of the apartheid ideological structure. The government declared in each case that the traditional tenet was obsolete, inconsistent with the facts, unjust. Even the Bantustans, the cement that gave a sense of totality and moral purpose to the old order, were denied and relegated to a narrow instrumental role. The state now proclaimed, in effect, the death of an ideological construction that affirmed the historic entanglement of state and markets.

First, the government declared that state efforts to bar the development of a permanent, vital African urban community were a failure. In a tone reminiscent of my earlier narrative, the SABC underlined the inefficacy and contradictory aspects of state policy.

> The traditional influx control system is ineffective. Despite being enforced by a large bureaucratic machinery and tens of thousands of prosecutions annually, it has made no discernible difference to the rate of urbanisation of the black people—a rate dictated on the one hand by the need to earn a livelihood and on the other by the need for labour in a growing economy. . . .
>
> [The] effects [of influx control] have been negative in virtually all aspects. It is no exaggeration to say that trying to make the system effective by applying it even more rigorously could be done only by courting disaster: ruthless repression, economic depression, mass famine in the rural areas and unmanageable social unrest.

The SABC pointed to Crossroads and other such uncontrolled urban settlements and concluded, "Clearly the policy of influx control has failed."[19]

The other side of failed controls on urbanization is a failed policy of "homeland development." Originally, the Bantustans were intended "to accommodate virtually all the original members of their nations" and make possible the partition of South Africa. But, according to the SABC, "that expectation was false." The Bantustans could provide "work and living space" for no more "than a fraction of the Black peoples in the national states," thus rendering "the original partition aims obsolete." The attempt to affect a "mass physical separation of the peoples . . . became futile, and increasingly destructive of economic growth, social stability and viable political solutions."[20] Consequently, the public would have to face up to a "major sociopolitical reality"—"the growth of urban Black communities" and the citizenship claims of Africans within a new constitutional system.[21]

There was little room now for "essentially exclusive" holidays, like Republic Day. Black and white peoples would have to come to terms with the broader foundations of the reconstructed South African state.

> The fact had to be faced: the Republic was for all its peoples. However, if the demand for group self-determination was to be met, it had to be done

in a system that would simultaneously reflect the interdependence of the communities. What was clearly needed was an accommodation of the diversity in a common loyalty to the Republic.[22]

The SABC has not sought to replace apartheid with some new grand construction; its strategy instead is to lower the expectation for grand and coherent ideological formulas so that all groups can focus on narrower principles that would not require remaking the state and society. The SABC took note of the "pervading confusion—cross-purposes over goals, motives and methods . . . the lack of clarity about the essentials," as the apartheid formula lost its hold on public thinking. The public discourse is cluttered by "dogmas and sacred cows in our politics—among White, Brown and Black" that have been "elevated to the status of basic principles." The "accretion" of these dogmas has sown conflict and confusion that now may only be dispelled by discarding outdated principles and lowering expectations. The need for coherence and order can be satisfied, the SABC suggested, by affirming two simple and generally accepted principles: "group identity and interdependence."[23]

In affirming apartheid's death, the SABC moved to depoliticize ethnicity, a first principle in apartheid ideology that had set the stage for political conflict on a grand scale. The main committee report of the Human Sciences Research Council (HSRC) in 1985, drawing on a broad spectrum of state and academic opinion and calling upon "scientific principles," declared that ethnic groups are "not valid legal entities." Apartheid policies since 1948 had politicized ethnicity and thus politicized society. "Political ordering became an end in itself." It gave rise, consequently, to a "legitimacy crisis involving the whole socio-political system." Now, South Africa would move away from "apartheid measures . . . that legally entrench certain rights and privileges for selected groups at the expense of others."[24]

The SABC and the Human Sciences Research Council, in affirming apartheid's death, have made no effort to substitute some new set of ideas that would order state and society. They simply have negated the traditional construction that was exclusive, obtrusive, and politicizing.

Denationalizing Political Struggles

The government, led by the Ministry of Constitutional Development, has sought to break the unmediated encounter between the national state and the African citizenry. To untangle the combatants, the government has devolved its functions and politics to lower levels where conflict is more diffuse and manageable and reinforced the diffusion of power through regionalization, which gives greater latitude to market, rather than political and coercive, processes. This two-pronged reconstruction, if successful, will remove the national state as a primary site of struggle, create a complex of institutions through which political demands are mediated, and reduce state reliance on coercive methods.

African local authorities, the new town and village councils, were the first piece in this strategy—Africans were to gain extended powers to regulate local affairs. But, as we saw earlier, the African communities boycotted the local elections and then drove out those few leaders who chose to participate.[25] Despite the fact that local government existed, in many cases, in name only, the central government remained insistent that African politics be localized. The state president, even as he looked back on ten months of untiring turmoil in the townships, rejected any national solution and pointed stubbornly to the local option: "I believe that the basis for democracy is local government. Without proper local government no democracy can really exist. What we are now doing is to bring about local authorities for black communities in the urban areas." He was no doubt heeding the warning uttered by the SABC at the end of 1984: "The alternative is constant and intolerable competition among groups for power at the centre of the system."[26]

Of more importance than the local authorities, given recent events, are the regional structures now being formed to accommodate African participation in labor markets and state administration. Here, the government has sought to give greater play to economic processes, reduce the visible central state presence, and allow multiracial forums to emerge in technical areas.

The eight development regions (established in 1981 and 1982) cut across the rigidities of Bantustan boundaries and seek to define economic regions that integrate white metropolitan, township, commuter, and Bantustan areas. Unlike past decentralization programs that depended on strict political locational criteria, sanctions against urban employers (Physical Planning Act), and strict application of influx controls, this program claims to rely more on markets and incentives. The government still seeks to manage the emerging African working class but within economic regions and by employing policies that minimize evident coercion.[27]

By working with "natural" regions, employing fewer development points, and offering strong economic incentives, the government hopes that industry will be encouraged on economic grounds to disperse toward the Bantustans. The incentives in high priority areas, such as the Eastern Cape/ Ciskei area, are quite staggering: cash payments of R 110 per worker for seven years; 60 percent rail rebates; 50 percent discounts on harbor charges; training grants, relocation allowances, and subsidies for overhead costs (electricity, rent, and housing). Although the program is costly, there is some evidence that these escalating incentives have produced some job creation near the Bantustans where earlier efforts failed. With administration boards dispersing their new housing units to commuter areas and to more distant townships, like Khayelitsha in the Cape flats (Development Region A) and

Bronkhorstspruit in KwaNdebele (Development Region H), "natural" forces constraining the development of African urban concentration are created.[28]

These regions have recently taken on political importance because proposed regional service councils and new regional administrators will now replace the provinces as the second tier of government. It is at this level that the national government has held out the prospect of multiracial participation, and as P. W. Botha affirmed, "From there we will move into the future."[29] But it is also at this level that the government has sought to swallow up and depoliticize social conflict. The regional service councils encompass all local authorities within particular regions—white local authorities, African town and village councils, Indian and colored management committees, and so on—and are responsible for basic local functions: water, electricity, roads, refuse, fire, and health services. But the councils' emphasis is on functional administration under white control, not on politics, multiracial or otherwise. (The inclusion of African local authorities in the Regional Services Councils was belated in any case, necessitated by the urban disorders of 1984 and 1985 that led to the collapse of the third tier of government in African areas.) Representation on the councils is based on each authority's financial contributions, thus ensuring that white local authorities are fully dominant. Decisions require a two-thirds majority, which blocks any future coalitions that might impose on the white towns. The structure of decisionmaking moves the councils, therefore, either toward white dominance or toward consensus (presumably nonconflictual) decisionmaking. The administrator for the region is not elected by or responsible to the council, as he is appointed by the central government. The appointed administrators have wide-ranging powers—they are able to act where the council fails to and are able to appoint representatives when local authorities are uncooperative or moribund.[30]

The regional councils represent a form of local participation and devolution of functions and, therefore, serve to broaden the racial character of governmental institutions and localize participation. At the same time, they fragment and localize African politics, encourage consensual modes of behavior, and maintain white dominance; they provide renewed scope for central state authority, even as they divert attention from the national polity.[31]

Of course, the viability of such institutions and depoliticization depends on the willingness of Africans to create town councils or accept appointment to the councils. The history of recent unrest is not altogether auspicious for such collaboration. Indeed, even some businessmen who otherwise support federal solutions have become skeptical about such institutional shuffling and devolution. What is "worrisome," one association leader points out, "is the credibility of the regional service councils in black eyes." As long as government at "central level" is illegitimate, it cannot easily persuade the African majority of the value of "devolution" (Prominent Business Association).

Consociational Elements

White South Africa's public discourse since the late 1970s has been laden with an obscurantist preoccupation with "consociational democratic" theorizing. That discourse has had little bearing on the African majority, as they, for the most part, have been left out of the process. The first report of the Constitutional Committee of the President's Council pointedly denied that consociational arrangements could include Africans: "An all embracing consociational system would lead to Black domination," given vast "cultural differences, relative numbers, conflicting interests and divergent political objectives."[32] Little wonder, then, that urban Africans responded to elections for the new tricameral legislature, from which they were excluded, by destroying the separate and localized political arrangements provided for them.

Still, the new constitution forms part of a process incorporating consociational elements and aimed at narrowing the scope for politics. In the new constitution, there are mechanisms that depend on either consensual or technocratic processes (leaving, of course, the ultimate decisionmaking power with the white state president). Joint standing committees bring representatives of the three chambers together, and these, according to the SABC, "are the major instruments for conducting consensus politics." Where the chambers cannot reach consensus, the state president may refer matters to the President's Council. Here, appointed members "of the highest standing," "political, social and economic experts," act as the "arbiter of last resort."[33] Almost from the outset of the constitutional process, the President's Council has been conceived as a technocratic appendage to the government and state president that would bring expert, nonpolitical considerations to bear on the legislative process. In the Schlebusch Commission (1979), the President's Council was defined as sixty "nationally acknowledged experts," and, later, the new council would itself reproduce these criteria: "The President's Council requires people with political skills, a capacity for dispassionate judgement, and specialized forms of knowledge." Its reports and recommendations are laden with academic/expert detours and citations, leaving the impression that public choices are circumscribed or dictated by scientific necessity.[34]

The recommendation for African representation emerged from the President's Council as a residual necessity, realized through the Bantustans and "partition," an advisory black council, and local government. None of those elements, whatever their expert foundations, has survived the recent political process, although the state president now speaks of a potential forum, the Statutory Council, for future discussion. The regional councils, however, bound by a two-thirds decision rule and broad participation, are supposed to bring consensual decisionmaking and a narrowed political discourse to Africans at a local level.

Reconstructing Civil Society: The African Labor Unions

The Wiehahn Commission in 1979 recommended that African workers be permitted to join legally constituted and recognized trade unions. The report and the government white paper noted that orderly labor relations in the republic were threatened by independent African organizations that failed to conform to rules prevailing within the established industrial labor framework and that threatened to take up issues outside the scope of conventional trade union practice. With a backdrop of general strikes in 1973 and 1974 and spreading work stoppages before the Soweto unrest in 1976, the commission chose to recommend legal incorporation.[35]

The government sought to circumscribe these incipient African organizations—to limit their membership to the urbanized section of the working population (excluding migrants), to force them to mirror South Africa's social segregation (barring multiracial unions), to limit their political involvement (barring party political activity), to force them to register and submit their finances and membership lists to state scrutiny, and finally, to foster compliant parallel unions organized by established white and colored unions. The African unions were to be institutionalized within industrial councils posing economic issues within the long-standing industrial conciliation machinery. The unions would not be permitted to emerge as diffuse organizations with ambitious social programs prepared to make the connection between African society and the political order. Little wonder, then, that critics described the labor reforms as a tool to wrest control from the independent unions.[36]

But African workers, sometimes supported by employers, remade the labor environment despite government intentions. The unions organized migrants and workers across the race lines, blocked the growth of compliant parallel unions, declined to be incorporated into the industrial conciliation machinery, and established a varied political program that has periodically brought them into the political fray. In the seven year period from 1979 to 1986, the African labor movement grew from fifty thousand to more than seven hundred fifty thousand members and spread even to the gold mines and government sector. Strike activity jumped from less than twenty thousand African worker days lost at the time of Wiehahn to three hundred thousand in 1982 and nearly 1 million in 1983, four times the scale of strike activity registered during the 1973 Durban general strikes.[37]

Some unions, particularly those in the eastern and western Cape, articulated political goals. But on a larger scale, the major African federations encompassing the great majority of organized African workers campaigned in support of the boycott of the tricameral parliamentary elections and, later, called a successful two-day general strike in response to the military occupation of Sebokeng. With the founding of the Confederation of South African Trade Unions (COSATU), with nearly a half million affiliated members, the independent unions gained new strength and political capacity. The confederation issued an ultimatum to the government demanding an end to passes within six months, and later it was instrumental in the massive May Day strike of 1986.

The government sought to create an institutional framework in society that would contain, absorb, and channel the emergent African unions. That goal seems on its face to have been unrealized, as African unions proved expansive in membership and goals and, indeed, forged potential avenues to the political realm.

Nevertheless, in this period of union growth and political instability, political institutions and coercive machinery have to some extent pulled back from their direct and visible role in the workplace. The political leadership has been sorely tempted, of course, and it is possible to point to important instances of political interference: arrests of union activists under the Intimidation and Trespassing acts, the "endorsing out" of striking migrant workers and their shipment back to the Bantustans, the detention of union leaders, including the heads of the principal federations, and the attempts, together with Ciskei collaborative officials, to smash the largest general workers union (the South African Allied Workers Union). Yet, at the same time, the Industrial Court and the Department of Manpower Utilization have helped carve out a legal space where African unions have been able to organize and achieve immense collective bargaining advances. The African unions increasingly have taken advantage of litigation and appeals to the Industrial Court, and some were joining industrial councils such as the Metal and Allied Workers, which joined the powerful national industrial council for the iron and steel industry.[38] In the same period, the security agencies drastically cut back on the detention of union leaders (fifty-one in 1984, 4 percent of all detentions) and seemed in 1983, as a matter of policy, to pull back from the scene of work stoppages, despite the spread of strike activity.[39]

State efforts to reconstruct South Africa's labor institutions yielded contradictory and uncertain results for the disentanglement of state and society. Areas of industrial "self-governance" have emerged where officials have placed restraints on the coercive machinery. Employers believe that, through the private realm of industrial relations, they have established their independence from the state. The bargaining process has gained "integrity," meaning autonomy from politics. Although the HSRC investigation applauded the changes in the labor field, it called for greater autonomy, so that the employer might emerge more credible and the state more removed: "[The] Government continues to feature too large as a party in the conflict. As long as labour conflict is not totally privatized, as is the case in the USA, the Government will too often be seen as interfering in favour of the employer."[40]

Yet at the same time, the African unions have emerged as an expansive force in civil society, absorbing broad strata of the African workers and threatening to politicize the workplace. Even employers worry that, in the absence of political outlets at the national level, the unions and workplace will become the terrain for politics.

The Politicization of South Africa

Leaders of the South African state, witnessing the rising costs of apartheid, the growing contradictions in state practice, and the increasing evidence of African disaffection and resistance, have devoted enormous energy and invention to legitimating this social order. They have tried to forge a private realm where new sources of wealth and public values could operate. Business enterprise and market principles have gained new prestige. Indeed, the government has deregulated in a range of areas, from monetary controls and job color bars to personal intimacy.[41] They have tried to create "free" spaces where market principles and private exchanges could be determinate as in the case of "urban insiders" seeking work, employers seeking to locate their factories, African trade unions seeking to bargain, and the African family trying to find a home.

At the same time, South Africa's leaders have moved systematically to narrow the perceived scope of state intrusions on civil society. They have tried to devolve state regulation to lower tiers of government, to private employers, to black institutions, and to collaborative elites. In a more fundamental way, they have tried to deny politics by repudiating broad principles of governance, including apartheid, narrowing the scope for public choice, and resorting to technocratic rationales and consensual decision rules.

But paralleling the legitimation project that seeks to divert African eyes (and ours) downward to civil society are other projects and processes that are further politicizing South Africa, that further entangle rather than separate the worlds of politics and economics. In North America and Europe, the market as an institution and a set of rules and values emerged haltingly during the centuries and only unevenly wedded working populations to the capitalist economic orders. But in South Africa, there is little evidence, despite attempts to reconstruct the state and its dominant ideology, that the market will be allowed to emerge through the heavy pall of politics.

The reconstruction process, although sometimes relinquishing conventional repressive practices, has offered new state contrivances that reassert the legal-political definition of groups in society and that seek to regulate the movements of an emergent working class. The new constitution, for example, entrenches racial-national groupings by creating separate parliamentary chambers; it enshrines a decision principle, "own affairs," that gives various ethnic groups autonomy in areas of housing, culture, education, and, by one account, even the "wealth that they have built up."[42] The state reconstruction incorporates, rather than abandons, the segregated African townships and ethnic "homelands." Although apartheid is said to be "dead," the state president, against a backdrop of unrelieved unrest, busies himself with relocation and the "independence" of KwaNdebele, a newly fashioned ethnic labor reserve for the Witwatersrand.

The much heralded abolition of passes—as we noted, *following* the effective breakdown of the machinery of control—has been accompanied by new policies to control and limit urbanization. Administration boards, for example, have expanded their labor recruitment functions in the Bantustans and continue with development projects that shift infrastructure, schools, and industrial areas to Bantustans and "deconcentration" points. Board officials, supposedly relics of the old order, are now being reconstructed as "the only officials who can think on a regional basis." As one official put it, "We have a culture of regional administration" (AB: East Rand; also AB: West Rand and CC: Witwatersrand). Although police and inspectors may no longer harass workers on the street, officials speak of "more effective," more indirect methods: subsidized wages for relocating employers, provision of facilities in distant commuter areas, the privatization of housing amid a massive housing shortage, severe limits on land in urban areas, the use of anti-squatting laws, and the maintenance of racial group areas. Africans, one prominent official notes, can choose between "squalor" and "cardboard" in squatter locations and a "decent life which one can build" outside the urban areas (AB: West Rand).

The government has sought to play down the most direct intrusions on the market and the most direct encounters between the state and workers—the influx control and pass laws that placed hundreds of thousands in jail each year and that, in the view of the HSRC and the President's Council, inflamed African opinion.[43] In that, the government addressed the most visible aspects of market control. Yet, there is little in this story to suggest that the government has moved to lessen the politicization of society and markets.

South Africa lives today with the legacy of this illegitimate order, a legacy that includes a disaffected populace ill prepared to examine the nuances of concessions in state reconstruction. The consequence is rising disorder and rising repression. The army in the African townships is the new form of state presence that overshadows the bureaucratic and labor-repressive machinery once dominant in the lives of black South Africans.

Sebokeng, where the military first entered the townships with house-to-house searches and soccer balls, proved not to be an exceptional event, as, during two years, military forces have been deployed in townships across South Africa. The state of emergency has come and gone, but not the military, the daily arrests, and the detentions. As "troops out" has become a common slogan of the African resistance, sprawled on walls and painted on t-shirts, the government has reaffirmed its commitment to a coercive order. In 1986, it sought new powers in law to detain, without trial, students and community and political activists.⁴⁴

Political leaders, Afrikaner intellectuals, and businessmen now speak freely of new participatory and unitary state institutions, but none has begun to fashion a state that might elicit broad support in society. None has begun to address seriously the ways this state is partial. It is no great surprise that the present government has offered Africans little more than a Statutory Council with uncertain powers and regional service councils where the African role is limited by an appointed administrator, a wealth-based voting formula, and various checking mechanisms.

More striking is the role of businessmen who have combined calls for "dramatic action" with proposals that would largely entrench white political and economic privilege. The Afrikaanse Handelsinstituut (AHI) and the Chamber of Mines have proved to be the most cautious. The AHI has largely concentrated on privatization and local government without much attention to national political structures and political repression. It pulled back belatedly from its support for influx control—indeed, after the government announced its intention to abolish passes—and issued a joint statement with the minister of police supporting detention as a means to protect the economy and orderly development.⁴⁵ Although most business associations—including the Federated Chamber of Industries (FCI), the Association of Chambers of Commerce (Assocom), the National African Chamber of Commerce (NAFCOC), the Urban Foundation, and even AHI—prepared joint pronouncements and appeals during the unrest, the Chamber of Mines has largely pulled back from the public discourse. It joined other business groups at the time of Senator Edward Kennedy's visit to South Africa but subsequently declined to become involved on political and security matters, including the appeal for Nelson Mandela's release (Prominent Business Association). Harry Oppenheimer, former chairman of Anglo-American, and Peter Gush, the current head of the gold division, emphasized the primacy of minority rights and questioned majority rule as "unrealistic and unacceptable."⁴⁶

Assocom turned to Jan Lombard, as had the sugar growers at an earlier point, to help fashion a political program for commerce. Although committed to the abolition of race discrimination, the Assocom report affirmed "the norms of the existing common law of South Africa" as the best route to political and economic progress. As a prior condition for negotiation, the report proposed that the parties accept "personal freedom," "freedom of property and contract," and "personal culpability"—the basic tenets of South Africa's common law. That body of practice, the report maintained, favors the "avoidance of excessive taxation," "constraints on the freedom of action of political institutions," "logical extensions of the market system principles," and the "basic federal principle of public law."[47] Although Assocom supported new political initiatives, the imminence of more far-reaching change brought out a political imagination focused on protecting property and limiting the capacities of a potentially black-run state.

The FCI seemed willing to venture further into the political process than the others, calling for an end to a broad range of state practices, including the state of emergency, detentions without trial, influx control, and the Group Areas Act. Here, business seemed to recognize that fractured and localized initiatives would not win African support or acquiescence without some change in the character of the central state. The FCI's "business charter" called for "power sharing at central level in a single institution." Majority rule, however, was not addressed specifically, although other business concerns, such as lower taxes and government spending, managed to become principles in the FCI's political program.[48]

None of these business statements about politics reflects on the ways this social order, forged by the state and private economy, is partial: that is, how this social order maintains itself through the distribution of property that makes commercial agriculture and industrial capitalism a white preserve; the structures of segregation that artificially divided Africans between the modern economy and impoverished reserves, that keep Africans in distant townships and commuter towns and whites in their own group areas; the patterns of inequality that leave many Africans on the margins of life and the wage economy and leave whites to monopolize the upper strata of employment and income; and a political structure that leaves whites in control of the state presidency, the lawmaking bodies, the bureaucracies, and the army.

Conclusion

By the end of May 1986, more than thirty thousand Africans had fled the sprawling squatter community of Crossroads outside Cape Town, their corrugated iron and cardboard homes lost to fire and the work of vigilantes. More than thirty of their comrades were dead. Since 1975, Crossroads had come to represent African defiance: African migrants from the Transkei who refused to heed state directives and who, again and again, chanced arrest to seek work; workers who united and housed their families despite state policies that denied the African presence in the western Cape; a community that organized to fight the nightly raids, the pass arrests, the bulldozers that sought to level their shanties. Crossroads had grown to more than one hundred thousand people, illegally present but unwilling to be bused back to the Bantustans or moved to a more distant relocation area in the Cape flats, Khayelitsha.

But now, vigilantes allied with collaborative elements and supported by the police have managed what the state could not accomplish through direct means—the dislocation and removal of African squatters. Perhaps this is the new South Africa where the state seems distant and African collaborators, local institutions, and circumstances conspire to manage the African majority. Perhaps in this social order, even the illegitimate can be legitimated.

But the battle for Crossroads and for South Africa, for a new and legitimate order, is ongoing. South Africa is a politicized society where, as we have seen since Sebokeng, the majority has turned to politics.

Notes

The parenthetical citations in the text refer to interviews conducted by the author between 1980 and 1985. The following abbreviations are used to reference positions with the South African state: DL (director of labor), AB (administration board chief director or chairman), CC (chief commissioner), and LB (labor bureau official). To ensure the anonymity of business leaders interviewed for this project, I use the vague reference, Prominent Business Association.

1. This account depends on the following sources: Lawrence Schlemmer, "South Africa's Urban Crisis," and Graham Howe, "Cycles of Civil Unrest 1976/84." *Indicator* 3 (Winter 1985), "Political Monitor," 11–14; "Very Vicious Circle." *Economist* (July 27, 1985), 36–37; Johannes Rantete, *The Third Day of September: An Eyewitness Account of the Sebokeng Rebellion of 1984* (Johannesburg: Ravan Press, 1984); *New York Times*, 24 October 1984, 14 April 1984, and 4 August 1985; *Washington Post*, 11 March 1985, 23–25 March 1985, and 17 May 1985; and *The Weekly Mail*, November through May 1986.

2. Howe, "Cycles of Civil Unrest," 12; "Very Vicious Circle," 36.

3. The Van der Walt Commission, reported in the *Weekly Mail*, 2–8 May 1986, 8–9.

4. South African Institute of Race Relations (SAIRR), *Annual Survey of Race Relations* (Johannesburg: SAIRR, 1985), 103–104. Business did not oppose the state of emergency (*Financial Mail*, 26 July 1985), and the AHI resisted the lifting of influx control (*Financial Mail*, 23 November 1984).

5. See Anglo-American Corporation, "Statement by the Chairman Mr. G. W. H. Relly" (1985), 4–5; *Sunday Times*, 2 June 1985; *Cape Times*, 25 May 1985; and *Financial Mail*, 23 November 1984.

6. *Sunday Times*, 2 June 1985.

7. *Financial Mail*, 26 July 1985, 35.

8. *Natal Mercury*, 20 June 1985; and *Financial Mail*, 14 June 1985. Later in this chapter, I consider the specifics of the business proposals and the limited vision for political change.

9. *The Citizen*, 22 January 1986.

10. Reported in Lawrence Schlemmer, "African Political Rights: Part Two," *Indicator* 2 (January 1985), "Political Monitor," 2. Botha reaffirmed the government's openness on the citizenship question in April 1985 (*Citizen*, 20 April 1985).

11. *The Star,* 8 May 1985.

12. SABC, 27 December 1984.

13. SABC, 25 January 1985.

14. SABC, 29 January 1985.

15. SABC, 23 April 1985.

16. *The Argus,* 3 February 1986.

17. *Weekly Mail,* 2–8 May 1986; and *The Citizen,* 30 April 1986.

18. The theoretical issues raised here are considered in more detail in Stanley B. Greenberg, *Legitimating the Illegitimate* (Berkeley: University of California Press, forthcoming).

19. SABC, 29–30 January 1985.

20. SABC, 6 January 1985, 29 January 1985, and 14 May 1985.

21. SABC, 23 April 1985, and 14 May 1985.

22. SABC, 6 January 1985.

23. SABC, 14 February 1985.

24. South Africa, Main Committee, Human Sciences Research Council (HSRC), *The South African Society: Realities and Future Prospects* (Pretoria: HSRC, 1985), 64, 147; and SABC, 5 February 1986.

25. See Heather Hughes and Jeremy Grest, "The Local State," in South African Review Service (SARS), *South African Review I* (Johannesburg: Ravan Press, 1983), 130–131; and William Cobbett, et al., "Regionalism, Federalism and the Reconstruction of the South African State," *South African Labour Bulletin* 10, no. 5 (April 1985):95–97.

26. *Natal Mercury,* 27 May 1985; and SABC, 20 December 1984.

27. Cobbett refers to the "formation of regional proletariats" ("Regionalism," 101).

28. See Helen Zille, "Restructuring the Industrial Decentralisation Strategy," in SARS, *South African Review I,* 60–65; Gavin Maasdorp, "Co-ordinated Regional Development: Hope for the Good Hope Proposals?" in Hermann Giliomee and Lawrence Schlemmer, eds., *Up Against the Fences: Poverty, Passes and Privilege in South Africa* (Cape Town: David Philip, 1985), 223–233; and South Africa, *White Paper on Industrial Development Strategy in the Republic of South Africa* (Cape Town: Government Printers, 1985), 23–25.

The larger employers, such as the Anglo-American Corporation, have not been persuaded of the economic sense in such measures, even if the government relies on incentive and market processes rather than coercive and regulatory instruments. See H. F. Oppenheimer, "Reflections on the Government's Industrial Decentralisation Policy" and Gaven Relly, "Influx Control and Economic Growth," in Giliomee, *Up Against the Fences,* 293–302.

29. *Natal Mercury,* 27 May 1985.

30. *Argus,* 9 May 1985; and *Natal Mercury,* 10 May 1985.

31. With the introduction of the regional councils, the minister of cooperation and development has shown renewed interest in the *Buthelezi Commission Report* and its proposals for a Natal-KwaZulu regional dispensation (*Natal Mercury,* 4 May 1985).

32. South Africa, *First Report of the Constitutional Committee of the President's Council* (Cape Town: Government Printers, 1982), 19, 44. This work, concerned

primarily with the administrative structure for influx control, has not devoted much attention to other black groups. Nonetheless, it is important to note that the overwhelming majority of coloreds and Indians (more than 80 percent) boycotted the elections for the new Parliament and that black candidates and MPs have also been victims of community violence. Ebrahim Patel, *Legitimacy and Statistics: A Critical Analysis of the First Tri-Cameral Parliamentary Elections,* Southern African Labour and Development Research Unit, Working Paper No. 61 (Cape Town: University of Cape Town, January 1985); *The Star,* 20 July 1984; and *Sunday Times,* 22 July 1984.

33. SABC, 16 January 1985 and 8 September 1984.

34. South Africa, *First Report,* 80; also see L. J. Boulle, *South Africa and the Consociational Option: A Constitutional Analysis* (Cape Town: Juta, 1984), 158, 174.

35. South Africa, *Report of the Industrial Legislation Commission of Inquiry* (Cape Town: Government Printers, 1984).

36. General Workers' Union, "Reply," *South African Labour Bulletin* 7 (November 1981):18.

37. SAIRR, *Annual Survey of Race Relations* (Johannesburg: SAIRR, 1984), 186–187.

38. Nicholas Haysom, "The Industrial Court: Institutionalising Industrial Conflict" in SARS, *South African Review II* (Johannesburg: SARS, 1984), 111.

39. Ibid., p. 205; Max Coleman and David Webster, "Repression and Detention in South Africa," in *South African Review III* (Johannesburg: Ravan Press, 1986), 117–118.

40. Johan C. van Zyl (Federated Chamber of Industries), "Business and the Process of Change in South Africa." June 20, 1985, 4, 7–8; and South Africa, HSRC, *The South African Reality* (Pretoria: HSRC, n.d.), 111–113.

41. The SABC refers to the repeal of the Immorality and Mixed Marriages acts as the "deregulation of intimacy" (17 April 1985).

42. Account of meeting with the state president (leader, Progressive Federal party).

43. HSRC, *The South African Reality,* 126; and South Africa, Committee for Constitutional Affairs, President's Council, *An Urbanisation Strategy for the Republic of South Africa* (Cape Town: Government Printers, 1985), 149–150.

44. Students, teachers, community and political workers constituted more than 70 percent of the 1,149 detentions in 1985 (Coleman and Webster, "Repression and Detentions," 117); also see *New York Times* 25 May 1986.

45. SAIRR, *Annual Survey of Race Relations* (Johannesburg: SAIRR, 1985), 104; and *Business Day,* 21 March 1986.

46. Ibid., 105.

47. Assocom, *Removal of Discrimination Against Blacks in the Political Economy of the Republic of South Africa* (1985, memorandum), 4–6, 27–33, 83.

48. *The Weekly Mail,* 24–30 January 1986.

5

SIMON BEKKER
RICHARD HUMPHRIES

State Control over African Labor

In this chapter, Simon Bekker and Richard Humphries provide an account of South Africa's complex and dehumanizing system of influx control. A supreme violation of the principle of freedom of movement, influx control is a manifestation of the state's desire to control (almost) every aspect of African society. The authors provide an analysis of the comprehensive regulatory and policing functions of the labor bureaucracies—the administration boards—and the staggering complexity of state intervention in the labor market in urban and homeland South Africa. The failures and contradictions of the system are analyzed, and the authors are compelled to agree that the system of influx control became too difficult for the labor bureaucracies to manage, which resulted in the system's partial and problematic abolition by government in 1986. However, the government still controls African urbanization and homeland development and does not intend to fully abandon its interference in the African labor market. Indeed, the end of influx control really means its modernization—that is, the introduction of more subtle or less politically overt forms of labor control. Whether the new strategy will succeed is doubtful, given the incapacity of the existing regime to realize any of its major political objectives in the sphere of African governance and control.

W. G. J.

The history of South Africa's modern economy began in the mining sector. Institutions of labor repression, of massive state intervention in the labor market, were first developed and elaborated there. Labor migrancy, single-sex compound housing, and the policing of labor movement became the familiar phenomena of mining and the everyday burden of African workers. The control of African workers in the mines was in time extended also to towns and, later, to the republic as a whole.[1] The ideology and policy of apartheid came after 1948, partly as a justification of a state system of labor and movement control that had already taken root in practice and law.

Until the 1970s, state intervention in the labor market affected all Africans equally, regardless of their class and status positions in society. The state's police and labor bureaucracies did not care to discriminate between the various social categories of Africans in the pass raids, daily prosecutions, and brief periods of incarceration used to control the African population.[2] By the late 1970s, this model of control fell into disfavor, in and outside of government, for two reasons. On the one hand, political developments on the subcontinent—the decolonization of Angola, Mozambique, and Zimbabwe, the Soweto revolts of 1976—focused international attention on the system of apartheid; African labor control was singled out for particularly hostile criticism. On the other hand, the domestic business community lobbied for a freer labor market, arguing essentially that the economy required a more mobile African labor force in order to prosper. For these reasons, the government was willing to countenance changes in the labor control system.

The changes were formulated by a government-appointed commission, commonly known as the Riekert Commission, named after its principal investigator.[3] The commission called for a modification of labor control, not its abolition. One aspect of the revised system increased the restrictions for Africans living in the homelands and in the countryside. For these African workers, access to urban employment continued to be regarded as temporary. They were to return to their original residences once their contracts expired, or, if they commuted from the homelands, once their daily tasks were done. For those Africans who took up residence and employment in the republic's urban areas without permission, prosecution (of both employer and employee) and eviction were applied more effectively than before. Thus, Africans from homelands and rural areas faced a more intensified and punitive continuation of the traditional system of labor control.

The other aspect of the revised system freed Africans who were permanent urban residents and were recognized as such by the government from some forms of control. In the words of the Department of Cooperation and Development (DCD), the ministry in charge of African affairs, urban Africans were "permanent urban dwellers whose movements outside of the National States will be unrestricted."[4] Workers from this group were to receive the same treatment as urban workers of other colors. These workers now were defined in the government's parlance as "urban insiders," and the revised system freed them from labor control in the abstract.

As the government and its labor control agencies soon discovered, the central problem with the revised system was that the policing and control of some African workers inevitably meant the policing and control of all African workers. The urban African workers, freed from control in the abstract, still were subject to pass checks. This problem—which soon turned into a major contradiction—landed in the lap of the administration boards, the government agencies responsible for African labor control.[5] The boards had to implement the revised policy and develop an effective means of sorting out the urban African workers from the rural and homeland African workers, so as to free the former from and subject the latter more stringently to labor control. The boards had great difficulty in realizing this objective.

The boards' efforts to implement the revised policy failed, in the sense that the boards lost control of the African population and were unable to achieve the objectives set under the revised policy. In July 1986, the government repealed legislation governing influx control and dismantled the administration boards. However, Africans are still restricted to their townships, and their ability to live in cities is still circumscribed by the availability of land, housing, employment, and by the enforcement of squatting and law and order legislation. The end of influx control and the administration boards does not mean the end of government control of African movement and residence in cities. Indeed, one could view the abolition of influx control as its modernization—that is to say, the putting in place of more subtle and less politically overt mechanisms of African movement and settlement controls.

As administration boards are being dismantled, so their functions are being reallocated to other government agencies. It is not clear at the time of this writing which agencies are receiving what functions, but an entirely new agency, the Regional Service Council (RSC), ostensibly will control African housing, township administration, and employment, all matters affecting the settlement of Africans in cities. The functions of administration boards are thus being reallocated rather than abolished, which is why a study of their role in the control of the African population is of special importance.

This chapter investigates the most recent history of the administration boards and their policies, in part to document the nature and effect of influx control policies on the African population and to give an account of their failure to achieve regime objectives. Present government policies with regard to African urbanization and settlement can only be understood, we argue, by close scrutiny of the history immediately preceding the abolition of influx control and administration boards and by tracing the latter's functions to the present (1986) period.

Sorting Africans Out

A primary function of administration boards was to ensure that those Africans who in terms of influx control laws were not supposed to be in cities were kept out of cities.[6] Created in 1972 and 1973 (twenty-two boards were created, then reduced to fourteen in 1979), the boards were charged with the responsibility to channel or allocate African labor from the homelands to employers in the cities; repatriate unemployed and illegally employed African workers from the cities to the homelands; and resettle whole communities of Africans living in so-called white areas to the homelands. These were the main but not all of the functions. Essentially the role of the boards was to regulate and police the flow of African labor in the labor market.

A major distinction made by the boards in the labor market was—and still is—between Africans who were not considered permanent residents of the republic, meaning Africans from homelands, and those who were. During the 1970s, boards allocated work to Africans on the basis of the urban-homeland distinction. First in line for jobs within a specific town were Africans who qualified as permanent residents in that town. Second preference was offered to Africans resident in a specified neighboring region, including the homelands, a strategy known as labor zoning. Although these strategies were never formalized in law, they were common practice.[7] The Riekert Commission reinforced this division between urban and homeland Africans.

Permanent Residents

In theory, Africans who had permanent residence rights (in legal terms, they had or were qualified for so-called Section 10 rights under the Blacks [Urban Areas] Consolidation Act of 1945), were first in line for jobs.[8] In the early 1980s, three developments created problems for the way in which the board labor bureaus placed permanent urban residents at the front of the job line. First, since the Riekert Commission recommended that permanently resident Africans ought to be free of board control, the boards had no accurate register of who was and was not permanent, with the result that jobs were allocated on a first-come, first-serve basis.[9] Second, employers of labor did not necessarily go along with this system of preferential labor allocation. In the 1980s, the boards tended to give priority to employer requests.[10] Thus, for example, the wish of an industrialist in the Eastern Cape to employ contract workers from rural Ciskei took precedence over the position that registered urban African work seekers in East London and King William's Town were supposed to have in the job line.[11]

The third development had to do with rapid expansion in the 1970s of homeland dormitory towns and the concomitant increase in frontier commuters—residents of homeland towns who commute daily to jobs in the republic.[12] These commuters did not qualify for permanent residence under Section 10 of the Blacks (Urban Areas) Consolidation Act. In fact, this qualification in many cases had previously been surrendered. Mdantsane residents who moved from Duncan Village in East London, Seshego residents who moved from Pietersburg, or KwaMashu residents after this township was incorporated in KwaZulu are cases of communities that were deprived en masse of their Section 10 rights. The change in status caused tremendous administrative difficulties because these "residents turned commuters" had to be reprocessed.[13] The boards' solution to the problem was to give them back their Section 10 rights, but on an ad hoc basis, which easily could be taken away again. Known as the "administrative Section 10" procedure, this approach had considerable currency and was widely applied.[14]

The frontier commuters, those variously affected by the administrative Section 10 procedure, were divided into two classes. First, there were those commuters who were granted authorization to enter the urban areas of the republic that are close to the commuters' homeland townships in order to seek employment in those areas. Once these persons obtained authorization from a labor bureau, they were viewed as administrative Section 10 qualifiers. The second group was composed of frontier commuters who entered after they had obtained a contract of employment. These persons were then treated by labor bureau officials as contract workers, obliged to reapply in their homeland if they wished to obtain new jobs.[15] The latter group therefore was not granted administrative Section 10 rights.

In practice, boards granted administrative Section 10 qualifications to many persons who lost proper Section 10 qualifications. In the Western Transvaal, for instance, the board developed a number of dormitory towns in the homeland of Bophuthatswana. Commuters from these towns who were qualifying residents in the Western Transvaal before their move were granted administrative Section 10 qualifications. Commuters who left other areas of Bophuthatswana to take up residence in the same towns were treated as contract commuters.[16]

This administrative practice also has been applied to residents in certain dormitory towns falling outside board areas of jurisdiction. Authorization has been granted within Durban to all bona fide residents of KwaMashu and Umlazi (in which residents did not enjoy Section 10 qualifications prior to incorporation),[17] within Pretoria and Bloemfontein, to residents of the townships of Soshanguve[18] and Botshabelo (Onverwacht),[19] both of which are administered by DCD as South African Development Trust (SADT) areas, and in a number of others.[20] In the case of Botshabelo, which is situated a considerable distance from Bloemfontein, authorization was granted to residents seeking work solely on a commuter basis and solely in Bloemfontein, not in other urban areas falling under the jurisdiction of the responsible Southern Orange Free State Administration Board.[21]

The all too many exceptions, qualifications, and ad hoc granting of Section 10 rights systematically violated the system of preferential labor allocation and made the practice extremely difficult to implement and keep under control. In certain cases, Section 10 and administrative Section 10 holders were placed side by side in the job line. In other cases, the boards could not discriminate effectively between permanent residents and homeland residents. Those who were theoretically in front of the job line in practice often were not and, which is the same thing, those at the end of line often were up front. The system of preferential labor allocation did not work that well—bureaucratically it had become a tangled web—and, given the pervasive and widespread inefficiencies that came with the system, was abandoned in practice by the boards.

Homeland Residents

A corollary of preferential work allocation in cities was recruitment practices in the homelands, known in board and government circles as labor zoning. The Riekert Commission, which recommended that its implementation be left to the discretion of each board,[22] defined labor zoning as "the admission of contract workers from a specific Black state or states to the area of jurisdiction of a particular administration board."[23] Within the Western Transvaal, for example, contract workers employed in the board area were solely recruited in the homeland of Bophuthatswana, a practice with a long history going back to preboard days in the 1960s.[24] The Port Natal Administration Board, as another example, introduced a system of linking "feeder regions" in the homeland of KwaZulu to four receiving regions in their board area. KwaZulu residents seeking work in the republic were treated preferentially by board labor bureaus if they resided in one of the feeder regions and accepted work in its twin receiving region in Natal.[25] In the Eastern Cape Administration Board, as a final example, agreement was reached between the Ciskei government and the Eastern Cape Administration Board on similar zoning agreements.[26] Labor zoning, therefore, moved beyond a simple link between homeland and board to links among regions within each entity.

Two justifications were offered by the DCD for this preferential strategy of labor zoning. The first was that labor zoning was an effective indirect means of implementing influx control.[27] Labor zoning canalized African labor into predefined destinations in a way that was predictable and controllable. A second justification defined labor zoning as a more efficient system of allocating workers to jobs because it minimized the distance between workers' homes and workplaces and thereby promoted the development of a commuter, rather than a contract, labor force. Labor zoning was, in principle, a homeland counterpart to the urban practices of controlling and limiting the presence of Africans in cities.

The labor zoning strategy that linked homeland regions to board regions, however, suffered from a significant weakness. For the strategy to be successful, labor and movement control was required within homelands so that the recruitment and the migration of people from one homeland region to another could be regulated and controlled. Although such a system has existed for many years, operated by tribal authorities and (since 1968)[28] by tribal labor bureaus, it is clear from the evidence that the system failed to achieve these objectives.[29] In a particular tribal authority area in the jurisdiction of Ciskei, for instance, a survey of one village established that its residents worked as commuters in East London. This was in direct contravention of the Eastern Cape Administration Board labor zoning agreement with the Ciskei government.[30]

The contradiction of this system of control of African labor affected more than the board policy of labor zoning. The labor bureau system also was designed to process, as a matter of routine, contracts offered to homeland workers who then took up employment throughout the republic. There was, therefore, substantial cooperation between boards on recruitment from homelands. Inadequate control—which follows from the fact that the tribal labor bureaus had broken down and were in effect not functioning at all—of these recruitment procedures affected the efficiency of the contract labor system in the country as a whole.[31] The boards' answer to the problem in the system can be found in the development, first, of assembly centers (government-run places where African workers assemble and are processed) and, second, of mobile labor bureaus.

Assembly centers were intended as a partial solution. Situated close to homeland borders, the centers operated joint board-homeland labor bureaus. As stated in the Riekert white paper, these centers were to be administered by board officials and homeland government officials (homeland officials processed employment contract attestations) and could be approached by prospective employers to supply, at a fee, the commuter workers they required.[32] A number of boards opened assembly centers, some of them situated within homelands.[33] In greater Durban the Port Natal Administration Board operated labor bureaus in both KwaMashu and Umlazi in KwaZulu that performed functions similar to assembly centers. The Department of Manpower also has been involved in the operation of these centers because a number undertake guidance and placement functions for administrative Section 10 commuters.[34]

Due to their location, these centers could not take over the functions of those tribal labor bureaus situated at some distance from homeland boundaries. Consequently, the Northern Transvaal Administration Board developed a mobile labor bureau system that undertook, in remote rural homeland areas, the same activities as assembly centers. Officials of the mobile units maintained constant radio contact with their board head office and during a four-month period recruited more than fifteen hundred contract workers. They claimed that contract workers arrived and could arrive at their places of employment on the Witwatersrand two days after employer requisitions were received.[35] Both assembly centers and mobile bureaus require homeland government approval, which was given, to operate.[36] Under such circumstances, the establishment of these institutions extended into homelands effective board powers of labor regulation.

The dismantling of administration boards now taking place also means, in principle if not necessarily in fact, that the institutions governing labor in the homelands will also either be dismantled or transferred to other government agencies. It is probable that labor zoning will be transferred to another agency because government is still concerned about controlling labor movement from the homelands to cities, as the proposed Aliens Act suggests. This new legislation before Parliament in 1986 defines Africans from nominally independent homelands as aliens, non–South African citizens, which means that a new government agency can refuse entry to or allocate to specific cities and regions Africans coming from these homelands seeking work in the republic.[37]

Influx Control

The strategy of influx control served two racial objectives. The first was to regulate and police the process of African urbanization—that is, the migration of Africans from rural and homeland South Africa to its towns and cities. The second was to resettle as many African communities in the republic as possible back to the homelands. The boards were involved in both aspects of the strategy, and, in 1985, were still in the business of resettling African communities.

With regard to African urbanization, the boards were to identify and evict Africans illegally present in cities, those who left their homelands or rural areas without proper authorization. With regard to homelands, it was the boards' responsibility to encourage or forcibly resettle African communities resident in so-called white areas back into the homelands.

Policing Illegal Africans

Influx control was by definition directed at Africans who entered cities illegally and not at permanent residents. The Blacks (Urban Areas) Consolidation Act of 1945 (Section 10 in particular) and the Black Labor Act of 1964 defined the conditions of legal and illegal presence. To be legally present in a city, all Africans were obliged to obtain authorization notarized in a book, known colloquially as a passbook, from board officials in each of three life domains. Africans had to get authorization to be in a city beyond a seventy-two-hour period; they had to get work, and they had to get housing. Both the African person and the board had to keep documentary proof of authorization of the affected person's situation at all times.

The crucial institutions used by boards to govern influx were Section 10, which included the seventy-two-hour provision, the registration of labor, and the provision of accommodation. Since 1979, a series of commissions and committees of inquiry made recommendations aimed at changing these institutions and the system of urban influx regulation. The Riekert Commission recommended the repeal of the seventy-two-hour provision of Section 10.[38] This provision referred to the length of time a nonqualifying African may remain in an urban area in the republic before his or her presence was considered illegal. The commission recommended the abolition of curfew and night-permit regulations, which controlled the presence of Africans outside their areas.[39] These latter controls referred to the regulation of Africans in white, colored, and Indian urban areas (including the central business districts), not in urban areas as such. Finally, on this score, the Riekert Commission recommended that policing on the street be abandoned in favor of board control of employment and housing.

Traditionally, the policing of Africans in the three life domains—physical presence, employment, and housing—was the responsibility of a number of officials. Board inspectors, together with members of the South African Police (SAP), identified and arrested Africans whose presence in urban areas was considered illegal; inspectors, together with labor bureau officials, undertook the same duties with regard to illegal employment; and inspectors, together with township managers, policed contravention of approved accommodation practices. Employers of unregistered workers were fined and the workers arrested. In the case of accommodation, officials were empowered to take action against persons accommodated without permission in approved houses and in structures that had not been approved, such as squatter shacks. Inspectors, in their capacity as peace officers, had the power to interrogate and, if they deemed necessary, arrest Africans on the street, in their places of employment, and in their houses.[40] Suspected offenders were required to prove their innocence by producing documents of authorization or passes—board and other officials were required far less often to prove guilt.[41]

The specific recommendation of the Riekert Commission was to abolish one part of this overall policing network—policing on the street—so as to free permanent residents from police and board harassment. Thus, the commission wanted to modify and manipulate the system, not abolish it, as a way of making it less visibly oppressive. But the manipulation of the system had its own deep problems, as illustrated in part by the confused debate among state officials in response to the recommendation.

The debate divided along two lines of argument. The traditionalist argument was that in order to control urbanization there was no choice but to maintain street and other forms of policing. If Africans were illegally in cities, the argument went, they had to be identified and evicted. To do this, there had to be an enforceable restriction—such as the seventy-two-hour provision, curfew regulations, and passes. Thus, the argument of the traditionalists was that either you have policing or you don't, and some officials preferred the former. To be effective, therefore, officials were obliged to throw their police net as wide as possible, catching and holding the "guilty" and the "innocent" alike.[42]

The other argument in government circles was that policing on the streets was wholly ineffective. With regard to the seventy-two-hour provision, Africans accosted on the street could simply state that they have indeed been there within the specified period, leaving policing officials with no independent way of checking the truth of the claim. Many Africans evaded street policing, came to cities regardless of street policing, or flooded the jails; in other words, policing on the street did not effectively do what it was supposed to do, which was to curb the urbanization of the unwanted. Thus, those of this persuasion argued that policing the workplace and housing ought to be an adequate, less discriminatory form of regulating urban influx.

In time, the latter argument prevailed in government circles, and influx control in the narrow sense of policing on the street was abandoned in 1986. The administration boards were the first to point out that policing was not effective, that thousands of Africans evaded their nets, and that urbanization proceeded regardless of the massive policing network of the boards. At first, the government insisted that Africans coming to cities have employment and housing, but these requirements were softened as well because some form of policing was necessary to regulate housing and employment.[43]

This is not to say that influx control has ended but that the traditional form of influx control based on policing on the street is coming to an end. There are a number of ways in which government can and does at this time curb the flow of Africans to the cities. First, Africans have to live in their group areas—the townships—and can only erect squatter settlements in areas and under conditions approved by government. Limited land in cities and an unwillingness on the part of government to grant more land for African settlement mean that many will be in cities without accommodation. Second, legislation that strictly speaking has little to do with influx control can be used to evict from cities those people without accommodation, such as, for example, "antisquatting" and "disturbing the peace" legislation. Indeed, since the end of 1985 the DCD has been in the process of fashioning such a strategy, one less self-evidently aimed at Africans and with less political overtones. However, as with other forms of influx control, this strategy only contains the problem—it does not remedy it.

Resettlement

Administration boards have used their control of the African labor market to create alternatives to city residence in the homelands. A policy of dormitory township development linked to the freezing of housing development in the republic's towns close to homelands made possible the manipulation of accommodation preference to promote resettlement. As a corollary of promoting housing alternative in homelands, African communities with long-standing residence and roots in the republic have been approached with requests to leave the republic for new homes in the homelands. In some cases, when the requests were turned down, residents were forced to move.

The boards have played an important part in implementing this policy. As agents of the SADT, most boards have been involved directly in homeland township development.[44] Most boards, moreover, implemented DCD directives to freeze housing development in certain republican towns and cities.[45] Finally, boards have supervised the coercive resettlement of a number of African communities, of which the following cases are examples.

It has been government policy to resettle residents from Duncan Village in East London to Madantsane, the largest of Ciskei homeland's towns. Beginning in the early 1980s, new housing stock was established in this dormitory town. A fixed percentage of all new houses was earmarked for Duncan Village residents, and board officials responsible for Duncan Village supervised the allocation of these houses to residents who were then required to move.[46]

In the Northern Transvaal, the board policy was to resettle into homelands all Africans in the board's area of jurisdiction. Board officials undertook a major project to persuade members of a community living close to Ellisras, an informal settlement lacking in services, to move 72 miles to the township of Steyloop in the Lebowa homeland. Leading members of the community were taken to Steyloop by board officials and were shown the superior water supply and educational facilities in that area. The community moved to this township in the early 1980s.[47]

Examples of forcible expulsion of people from their homes, accomplished mainly by the demolition of backyard units or shacks, often have occurred, with great accompanying publicity. Demolitions in Crossroads in Cape Town have been and remain an international focus of attention, and demolitions in Glenmore in the Eastern Cape have been given considerable domestic publicity. During 1982, the East Rand Administration Board sent 8,000 families living illegally in Katlehong back to the homelands and demolished their backyard units.[48] More broadly, the aptly named Surplus Peoples Project of the University of Cape Town established that 234,639 Africans and 33,517 African families have been resettled by the boards through 1985.[49]

Due in part to international criticism, the minister of DCD announced in 1985 that all coercive resettlement would henceforth cease. The DCD increasingly began to rely on noncoercive means, of the sort described in this section, to persuade people to move. The idea is to keep resettlement out of the glare of public and especially international attention without necessarily abandoning the policy. Although the resettlement process is almost complete—that is, the majority of people government wanted to see resettled have been resettled—there is no reason to suppose that the process will cease, even in the absence of administration boards.

Pockets of Privilege

The Riekert Commission recommended that Africans with permanent city rights be liberated from influx control and, in effect, be permitted to become privileged workers in the African labor market. Government embraced the idea, and by 1983 a range of privileges was being offered, at least in principle. The Riekert white paper offered commercial involvement to urban Africans free of board control;[50] the Viljoen Committee proposed a process of housing development that included a ninety-nine-year leasehold and that was free of much of the bureaucratic control of the past; and a new piece of legislation gave representative government to Africans on a local level, the so-called community councils (see the discussion of community councils and their fate in Chapter 3).[51] For urban Africans, the so-called "insiders," this was the new deal.

Senior officials in administration boards underwrote both the policy and the values that supported the new deal. They were responsible, however, for control of all Africans in their areas of jurisdiction and therefore were aware of the problems involved in trying to discriminate between those for whom control had to be lessened and those for whom it had to be intensified. They also were aware of the fact that permanent urban African communities are smaller than other African communities and often live in small towns that offer few opportunities for prosperity and a better quality of life.

The problem was particularly acute for the board departments of labor, which in practice were involved in implementing policy. Officials in these departments were responsible for achieving the dual goals of allocating labor to the economy and controlling African influx into cities. The new deal required the freeing of qualifying urban work seekers from restrictions that were inherent and systematically entrenched in the overall system of control. These workers were to be treated in the same color-blind fashion as were other workers in the cities and towns of the republic. Simultaneously, commuters and contract workers as well as African work seekers and workers in urban areas without board permission had to be treated in the traditional fashion of influx control.

The new policy, contradictions and all, was put into practice between 1983 and 1985. Permanent residents were free to find work and change jobs within towns and cities in the board areas, without registration with or authorization from the boards.[52] They were no longer obliged, as they used to be, to register at the board labor bureau as work seekers.[53] In the urban labor market, urban Africans in principle and in policy were free from board control.

The employers of permanent African urban residents were no longer obliged to give them or the board documentary proof of employment.[54] Employers themselves, however, were required to keep a register that included the personal particulars of their African employees, to provide the board with employment information on which basis a fee was charged by the board for services rendered, and to pay the fees.[55] The employer, not the African worker, was liable for any violations of the regulations. Under the new system, urban Africans were provided with a working environment free of board intervention and control.

In practice, matters were not so straightforward. For one thing, urban Africans still had to obtain housing in order to be in a board urban area.[56] Boards, therefore, had to monitor housing allocation to Africans, a control function directed at those ostensibly free from control. For another, board inspectors continued, and had to continue by virtue of the system's logic, to control the employment, housing, and presence of all Africans in urban areas. Indeed, regardless of the new deal, a permanent resident with full privileges continued to run the average risk of being approached on the street by a policeman or a board inspector. If he or she, for whatever reason, failed to present a passbook that was in proper order, he or she ran the further risk of being arrested and referred to so-called aid centers, which were employment centers, or to the courts, a process that more likely meant a few days in jail. In practice, the new deal was no new deal at all.

The attempt of the Riekert Commission to modify the system of influx control so as to create pockets of privileges for permanently resident Africans in urban areas was difficult in the face of a system premised on the principle of subjecting all Africans to systematic control. In 1986, after a full two years of living through the anomalous situation of attempting to reform the irreformable, government abandoned the policy of policing on the street.

However, the boards and their as-yet-unknown successors still control the land and housing that Africans must have in order to be safe from harassment and insecurity. By the manipulation of these resources and by using squatting and law and order legislation, African urbanization is still government regulated, although in ways less overtly coercive than has been the case previously. For Africans on the move, life under apartheid keeps them on the move.

Conclusion

Before 1980, South African government control of the African labor market, as reflected in statute, regulation, and administration, was comprehensive, as was the complementary ideology of apartheid. Once it was decided to revise or "reform" the system of control, a revision that required the differential treatment of two groups of Africans—urban residents and all others—contradictions surfaced. It soon became apparent that the contradictions were fundamentally rooted in the system itself and that influx control, broadly understood as government control of the movement, employment, and housing of Africans in homeland and nonhomeland South Africa, cannot be tinkered with without setting in motion processes that result in the collapse of the entire system of control.

The result is a wholly confused, incoherent, ad hoc set of government policies and practices. Preferential work allocation has been abandoned, policing on the street is no longer practiced, but indirect control of African presence in cities, housing, and employment still continues. Resettlement (which in principle is frowned upon by government), having done its work, still continues. The promotion of homeland development, of providing alternative work and housing there, has not ended either. Government remains wholly involved in African urbanization.

The forces of internal black opposition, external political pressures, and structural economic transformations that have induced the government to introduce the reforms are irreversibly gathering momentum. As the government reacts to these forces and seeks strategies to sustain efficient allocation of labor to the economy while trying to lessen its hold on the labor market, it finds itself burdened with an ideology and with an apparatus rapidly losing legitimacy and strength. The demise of the comprehensive model of government labor control is an important influence, if not cause, for the rapid erosion of the ideology and policies of apartheid.

Notes

1. The term *republic* is used to refer exclusively to those areas of greater South Africa that do not fall under the jurisdiction of dependent or independent homeland governments. This region coincides with the areas of jurisdiction of administration boards, and the use of the term republic is seen by the authors as preferable to the anomalous phrase "white South Africa," even though the former's use is inaccurate in terms of South African law.

2. Passbooks were documents in which the personal particulars, especially employment and residence, of the bearer were notarized. Passbooks had to be with the bearer at all times and shown on demand. If the bearer failed to produce a passbook or if it was not in proper order, he or she would be arrested, processed through

a special court system, and either fined, jailed, or both, depending on the severity of the transgression.

3. South Africa, *Report of the Commission of Inquiry into Legislation Affecting the Utilisation of Manpower* (Pretoria: Government Printer, 1979). Text is hereafter referred to as the *Riekert Commission,* after the principal investigator.

4. South Africa, Department of Cooperation and Development (DCD), *Report of the Department of Cooperation and Development* (Pretoria: Government Printers, 1982), 33. The statutory provision allowing an African to take up permanent residence in a republican area is found in Section 10 of the Black (Urban Areas) Consolidation Act. In 1982, there were approximately 3.5 million Africans who so qualified. See Simon Bekker and Richard Humphries, *From Control to Confusion* (Johannesburg: Shuter and Shooter, 1985), Chapter 3.

5. Administration boards were government agencies responsible for the control of Africans in urban, rural, and, to some extent, homeland areas. In 1972 and 1973, when the boards were introduced, there were twenty-two boards; in the light of the Riekert Commission's call for their rationalization, the boards were reduced to fourteen in 1979.

6. The primary influx control law was the Blacks (Urban Areas) Consolidation Act of 1945.

7. Interviews with board director of labor. Also see *Riekert Commission,* para. 7.986.

8. Section 10 rights was a clause in the Blacks (Urban Areas) Consolidation Act that specified criteria for urban residence. Individuals who qualified for urban residence thus have, as it is popularly termed, Section 10 rights.

9. South Africa, "Black Labour Regulations," *Government Gazette* (Pretoria: Government Printer, GNR 1892/1965. VII, 10, 1965).

10. Interviews with board officials in the Western Transvaal.

11. South Africa, East Cape Administration Board, Port Elizabeth, Circular G12/6/6/2 (August 1982).

12. See Anthony Lemon, "Migrant Labour and Frontier Commuters," in D. M. Smith, ed., *Living Under Apartheid* (London: George Allen and Unwin, 1982), 54–69.

13. Because the Office of the Chief Commissioner is responsible for processing contracts offered homeland workers, severe bottlenecks would occur, for example, in Durban and Pietermaritzburg.

14. The term itself is widely used by board officials.

15. See South Africa, Department of Manpower, circular 12/12/2/6 (1982).

16. Interview with senior board officials.

17. Umlazi had been administered as a SADT area before incorporation into KwaZulu.

18. The dormitory town north of Pretoria has an estimated population of sixty-three thousand. Its name is an acronym for Sotho, Shangaan, Nguni, and Venda.

19. This new township is situated between Bloemfontein and Thabanchu and has an estimated population of one hundred ten thousand. Residents are mainly South Sotho speaking, and many settled in Botshabelo after they left Thabanchu. The township is a considerable distance from the homeland of QwaQwa.

20. "Administrative Section 10" procedures have been introduced in certain towns within the Eastern Cape and Northern Transvaal boards of jurisdiction.

21. Interviews with board officials.

22. *Riekert Commission,* para. 7.65.

23. Ibid., para. 4.216. In government publications, "black states" is usually a reference to homelands but often refers to the sovereign neighboring states of Lesotho, Swaziland, and Botswana.

24. Richard Humphries, "The Origins and Subsequent Development of Administration Boards" (M.A. diss., Rhodes University, 1983), 147.

25. Interviews with board officials.

26. Simon Bekker et al. *Tsweletswele* (Grahamstown: Rhodes University, 1983), 59–60.

27. Humphries, "Origins," 134, 147.

28. Ibid., 132.

29. *Riekert Commission,* para. 4.34.

30. Bekker, *Tsweletswele,* 59–60.

31. Stanley Greenberg and Hermann Giliomee, "Managing Influx Control from the Rural End: The Black Homelands and the Underbelly of Privilege," in Hermann Giliomee and Lawrence Schlemmer, eds., *Up Against the Fences: Poverty, Passes and Privilege in South Africa* (Cape Town, David Philip, 1985), 68–84.

32. South Africa, *White Paper on the Report of the Commission of Inquiry into Legislation Affecting the Utilisation of Manpower* (Pretoria: Government Printers, 1979), para. 1.3.

33. See South Africa, Department of Manpower, circular (1982); and South Africa, Eastern Transvaal Administration Board, *Chairman's Annual Report* (Nelspruit: Eastern Transvaal Administration Board, 1981).

34. See South Africa, Department of Manpower, circular.

35. Interviews with board officials.

36. *Riekert Commission,* para. 7.18.

37. *Cape Times,* 29 July 1986, 3.

38. *Riekert Commission,* para. 7.60.

39. Ibid., para. 7.87.

40. South Africa, Eastern Transvaal Administration Board, *Instruction Manual* (Nelspruit: Eastern Transvaal Administration Board, n.d.), 1.

41. This can be seen from the wording of Section 10: "No Black shall remain for more than seventy-two hours in a prescribed area unless . . . "

42. See Giliomee, *Up Against the Fences,* 68–125.

43. *Leadership South Africa* (1st Quarter 1985):12; and *Financial Mail* (20 September 1985):42.

44. Bekker, *From Control to Confusion,* Chapter 2.

45. Ibid., Chapter 5.

46. Interviews with board officials.

47. Interviews with board officials.

48. South Africa, *Debates of the House of Assembly* (Cape Town: Government Printers, 1983), col. 8885.

49. Laurine Platzky and Cherryl Walker, eds., *The Surplus People: Forced Removals in South Africa* (Johannesburg: Ravan Press, 1985), 14.

50. *Riekert Commission,* para. 7.66f.

51. South Africa, *The Black Local Authorities Act, No. 102* (Pretoria: Government Printers, 1982).

52. South Africa, "Black Labour Regulations," VIII, 16, 4.

53. Ibid., 10, 1.

54. Ibid., 15, 2(d).

55. Ibid., VI, 6, 1; and South Africa, Central Transvaal Administration Board, circular ST19/2/2 24 (April 1981), 3.

56. South Africa, "Black Labour Regulations," VIII, 14, 4(a).

6

HUGH CORDER

The Supreme Court: Arena of Struggle?

The judiciary in South Africa constitutes without doubt the most neglected branch of the triaspolitica in terms of public scrutiny and academic inquiry. For this reason and because of the judiciary's formal absence from the constitutional process (as is found in the Westminster constitutional model), the Supreme Court has long enjoyed a reputation for the independent administration of justice and has somehow escaped being tainted by apartheid. In recent years, there has been a steady stream of analytical studies of the judicial process, all of which have indicated that the courts must admit a greater culpability for the promulgation of discriminatory practices and racial domination than was previously acknowledged. This has led to a crisis in the credibility and legitimacy of the courts and the judicial process.

With these observations in mind, Hugh Corder gives an account of how the Supreme Court has aided the execution of state policy by its judgments and extracurial actions. The part the Supreme Court continues to play in the current "reform" phase and its likely future role are analyzed in the light of the materialist debate on the role of the rule of law in the state and civil society. By argument and case examination (recent Supreme Court cases), Corder concludes that the attempt to disentangle the judiciary from apartheid is a problematic, even a fruitless, exercise.

W. G. J.

Our legal system cannot be outclassed. . . . There are attacks, incriminations and accusations that our judgments in law are not objective and independent. I am convinced and satisfied we can boast and also be thankful we have always had men who not only maintain our legal system, but have also expanded and improved the system. . . . To say our courts are just and impartial is not saying much. The truth is that there are no courts anywhere in the world whose judges' and magistrates' integrity is higher than ours.[1]

H. J. Coetsee, Minister of Justice

The social service which the judge renders to the community is the removal of a sense of injustice. To perform this service the essential quality which he needs is impartiality and next after that the appearance of impartiality. I put impartiality before the appearance of it simply because without the reality the appearance would not endure. In truth, within the context of service to the community the appearance is the more important of the two. The judge who gives the right judgment while appearing not to do so may be thrice blessed in heaven, but on earth he is no use at all.[2]

Lord Devlin

The judiciary in South Africa has always occupied a lofty if at times uncomfortable throne in the palace of state. In the past, the Supreme Court has won for itself a remarkably firm and widespread reputation for impartiality and fairness, among friend and foe, at home and abroad. Mysteriously, the court's judges have largely escaped being tainted by the stench of apartheid, although isolated instances of judicially sanctioned injustice have been pointed out by critics. The recent past, however, has seen several substantially critical treatments of the judicial record.

This chapter seeks to examine three major issues: to determine whether the judiciary's reputation for impartiality survives a thorough scrutiny of the record; to review the main approaches in the literature on the judicial function; and to speculate on the corporate role the judiciary fulfills in the South African state. By way of illustration, a tentative account of judicial reaction to the state of emergency is attempted. These aspects of the judicial process are approached in the light of the historical background of the judicial system and with particular attention to the potential use of the courts to further the broadly political objectives of both opponents and supporters of the current regime.

As the focus of discussion is the Supreme Court and the judiciary, the inferior courts and the magistracy are excluded. It is appropriate to focus only on the superior courts for several reasons, among them the leading part played by their judgments under the system of precedent, the ready availability of their pronouncements in the law reports, the existence of several thorough analyses of the attitudes of Supreme Court judges, and the *relatively* wide discretion judges exercise in determining the scope of legislation. In addition, the popular conception of the judiciary seems to concentrate on Supreme Court judges, even though some 85 percent of all criminal cases are heard in magistrates courts.[3] Magistrates, furthermore, are set apart from Supreme Court judges by virtue of their office as career civil servants and their administrative duties as functionaries of the state.[4] For reasons such as these, discussion has been confined to the Supreme Court alone.

Historical and Structural Background of the Court

For the purposes of analysis and discussion it is important to sketch the development and structure of the Supreme Court in South Africa.[5] Prior to union in 1910, each constituent colony or republic had its own supreme court, and only in the Orange Free State was there a judicial right to test legislation against the provisions of the constitution. Even though the law itself was primarily Roman-Dutch in origin, the British judicial approach predominated because the vast majority of South African judges were educated and trained in British-style institutions.[6] Rules of procedure and much of public law were also based on the British system of law.

The year 1910 saw the unification of the courts of the Cape, Natal, Orange Free State, and Transvaal into one Supreme Court of South Africa (as provincial divisions) and the creation of a single appellate division for the whole country, seated in the judicial capital, Bloemfontein. The appellate division's writ ran nationwide, although without original jurisdiction and, until 1950, subject to an appeal to the Judicial Committee of the Privy Council in London. Its preeminent position in the system of precedent and the caliber of appointed judges soon assured the appellate division a dominant and unifying role among often headstrong and conflicting provincial decisions.[7] Apart from a considerable increase in the number of judges appointed to the Supreme Court[8] and a further regionalization of jurisdiction,[9] this basic structure of the Supreme Court has remained unaltered.

Judges are appointed to the bench by the state president, customarily acting on the advice of his minister of justice. Any "fit and proper person" may be appointed to an office with security of tenure; judges may be dismissed only on an address of every House of Parliament, a situation that has never occurred. In practice, appointees usually come from the ranks of senior advocates practicing at the bar, with the rare exception of several government law advisers during the years. It appears that the minister of justice informally consults the judge president of the division in which the appointment is to be made and that the latter's recommendation is usually followed. The cabinet probably plays a more important part in the elevation of a judge to the judge presidency or the appellate division because of the political significance of these offices.

These procedures as well as the conventions governing the South African legal and social tradition have meant that all judges have belonged to the white group, and, with one exception, all have been male. Political factors have indisputably influenced the selection process, but on the whole those representative of what most whites would regard as more "extreme" political opinion have been passed over. In general, too, the division among English- and Afrikaans-speaking judges has been maintained in accordance with the relative size of the two groups, with the exception of the decade or so immediately after the accession to power of the National party in 1948. Antisemitism is thought to have affected appointments on several occasions.[10] It can be safely stated, therefore, that South African judges have been drawn overwhelmingly from the white, male, Protestant group, have received a fairly elite education and a cloistered training, and have been relatively old on appointment.[11] There can be no doubt that the comparatively low remuneration judges receive when set against the earnings of senior practicing advocates has induced several such potential appointees to delay their elevation to the bench until the prospect of retirement and old age made the pension and other benefits an attractive proposition. On the whole, however, there has been no shortage of candidates willing and able to fill the judicial office competently.

The Hoexter Commission recently has conducted a detailed inquiry into the structure and functioning of all the courts. The implementation of the commission's recommendations already has had a beneficial effect on the work load and efficiency of the Supreme Court. This and allied improvements in the functioning of the inferior courts should at least provide a formal administration of justice more suited to the needs of a wider range of South Africans than has been the case to date.[12]

Judicial review of legislation exists only insofar as the court is empowered to test whether certain strictly formal procedural matters have been observed by Parliament. As to substance, the legislature reigns supreme. Prosecutions in criminal matters in the Supreme Court are initiated by the attorney-general of the division concerned, who is a salaried state official, assisted by several state advocates. Advocates in private practice assume the defense of an accused who can afford legal representation, and there is a system of *pro deo* counsel for indigent accused charged with crimes that carry a possible death sentence. There is a paltry legal aid scheme administered by the Department of Justice. Strong informal links are maintained between the bench and bar at the seat of each division, but there is hardly ever formal contact between the judges of different divisions.

Against this background, the record of the Supreme Court judiciary during the years can now be summarized and assessed.

The Record of the Court Since 1910

The existence of three major studies, supplemented by several more particular and limited analyses of judicial attitudes as reflected in the case law during the past seventy-five years, makes it convenient to divide this review into three periods: 1910–1950, 1950–1980, and 1980–June 1985. This periodization has the added advantage of rough coincidence with substantial shifts in South African sociopolitical conditions. In each case, the approach of the appellate judiciary is assumed to be indicative of the country's general mood, although differences of opinion at regional level are noted.[13]

In respect to the period 1910 to 1950,[14] the Supreme Court judiciary appeared to assume a consciously conciliatory stance in an attempt to allay the suspicion and hostility that was still rife between English- and Afrikaans-speaking whites, so recently engaged in a vicious war.[15] Although the court did not overtly further race discrimination, there is no doubt that almost all judges at this time subscribed to the policy of segregation of blacks from whites, particularly in the case of Africans and Indians.[16] The court did strike a notably civil libertarian note to the benefit of several individuals during the years and was prepared on occasion to harshly criticize executive and legislative action,[17] but the fundamental premise of the judges seems to have been loyalty to the status quo.

This premise expressed itself in an anxiously cooptive attitude to a rebellious white working class, a generous understanding of the action of Afrikaner rebels, and a conception of black interests so overly paternalistic that it often bordered on racism.[18] Few great civil rights issues confronted the courts at this time, yet the implicit race prejudice and several legal principles adopted by the judges established a framework and atmosphere that did little to mollify the effect of apartheid legislation after 1948.[19] This period in the appellate division I characterized earlier as follows:

> In the final analysis, the overall picture which emerges is one of a group of men who saw their dominant role as the protectors of a stability in the social formation of which they formed an integral part. This conception of their task was, doubtless, influenced by their racial and class backgrounds, education, and training. The judges expressed it in terms of a positivistic acceptance of the concept of legislative sovereignty, despite a patently racist political structure, and of a desire to preserve the existing order of legal relations, notwithstanding its basis in manifest social inequalities. . . . There can be little argument that the picture of the appellate judiciary, as a body of fearless fighters for the less-privileged and unrepresented majority, is a myth.[20]

It is important, however, to note that at no stage or in any division has there been an allegation of conscious or deliberate bias or prejudice by the judiciary. Rather, the judicial approach can be said to have been formed by class background and the inherent limitations of the judicial function in the state. In other words, as U.S. legal realists have argued, each individual acts in a way fashioned by his or her personal circumstances and learned values. This accords, too, with a materialist conception of the judicial function—that it is likely to be exercised in the interests of the ruling group from which the judiciary has been drawn—but more of that later on in this discussion.

The second period, 1950 to 1980, saw the Supreme Court formally more involved in the political battles that took place between the ruling National party and those of less-conservative opinion.[21] The appellate division was thrust into conflict with the majority in Parliament early in the 1950s. The scope of one or two pieces of apartheid legislation was effectively invalidated on grounds of administrative law,[22] and the court used its limited power of judicial review to delay the passage of legislation that transferred colored voters to a separate voters roll.[23] However, through scarcely disguised evasion of constitutional strictures on government action and clear manipulation of the composition and quorum requirements of the appellate division, the government signaled its determination to execute its policy, and the judiciary had little option but to acquiesce.[24]

However, judicial appointments by the National party in the late 1950s and, perhaps, an increasing political consensus among whites gave rise in the 1960s to a generally unquestioning and sometimes enthusiastic judicial approach to the interpretation of apartheid legislation.[25] More importantly, the court refused on many occasions to come to the aid of those who suffered the effects of the security legislation that marked that decade, nor was there any attempt made to check the development of almost unlimited discretionary power in the hands of the executive.[26] In Forsyth's assessment, "The court has . . . shown, in general, a considerable preference for the executive interest over that of the individual."[27]

During this period there was also a strong tendency to prefer continental European doctrines in private law and thus to downgrade the importance of English legal principles.[28] This overall pattern continued in the 1970s, with the odd exception that showed that there were some judges[29] who were not "more Executive minded than the Executive."[30] After a detailed consideration of the aspects of the appellate division's performance in the period 1950 to 1980, Forsyth concluded:

> [T]he question . . . whether the Appellate Division judges have stood aside from the developments which have tainted much of the rest of the legal system, must be answered in the negative. Although the courts have seldom associated themselves directly with government policy, their decisions reveal that since . . . [1959] . . . the implementation of government policy has been substantially facilitated by a failure to keep the executive within the law.[31]

Dugard, too, after a more wide-ranging but less-detailed survey of the case law was of the opinion that most "South African judges . . . whether they support the Government or not . . . have one basic premise in common—loyalty to the status quo. . . . This is what is at the root of the accusation that the . . . judiciary has become 'establishment-minded.'"[32]

Again, it must be clearly reiterated that the judiciary has not pursued an *intentionally* biased or prejudiced policy. However, the evidence up to 1980 points to a judicial approach firmly in line with the overall strategy of the government of the day, notwithstanding several isolated exceptions in which individuals succeeded in preserving or establishing their legal rights against the state. Furthermore, it must be emphasized that the picture presented here is merely a summary of the chief sources. Much of the complexity of the subject matter is not adequately portrayed. The scope of this chapter precludes such an investigation, but reference to the sources cited will confirm the outline given above and will provide detailed treatment of many of the underlying complexities.

The third period, 1980 to the end of June 1985 (before the declaration of the state of emergency, to be dealt with separately), is more difficult to assess due to the absence of adequate studies and the relative lack of historical perspective. Analysis of judicial performance must therefore proceed on a different basis; there are at least three features of judicial conduct during these years that deserve attention.

First, in the area of the control of influx of Africans to the urban areas of South Africa, the courts have led the way in granting such rights on a wider scale than ever before under the apartheid system. They have done so at the provincial level, each time being affirmed on appeal, through the interpretation of subordinate legislation in such a way as to make it operate in favor of the individual African applicant concerned and contrary to avowed government policy and administrative practice.[33] As a result, the position of hundreds of thousands of African men, women, and children has been potentially alleviated. Although such a step might have been in line with one body of opinion in government circles, and although the government has subsequently adopted legislation that attenuates the effect of the courts' judgments, there can be little doubt that the impetus for beneficial change in this sphere received a substantial boost through the findings of the judges.[34]

Second, in the sphere of labor relations, major shifts have taken place since 1980 that substantially affect the role of the existing court and the use to which a "court" can be put. The large-scale organization of black workers into trade unions that occurred in the 1970s and the fact that the existing statutory industrial relations machinery made no provision for African workers induced the government to set up the Wiehahn Commission of Inquiry.[35] This commission recommended the establishment of an industrial court, which would replace the Supreme Court as arbiter in most labor relations matters and which would be far closer to a court of equity than the ordinary courts of law in South Africa. The government accepted this proposition as part of the new labor relations package, and the Industrial Court was set up for the rapid solution of labor disputes at low cost.

After initial teething troubles, some of which persist,[36] and in an atmosphere of fairly widespread misgivings on the part of trade unions, the Industrial Court has generally managed to achieve a reasonably high level of success in according economic rights to (mainly) black workers.[37] The independent trade union movement is careful not to allow the legal process to overshadow factory-based collective bargaining, but the movement is not averse to using the Industrial Court when this seems to be in its interests. This has been particularly evident in disputes about unfair labor practice,[38] unfair dismissals, and the protection of workers engaged in a legal strike.[39]

Although the jurisdiction of the Industrial Court is fairly wide ranging, the Supreme Court is not entirely excluded from labor matters.[40] In the exercise of its residual jurisdiction, the judiciary has inevitably been influenced by the practices and principles of the Industrial Court.[41] The result of this development has been a reorientation of the common law of employment away from the interests of employers alone and a reconsideration of the possible part the courts can play as a mechanism of conflict management and, even, as a protector of worker interests.[42]

Third, the whole question of state security gained, if possible, even greater prominence in the years since 1980. Internal resistance, in the form of educational boycotts and civic disturbances, and an increasing number of guerrilla attacks on (mainly) state targets by members of opposition groups led inevitably to a rapid increase in the number of trials under the country's security legislation. At the same time, the government became concerned with its image abroad as the pressure for international sanctions against South Africa began to mount. In order to regularize the security laws, a commission of inquiry was appointed once again, under the chairmanship of Judge of Appeal P. J. Rabie. This commission reported to Parliament in February 1982 and recommended a procedural streamlining of the security laws and the introduction of several formal safeguards for the rights of those acted against in terms of these laws. However, the commission's approach was greeted by trenchant criticism from opponents of the government, for it attempted to legitimate the use of the type of security legislation on the statute books by reference to the "total onslaught" argument popular in government circles at the time. As a result, the range and harshness of powers available to the executive and the police remained unaffected.[43]

Despite the clarity and order brought to security legislation by the Rabie Commission, the state instead began charging those accused of acts against the state with the common law crime of treason.[44] Suttner suggests several reasons for this shift in practice. Among these is the fact that guerrilla activities are certainly indictable under the charge of high treason; that various pretrial procedural advantages under allied legislation make the prosecution's task less difficult;[45] that the legitimacy of the government may be enhanced abroad by resorting to trial for a crime known to all countries rather than for peculiar local statutory crimes; and, finally, that the value of judicial "authentication" will thereby be increased.[46]

Whatever the motivation for this change in state prosecutorial practice, the approach of the Supreme Court judiciary to the relative weight of the interests of state and individual in security trials seems to have remained firmly on the side of the state. There have been one or two exceptions to this rule,[47] but the evidence that the courts have been prepared in general to give full expression to legislative intent in cases of this type is overwhelming.[48] In doing so, certain judges have taken it as their duty to inveigh against the motives and political ideas of the accused, which are possibly shared by large numbers of fellow South Africans.[49]

Thus, it would seem as though the Supreme Court judiciary in the period 1980 to June 1985 continued along the path outlined by its predecessors since 1910. Changes in the influx control and labor relations areas at this time can probably find their parallel in judicial interpretation of the first Industrial Conciliation Act of 1924.[50] The enforcement of apartheid laws has continued largely unabated,[51] and the status quo remains unchallenged by judicial decree.[52]

In sum, this outline of the record of the judiciary in South Africa since 1910 clearly indicates that while maintaining a formal impartiality, the Supreme Court has in effect consistently acted in the interests of the dominant group in the social structure of which it forms a part. The reasons for this approach by the judiciary and the implications of this approach for the political process in South Africa both now and in the future form the subject matter of the rest of this chapter.

The Judicial Process

Had this been written a decade ago, there would have been very little to report on the subject of the judicial function in South Africa. Government discussion of the role of the judiciary and of judicial attitudes to matters broadly political was stifled by a double cloak of silence. On the one hand, liberal opponents of the South African regime hesitated to criticize the branch of government that had been kindest to their cause and that was regarded with almost universal admiration, largely the result, it would seem, of the stance of the appellate judiciary in the first half of the 1950s. To many liberals, it would have seemed self-defeating to undermine the very institution that represented in the popular mind the likeliest channel for limiting the excesses of legislature and executive.

On the other hand, the circumspect and polite critical commentaries that appeared before 1975 were immediately greeted by the serving judiciary and by government ministers with the greatest hostility. Some works were banned,[53] one of the most persistent authors was convicted of contempt of court for his forthright criticism,[54] and other writers[55] were all taken to task by no less a figure than the chief justice, whose reactions were widely reported.[56] This created an atmosphere scarcely conducive to healthy and open debate, yet through the persistence of academics such as John Dugard and Barend van Niekerk, the subject remained alive and now has become an accepted matter for discussion, even in the leading law journals.[57] Of the contributions to the literature, we need take note only of the main arguments to date as well as some recent developments.

As far as the "traditional" debate is concerned, the leading exponent of a view critical of the judiciary is John Dugard.[58] He has during the years eloquently and persistently taken the judiciary to task for leaning too quickly and too far in the direction of the executive and for being slow to uphold principles of justice (which he maintains are fundamental to South Africa's Roman-Dutch common law) in the face of the ravages wrought by apartheid. In realist fashion, he is of the opinion that the major inarticulate premise of the judiciary is loyalty to the status quo, and he attributes a fair amount of the blame for this to a vulgar, Austinian positivism to which, he argues, the judiciary subscribes.[59] He would have it that the judge stands before a choice in a hard case, and he pleads for the exercise of that choice in a "realist-cum-value-oriented" fashion in order to uphold basic liberties.[60] Dugard bases his argument on a somewhat selective review of judicial attitudes in all divisions of the Supreme Court and concentrates on the post-1948 period. Sachs' study, on the other hand, is an extremely valuable attempt to consider the course the administration of justice has taken in all South African courts since 1652,[61] while several other researchers have chosen to be more limited but more detailed in their focus.[62] All of these writers have been variously critical of that lack of resolution—conspicuous, in their opinion—in the judicial record of resistance to those tendencies toward totalitarianism in the legislature and executive.

A second aspect of the traditional criticism of the judiciary has been the concentration by Cameron on the effect of the judicial career of Chief Justice L. C. Steyn on the overall approach of the South African courts. Based on a reading of all Judge Steyn's appellate judgments, Cameron concluded that Steyn had "a towering but parsimonious intellect; that he was a scrupulous but ungenerous judge; [and] that he was an unfettered but—of his own volition—executive-minded judge."[63] Reaction to this assessment was both rapid and critical,[64] but this frank method of analyzing the judicial function has proved valuable in its emphasis on the influence a judge's background and political preferences have on the development of the law.

Third, and not unsurprisingly within the traditional school, criticism of the attitudes of South African judges on issues of public interest has led to a call for resignation from judicial office in order to highlight the moral bankruptcy of the laws the judges have to administer. This argument was first propagated by the liberal Civil Rights League in Cape Town,[65] and it became the subject of heated debate in the press and in the law journals after Raymond Wacks assumed a similar stance in his inaugural lecture (that is, his inauguration as chair of a university department).[66] Wacks relied upon the thoughts of Ronald Dworkin to support his argument and maintained that the "principles" that underlay the South African legal system, to which judges were bound to resort, were grounded in injustice and inequality. It followed, he said, that the judges ought to resign.[67]

Reaction to Dworkin's argument has not been confined to the relevance or otherwise of his work in South Africa. The dominant viewpoint of the debate seems to be that, although the moral iniquity of much of the legislation the judiciary enforces is acknowledged, there remains some opportunity for a serving judge to mollify the harsher aspects of these laws.[68] Although the performance of the judiciary outlined above gives little hope that such an attitude will be adopted by the majority of judges, or that the ruling party will tolerate a massive subversion of its will, proponents of this view yet maintain that the isolated instances of relief achieved during the years make the enterprise worthwhile.

As can be expected, reaction to the types of criticism put forward by the traditional writers has come in the form of heated denunciations of such views and protestations of judicial impartiality and independence, from both politicians and judges.[69] But in more recent times a different type of critique of the judiciary's role in South Africa has come to the fore. Traces of this nontraditional view of the judicial process can be found in the work of Millner and Sachs,[70] but its current revival and extension can be attributed directly to a Marxist interpretation of the role played by law and the judiciary in society.

A somewhat crude instrumentalist position was assumed by the forerunners to the present debate,[71] but this has rapidly shifted to one that bears traces of the work of both E. P. Thompson and European structuralism.[72] In this view the state is seen as operating generally in the interests of the ruling classes but without doing so in a mechanical fashion. In Suttner's words, "[I]t is structured as a differentiated and contradictory unity."[73] Law and the judiciary function with a measure of autonomy within this general framework, which serves to explain how a judicial record overwhelmingly in support of the status quo can at the same time bear witness to several decisions that have permanently improved the position of workers and been to the detriment of ruling-class interests.

The legal and judicial systems are thus not seen as mere tools of the ruling class because these systems can be used by the working class in certain circumstances to confirm gains made through popular struggle.[74] Human rights are similarly not mere bourgeois obfuscatory devices, for a regime that governs through law and not by decree and that is forced to concede certain rights to its citizens is by that fact not absolutely free to do as it wishes.[75]

On the other hand, the ideological legitimacy that the regime wins for itself by allowing such a process far outweighs the inconveniences caused by such aberrant judicial decisions and by an insistence upon certain procedures and individual rights. The courts also provide the means whereby punishment can be meted out to those who do not obey the commands of the state and whereby the value systems of the ruling group permeate those of the population as a whole.[76]

This oversimplified and perhaps unfairly brief version of the complex set of views propagated by the nontraditional critics of the South African judiciary nevertheless gives an idea of the kind of approach increasingly assuming center stage in any discussion of judicial role.[77] This approach is used as the theoretical underpinning for speculation on the present and future role of the judiciary in South Africa in the concluding section of this chapter because the nontraditional method of analysis seems to be more successful in explaining apparent inconsistencies in judicial behavior; such an analysis also stresses the sociopolitical context in which the judiciary operates. But before such a task can be attempted, the current position of the courts under the state of emergency must be sketched.

The Bench and the State of Emergency

It has been noted above that the Supreme Court judiciary had managed to retain a fairly good reputation in the public mind for maintaining standards of justice and equality before the law, in spite of legislative and executive inroads into its jurisdiction and in spite of the judicial record itself. There were one or two dissenting voices abroad, however, and by the early 1980s it was clear that the judicial image had been tarnished in the eyes of many South Africans.[78] This was confirmed by the final report of the Hoexter Commission in 1984,[79] and by the 1985 Human Sciences Research Council's Report on Inter-Group Relations, which spoke of a crisis of legitimacy affecting the administration of justice.[80] This had been dramatically demonstrated in the case of State v. Hadebe and Others, in which the accused refused to participate any further in their trial after the judge ordered that it be held in camera.[81] In this action they questioned the legitimacy of the court as part of an "illegal regime," and by disrupting proceedings they echoed the actions of British suffragettes in the early part of this century[82] and went further than Nelson Mandela in his well-known objection to being tried by a white magistrate in 1962.[83]

Although this type of open defiance of the authority of the courts is rare, there is no doubt that influential sections of the legal profession were troubled by the increasing degradation of the traditions of South African law, as they perceived them, by the effects of apartheid legislation.[84] There were signs that certain judges shared this concern,[85] but the judiciary as a whole has been put severely to the test since the declaration of the state of emergency in the most populous areas of the country in July 1985. As a result of many challenges to official actions in the courts and of the hearing of several trials in the latter half of 1985 that arose out of civic disturbances since September 1984, it is of particular relevance for present purposes to assess judicial reactions during this period of crisis.

In several cases, the judiciary has taken a resoundingly firm and public stance against the abuse of executive power and in favor of the liberty of the subject. The judgments of the Natal Provincial Division are especially noteworthy here, and three reported judgments deserve particular attention. In *State v. Ramgobin and Others*,[86] a full bench of the Natal court applied a strict interpretation of the power granted to the attorney-general pursuant to Section 30 of the Internal Security Act[87] to order that no bail be granted to persons charged with certain offenses. The effect of this judgment was to induce the attorney-general to withdraw his "no-bail" order on the sixteen accused in the "UDF treason trial" in Pietermaritzburg, a very significant curtailment of an administrative power that had been used freely by the state since 1976.

This section of the act came under further, devastating attack by Judge President A. J. Milne when bail for the accused came to be fixed.[88] He repeated and endorsed the views expressed by the three judges in the earlier judgment and in the process expressed himself forcibly.

> [It is right that the Court should grant bail.] This is so, inter alia, because the courts in this country exercise their power entirely free from any direct or indirect pressure from the State, the Legislature or the executive branch of Government. . . . I wholly fail to see the purpose or necessity for the legislative curtailment of ancient and fundamental rights, nor can I see any occasion under which its use could be justified. I venture to suggest that serious consideration should be given to its repeal.[89]

It is some time since any bench has brought such forthright language to bear on security legislation. It is by now well known that charges against all but three of the accused were withdrawn by the state after a few weeks of a trial presided over by Judge Milne.[90]

Second, in *Mkhize v. Minister of Law and Order*, another full bench of the Natal court confirmed that it lay within the power of the Supreme Court to order a magistrate or district surgeon to visit a detainee held under Section 29 of the Internal Security Act in order to put to him/her certain questions.[91] The section prohibits anyone other than an official of the state in the course of his or her duties having access to such a detainee, although fortnightly visits by both a magistrate and district surgeon are specifically required. Although there was a further prohibition in the section that prevented the divulging of "official information" about the detainee, the court held that information gathered at the request of the court would not fall foul of the section. This decision opens a chink in the armor of secrecy surrounding detention without trial, and it is significant that in a choice between two conflicting precedents, the court decided in favor of the liberty of the subject.

Third, in *Hurley and Another v. Minister of Law and Order and Another,* Acting Deputy Judge President R. N. Leon took the enormously significant step of ordering the release of a Section 29 detainee.[92] This section empowers a police officer to detain a person "if he has reason to believe" such a person to have committed certain acts against the security of the state. In the past, the courts had taken an executive-minded approach in holding that a merely subjective belief on the part of the arresting officer was sufficient compliance with the requirements of the statute. On this occasion, Judge Leon found that the phrase "if he has reason to believe" meant a belief based upon reason and not upon what the officer *thinks* he has reason to believe. Thus, a stated belief by a senior police officer that the detainee, a Christian pacifist, constituted a violent threat to law and order and the state could hardly be termed a belief based on reason. Again, Judge Leon had to decide between conflicting precedents, and again he came down on the side of the liberty of the subject: "The first and most sacred duty of the Court . . . is to administer justice to those who seek it, high and low, rich and poor, Black and White."[93]

The decision of a full bench of the Eastern Cape Division in the unreported case of *Nkwinti v. Commissioner of Police and Others* runs along the same lines.[94] Here Judge D. Kannemeyer agreed that the jurisdiction of the court was not ousted by the regulations issued by the state president for the use of the forces of the state during the emergency. He declared invalid the further detention under emergency regulations of the applicant's husband as he had not been afforded the opportunity of being heard (one of the maxims of natural justice) before his detention was extended beyond the original fourteen-day period. In addition, Kannemeyer decided that the state president was not empowered to exclude such a right to be heard by regulation, although this right was not strictly in issue here.

Several other noteworthy decisions have been reported in the media, but no further details are at hand. Three of these bear mention: the granting by the Eastern Cape court of an interim order prohibiting the Port Elizabeth police from further assaults on detainees, subsequently made final; the nullifying by the Transvaal court of no-bail orders for the Pretoria treason trialists; and the restoration of Allan Boesak's passport after his release on bail by a magistrate in the Cape. (Boesak is a theologian and political activist—in stature, second to Desmond Tutu.) Each of these decisions indicates a determination on the part of the judiciary to uphold the rights of the individual in the face of increasingly arbitrary interference by the executive.

In addition, the judges have used their right to enter any prison at any time to visit persons detained under the state of emergency. In some cases, this has been done at the request of the minister of justice, but it has led to the release of several detained children in the Cape, at least. Security legislation detainees are not yet the beneficiaries of such visits, even though the statutory prohibition is worded in exactly the same way as in the emergency regulations.

This is but one aspect of judicial reaction to the exigencies of the times. On the other hand, there have been more than a few press reports of judgments in favor of the state in circumstances similar to the above cases. For example, Boesak's application for the return of his passport, after it had once more been removed by executive decree, failed, as did an application by the Cape Teachers' Professional Association for the invalidation of the regulations issued by the colored minister of education to close arbitrarily all colored schools in the Western Cape.[95]

In *Omar and Others v. Minister of Law and Order and Others,* the situation was essentially the same as that in Nkwinti's case above.[96] However, subsequent to joinder of issue in *Nkwinti,* the state president amended the detention regulations and purported to exclude a right to a hearing before further detention. The following question faced the Cape court: Was the state president empowered by the Public Safety Act to exclude by regulation the right of an emergency detainee to be heard before his period of detention was extended?[97] Judge Kannemeyer in *Nkwinti* was of the opinion that this power was not available to the state president, while a different full bench of the Eastern Cape Division had held that he was so empowered.[98] There were, therefore, two conflicting full bench decisions of the neighboring provincial division of the Supreme Court for the full bench in the Cape to consider as persuasive, although the *Nkwinti* judgment was not directly in point.

The court ruled, by two judges to one, in favor of the respondent minister. The judges in the majority continued along the path established by the judiciary during the past thirty years in holding that in view of the general policy of the act and the very wide discretion conferred on the state president, his power to exclude the right to be heard was by implication incorporated in the act.[99] Judge G. Friedman, in dissent, preferred the reasoning of Judge Kannemeyer in *Nkwinti* and declared the regulation that excluded a hearing invalid on the grounds that the enabling act did not authorize such exclusion[100] and by reason of the fact that the state president had not properly applied his mind to the matter.[101]

In the light of the evidence and its paucity, it is difficult to make a firm assessment of the reaction of the judiciary to the state of political crisis in which South Africa finds itself. What can perhaps be gleaned from the above account is that the stage has been reached at which a larger minority of judges is prepared to redirect the judicial role away from a close identification with sectional ruling class interests and toward those of the majority of the population. Whether such an assessment will stand the test of time remains to be seen. It seems, however, that just as the judiciary as a whole constitutes one of the contradictions in the unity of the state, so, too, does a certain section of the judiciary find itself in a contradictory relation with the judicial branch of government.

Conclusion: The Judiciary in the State

To distrust the judiciary marks the beginning of the end of society. Smash the present patterns of the institution, rebuild it on a different basis . . . but don't stop believing in it.

Honoré Balzac[102]

It is to be noted how lapses in the administration of justice make an especially disastrous impression on the public; the hegemonic apparatus is more sensitive in this sector, to which arbitrary actions on the part of the police and political administration may also be referred.

Antonio Gramsci[103]

The role of the judiciary in the South African state can be usefully approached from two perspectives, the international and the internal. Internationally, the existence and continued operation of a branch of government that has during the years made some brave decisions in favor of the rights of the regime's opponents is of utmost importance for the rulers of South Africa. In many ways, this factor sets the South African case apart from most other authoritarian and dictatorial regimes. Indeed, when the almost complete absence of democracy and freedom in the rest of the body politic is taken into account, the formal independence of the Supreme Court and its willingness on occasion to thwart legislative and executive initiatives are remarkable. Reaction in the overseas media to the dropping of the treason charges against the majority of those on trial in Pietermaritzburg in November 1985 both confirms the public image of judicial impartiality and is of considerable propagandist benefit to the state as a whole.

It seems clear that one of the salient features of the present struggle for political control in South Africa is the battle being waged between the state and resistance groups for legitimacy in the eyes of international capitalism.[104] From the point of view of the state, it is thus important to be able to argue that at least part of its governing structure is free and accessible to all inhabitants of the country. This would also partially explain why criticism of the judiciary is frowned upon in official circles; it is much more convenient for the government to point to spectacular reversals of government policy through the legal process, such as occurred in the influx control cases in the early 1980s. The legal profession and business leaders also have a direct stake in maintaining the image of an independent judiciary, although for different reasons.[105]

From an internal perspective, the situation is more complex. From the state's vantage point, toleration of a certain amount of independent action by the courts must occasionally be slightly discomforting and embarrassing. Legal battles cause delay in the implementation of policy, whatever the outcome, attract sometimes unwelcome publicity, and can lead to the abandonment of a particular scheme on rare occasions.[106]

On the other hand, it seems that the ideological and repressive functions of the courts far outweigh any possible inconvenience, at present. As Raymond Suttner has so clearly indicated, the judiciary's independent image can be of great use internally because it lends an atmosphere of fairness both to court procedures that often heavily discriminate against the accused and also to the implementation of unpopular and unjust policies.[107] Judicial commissions of inquiry are also useful to defuse a highly controversial issue and to give an "impartial" stamp of approval to contentious actions. Besides, if the legislature and executive do not care for the tenor of a particular judgment, legislation or administrative action can easily restore the status quo.[108]

Of particular use to any state is the stamping of certain behaviors as criminal as well as the authentication of state authority that invariably occurs through the device of the political trial.[109] However, while this phenomenon may be of use for purposes of convincing the whites and some blacks of the state's legitimate authority, Norton's general conclusion is no doubt correct for most blacks: "The South African political trial . . . while performing the pragmatic function of effective elimination of political opponents, fails to perform the most important ideological function of authenticating State action against its foes."[110] Suttner is in general agreement with this point,[111] yet it is significant that denial of the legitimacy of the court by the politically accused occurs very rarely.[112]

From this brief outline, it can be seen that the internal benefits the South African state gains by allowing the judiciary formal independence are considerable. Therefore, it must be asked what opponents of the regime can gain from the situation. Besides the fact that individuals have benefited from judicial curtailment of state action throughout the history of the South African Supreme Court, opposition groupings can use the legal process in other ways to advance their cause.

First, the sanction of the court can be useful as a public confirmation of gains made through popular action, and this in turn can serve as a precedent on a wider front. The attitude of much of the independent trade union movement reflects this strategy. Second, trials in open court can serve as useful rallying and motivating points for a particular organization and its members.

Third, trials can provide a great source of publicity for the aims of the opposition group concerned, both internally and internationally. Finally, the legal process can serve as an educative force not only for those directly concerned with the trial but also for the public at large, although this is complicated by the relatively censored media in South Africa.

Naturally, there are limits beyond which these benefits will be outweighed by repressive and ideological gains for the state.[113] It would seem, however, that the stage has not yet been reached in South Africa, and there are few groupings who would shun the courts altogether, as the rash of applications for Supreme Court intervention under the state of emergency indicates.[114] In addition, there appears to be a growing feeling that the legal process and the courts, albeit in altered form and practice, have the potential for providing a valuable bulwark against arbitrary power, from whatever quarter it comes.[115]

South Africa is not the kind of society in which impartiality is possible, yet the formal independence of the courts and the actions of the judiciary have to date ensured that a certain measure of "judicial space"[116] exists in that society. Kirchheimer, writing in 1961, said of South Africa: "Yet behind transparent power relations, the protective function of the legal order, even a thoroughly iniquitous one, is still in evidence. It is served by procedure rather than substance."[117] In all likelihood, this is still the case, but whether it will endure is a moot point. What is certain is the enduring and cautionary value of Balzac's words.[118]

Notes

Acknowledgements

I am indebted to Dennis Davis, Stephen Watson, and André du Toit for helpful suggestions and critical comment in the preparation of this chapter.

1. *Cape Times,* 11 January 1986.
2. Lord Patrick Devlin, *The Judge* (Oxford: Oxford University Press, 1979), 3.
3. South Africa, State President's Commission, *Commission of Inquiry into the Structure and Functioning of the Courts* (Pretoria: Government Printer, Final Report RP 78/1983), Part IV, para. 2.2.1.2.1. This text is hereafter referred to as the *Hoexter Commission.*
4. The Hoexter Commission, in ibid., para. 6.4(a), has recommended the separation of judicial from administrative magisterial functions, which has been accepted in principle by the government but not yet implemented.
5. Further details can be found in H. R. Hahlo and Ellison Kahn, *The South African Legal System and Its Background* (Cape Town: Juta, 1968), Chapter 7; and John Dugard, *Human Rights and the South African Legal Order* (Princeton, N. J.: Princeton University Press, 1978), Part 1.

6. See Hugh Corder, *Judges at Work* (Cape Town: Juta, 1984), chapters 1 and 2.

7. Ibid., Chapter 2.

8. As of December 1985, there was a total of 124 judges (plus several acting judges) of whom 14 were judges of appeal.

9. Further regionalization of jurisdiction occurred through the creation of local divisions and separate courts for the independent homelands.

10. See Christopher Forsyth, *In Danger for Their Talents* (Cape Town: Juta, 1985), 6, note 36.

11. Corder, *Judges*, Chapter 2; Dugard, *Human Rights*, Chapter 1; and Forsyth, *In Danger*, Chapter 1.

12. For an outline and discussion of the work of the commission, see Hugh Corder, "A Fragile Plant: The Judicial Branch of Government and the Hoexter Report," in D. J. van Vuuren et al., eds., *South Africa: A Plural Society in Transition* (Durban: Butterworths, 1985).

13. The studies of Corder, *Judges*, Dugard, *Human Rights*, and Forsyth, *In Danger*, all concentrate almost exclusively on the appellate division.

14. See Corder, *Judges*, in general; and Dugard, *Human Rights*, 303–328.

15. Corder, *Judges*, Chapter 4.

16. Ibid., chapters 6, 7, 8.

17. Ibid., Chapter 3.

18. Ibid., Chapter 5.

19. The removal of Africans from the common voters roll passed quietly through the courts. See ibid., 152–155.

20. Ibid., 237, 240.

21. See Forsyth, *In Danger*, in general; and Dugard, *Human Rights*, 317–360.

22. See, for example, *Rex v. Abdurahman*, 1950(3) SA 136 (AD); and *R v. Lusu*, 1953(2) SA 484 (AD). See Forsyth, *In Danger*, Chapter 2, Part 5.

23. See the now-famous cases of *Harris v. Minister of the Interior*, 1952(2) SA 428 (AD); *Minister of the Interior v. Harris*, 1952(4) SA 769 (AD); and *Collins v. Minister of the Interior*, 1957(1) SA 552 (AD).

24. See Forsyth, *In Danger*, Chapter 2, Part 2, for a general discussion.

25. See, for example, the Group Areas Act: *Minister of the Interior v. Lockhat*, 1961(2) SA 587 (AD); and *Rex v. Pitje*, 1960(4) SA 709 (AD). Also see Martin Legassick, "Legislation, Ideology and Economy in Post-1948 South Africa," *Journal of Southern African Studies* 1, no. 1 (1974):5.

26. See Dugard, *Human Rights*, 332–343; and Forsyth, *In Danger*, Chapter 3.

27. Forsyth, ibid., 78.

28. Ibid., Chapter 4.

29. See *Wood and Others v. Ondangwa Tribal Authority and Another*, 1975(2) SA 294 (AD); *Nxasana v. Minister of Justice*, 1976(3) SA 745 (DC); and the dissenting judgment of J. A. Corbett in *Goldberg and Others v. Minister of Prisons*, 1979(1) SA 14 (A).

30. A famous dictum of Lord Atkin in *Liversidge v. Anderson*, 1942, AC 206 (HL) at 244.

31. Forsyth, *In Danger*, 236.

32. Dugard, *Human Rights*, 380.

33. The three leading decisions are reported as *Komani, NO v. Bantu Affairs Administration Board, Peninsula Area*, 1980(4) SA 448 (A); *Oos-Randse Administrasieraad en 'n ander v. Rikhoto*, 1983(3) SA 595 (A); and *Black Affairs Administration Board, Western Cape and Another v. Mthiya*, 1985(4) SA 754 (A).

34. For a detailed overview of the legal position in regard to influx control, see Hugh Corder, "The Rights and Conditions of Entry into and Residence in Urban Areas by Africans," *Acta Juridica* (1984):45–64.

35. Part 1 of the commission's report appears as RP 47/1979 (Pretoria: Government Printer, 1979). An excellent contemporary review of the background and content of the report and a critique thereof are to be found in *South African Labour Bulletin* 5, no. 2 (August 1979).

36. For examples of court rulings in favor of the economic rights of blacks, see *Moses Nkadimeng v. Raleigh Cycles (SA) Ltd*, 1981 2 ILJ 34 (IC); and *National Union of Textile Workers v. Jaguar Shoes (Pty) Ltd*, 1985 6 ILJ 92 (IC). Also see D. M. Davis, "Refusing to Step Beyond the Confines of the Contract: The Jurisprudence of Adv. Erasmus, SC," *International Law Journal* 6 (1985):425.

37. See G. M. Budlender and D. M. Davis, "Labour Law, Influx Control and Citizenship: The Emerging Policy Conflict," *Acta Juridica* (1984):141–172.

38. Charles Nupen, "Unfair Labour Practices," *South African Labour Bulletin* 8, nos. 8 and 9 (double issue, September-October 1983):39–64.

39. See *Marievale Consolidated Ltd v. President on the Industrial Court and Others* (Transvaal, 1986, unreported).

40. See *SA Technical Officials' Association v. President of the Industrial Court and Others*, 1985(1) SA 597 (AD).

41. *National Union of Textile Workers v. Stag Packings (Pty) Ltd*, 1982(4) SA 151 (T); and also see the *Marievale* decision (note 39 above).

42. See Dennis Davis and Hugh Corder, "Poverty and Co-option: The Role of the Courts" (Paper presented at the conference of the Second Carnegie Inquiry into Poverty in Southern Africa, University of Cape Town, 1984).

43. See Centre for Applied Legal Studies (CALS), *Report on the Rabie Report* (Johannesburg: CALS, 1982), for a trenchant critique of the commission's findings and recommendations.

44. J. D. van der Merwe, "Die Betekenis van Skuld in Hoogverraadverhore, 1980–1985" ("The Meaning of Guilt in High Treason Trials, 1980–1985") (unpublished, 1986), 7; and Raymond Suttner, "The Role of the Judiciary in the South African Social Order" (unpublished, 1982/1983), 44.

45. In other words, detention and interrogation practices, less stringent evidential rules, refusal to grant bail, and splitting of charges all contribute to a heightened rate of conviction.

46. Suttner, "The Role of the Judiciary," 44, 45.

47. See *Sigaba v. Minister of Defence and Police and Another*, 1980(3) SA 535 (Tk); *Honey and Another v. Minister of Police and Others*, 1980(3) SA 800 (Tk); *United Democratic Front (Western Cape Region) v. Theron NO*, 1984(1) SA 315 (C); and *State v. Meer and Another*, 1981(1) SA 739 (N), for example.

48. See *State v. Meer and Another*, 1981(4) SA 604 (A); *State v. Lubisi*, 1982(3) SA 113 (A); *State v. Tsotsobe*, 1983(1) SA 856 (A); *State v. Hogan*, 1983(2) SA 46 (W); and *State v. Christie*, 1982(1) SA 464 (A).

49. See J. Van Dvk in *State v. Hogan*; and C. J. Rumpff in *State v. Meer,* 1984(4), for example.

50. Corder, *Judges,* Chapter 5.

51. *State v. Adams, State v. Werner,* 1981(1) SA 187 (A), although see *In re Duma,* 1983(4) SA 466 (N), in contrast.

52. Whether it is incumbent upon the judiciary to uphold the principles of justice in the face of legislative encroachment is a different question, one beyond the scope of this chapter. But see sources cited at note 12 for some discussion.

53. See, for example, M. A. Millner, "Apartheid and the South African Courts," *Current Legal Problems* 14 (1961):280; and Albie Sachs, *Justice in South Africa* (London: Chatto-Heinemann, 1973).

54. The late Barend van Niekerk. See *State v. Van Niekerk,* 1970(3) SA 655 (T) and 1972(3) SA 711 (AD).

55. See, for example, A. S. Mathews and R. C. Albino, "The Permanence of the Temporary—An Examination of the 90- and 180-day Detention Laws," *South African Law Journal* (SALJ) 83 (1966):16; C. J. R. Dugard, "The Judicial Process, Positivism and Civil Liberty," *SALJ* 88 (1971):181; and Edwin Cameron, "Legal Chauvinism, Executive-Mindedness and Justice—L. C. Steyn's Impact on South African Law," *SALJ* 99 (1982):38.

56. See L. C. Steyn, "Oor die saak van Regbank en Regsfakulteit" ("On the Responsibility of Bench and Law Faculty"), *Tydskrif vir Hedendaagse Romeins-Hollandse Reg* (Journal of Contemporary Roman-Dutch Law) 30 (1967):101; N. Ogilvie Thompson, "Centenary Celebrations of the Northern Cape Division," *SALJ* 89 (1972):23; and P. J. Rabie, "Regbank en Akademie" ("Bench and Academy"), *DE JURE* 16 (1983):21.

57. For a list of some of Dugard's and van Niekerk's contributions on this topic, see Corder, *Judges,* xxiv, xxv.

58. The most complete outline of Dugard's ideas is to be found in *Human Rights.*

59. Dugard has been taken to task on his understanding of positivism. See C. Forsyth and J. Schiller, "The Judicial Process, Positivism and Civil Liberty II," *SALJ* 98 (1981):218, to which he replied in "Some Realism About the Judicial Process and Positivism—A Reply," *SALJ* 98 (1981):372.

60. Dugard, *Human Rights,* Chapter 12.

61. Sachs, *Justice.*

62. See Corder, *Judges;* Forsyth, *In Danger;* and Michael Kuper, "The Supreme Court and Race Relations in South Africa," (B.A. thesis, University of Witwatersrand, 1965).

63. Cameron, "Legal Chauvinism," 40.

64. See, for example, Adrienne van Blerk, "The Irony of Labels," *SALJ* 99 (1982):365; and David Dyzenhaus, "L. C. Steyn in Perspective," *SALJ* 99 (1982):380.

65. Civil Rights League, "The Responsibility of Judges in Applying Unjust Laws in South Africa" (Cape Town: pamphlet, 1982).

66. The whole debate is reproduced in Lawyers for Human Rights, *Bulletin,* no. 3 (1984).

67. Raymond Wacks, "Judges and Injustice," *SALJ* 101 (1984):266.

68. See John Dugard, "Should Judges Resign? A Reply to Professor Wacks,"

SALJ 101 (1984):286; and David Dyzanhaus, "Judging the Judges and Ourselves," *SALJ* 100 (1983):496; and several subsequent articles on the subject by the same author in *SALJ.*

69. The remarks of the minister of justice at the head of this chapter, the articles cited in note 53 above, and C. J. Claassen, "Retain the Bar and Sidebar," *SALJ* 87 (1970):25, provide good examples.

70. See Corder, *Judges,* Chapter 5.

71. Put bluntly, the position maintained that law is an instrument in the hands of those who control the state. See R. R. Suttner, "Law, Justice, and the Nature of Man: Some Unwarranted Assumptions," *Acta Juridica* (1973):173; and D. M. Davis, "Human Rights—A Re-examination," *SALJ* 97 (1980):94.

72. See, for example, D. M. Davis, "Human Rights—A Rebutter," *SALJ* 97 (1980):616; D. M. Davis, "The Rule of Law and the Radical Debate," *Acta Juridica* (1981):65; and Raymond Suttner, "The Role of the Judiciary." Both writers use the concept of "relative autonomy" derived in the main from the work of Nicos Poulantzas.

73. Suttner, ibid., 62.

74. Compare the discussion of the Industrial Court above and the views of Yunus Mohamed, "Limitations of the Law—Legalism and Relocation," in Surplus Peoples Project (SPP), *Removals and the Law* (Grahamstown: SPP and AFRA, 1984).

75. See E. P. Thompson, *Whigs and Hunters* (Harmondsworth: Peregrine, 1977), 261.

76. See Suttner, "The Role of the Judiciary," 52–66.

77. See Corder, *Judges,* 242–244; and D. M. Davis, "Positivism and the Judicial Function," *SALJ* 102 (1985):103.

78. Richard Falk, "Observer's Report," in International Commission of Jurists, *Erosion of the Rule of Law in South Africa* (Geneva: International Commission of Jurists, 1968).

79. See Corder, "A Fragile Plant," 92–93.

80. South Africa, Human Sciences Research Council (HSRC), *South African Society: Realities and Future Prospects* (Pretoria: HSRC, 1985).

81. See the description of events in M. L. Norton, "The Political Trial in South Africa: The Quest for Legitimacy," *Natal University Law Review* 3, nos. 1/2 (1982-83):81–82.

82. See Albie Sachs, "The Myth of Judicial Neutrality: The Male Monopoly Cases," in P. Carlen, ed., *The Sociology of Law* (Staffordshire: University of Keele, 1976), 116–117.

83. Nelson Mandela, *The Struggle Is My Life* (London: International Defense and Aid Fund, 1978), 125–126.

84. Indicative of this concern is the foundation of a national organization, Lawyers for Human Rights, in 1980; a speech by a leading advocate, Sydney Kentridge, published as "The Pathology of a Legal System: Criminal Justice in South Africa," *University of Pennsylvania Law Review* 128 (1980):603; and sources cited by Suttner, "The Role of the Judiciary," in notes 270–272.

85. See Forsyth, *In Danger,* Chapter 4.

86. *South Africa Law Reports,* 1985(3) SA 587 (N).

87. Act no. 74, *Internal Security Act* (Cape Town: Government Gazette, 1982).

88. *State v. Ramgobin and Others,* 1985(4) SA 130 (N).

89. Ibid., 131 A and 131 I.

90. This was a turn of events that earned the judiciary enormous praise, both at home and abroad.

91. *South African Law Reports,* 1985(4) SA 147 (N).

92. Ibid., 709.

93. Ibid., 715 G.

94. Case no. M 1631/85 of November 1985.

95. This outcome and those of similar applications led the minister to state that he had the "authority" to restore order and discipline in the schools, *Cape Times,* 6 January 1986.

96. Unreported case no. 12101/85 of 20 December 1985.

97. Act no. 3, *Public Safety Act* (Cape Town: Government Gazette, 1953).

98. *Fanie v. Minister of Law and Order and Others,* 6 December 1985 (unreported).

99. Typed judgment of the court (Natal: unpublished, 1985), 22–23.

100. Judge Kannemeyer's typed judgment (unpublished) 26.

101. Ibid., 28.

102. Honoré Balzac, *Splendeurs et miseres des courtisanes* (The Grandeur and Misery of the Courtesans) (Paris: Garnier-Flammarion, 1968), 367.

103. Antonio Gamsci, *Selections from the Prison Notebooks* (London: Lawrence and Wishart, 1971), 246.

104. For a discussion of this issue, see Alex Erwin, "The Question of Unity," *South African Labour Bulletin* 11, no. 1 (1985):51.

105. For a more extended discussion, see Suttner, "The Role of the Judiciary," 42–45.

106. For example, the proposed incorporation of Ingwavuma into Swaziland was effectively halted by legal action of the KwaZulu authorities.

107. Suttner, "The Role of the Judiciary."

108. See the aftermath of the *Rikhoto* decision in Corder, "The Rights and Conditions of Entry," 54.

109. See Kirchheimer, *Political Justice.*

110. Norton, "The Political Trial," 97.

111. Suttner, "The Role of the Judiciary," 40–45.

112. See Falk, "Observer's Report."

113. See Mohamed, "Limitations of the Law."

114. See Ishmail Mohamed, "The Law and Poverty," *Carnegie Conference Paper,* no. 305 (1984).

115. See Raymond Suttner, "A Symbol that Will Haunt the Unjust," *Weekly Mail,* 6 December 1985; D. M. Davis, "SA's Courts—the Last Hope for Human Rights," *The Argus* (10 December 1985); and Hugh Corder, "Human Rights and Self-Interest—the South African Situation," *Cape Times,* 10 December 1985.

116. In the words of Kirchheimer, *Political Justice,* 425.

117. Ibid., 122.

118. See the epigraph at the beginning of this section.

7

WILLIAM A. MUNRO

The State and Sports:
Political Maneuvering in the Civil Order

In South Africa, the domain of the private is encumbered by myriad laws
and regulations that essentially grant the state the right to make public what
otherwise are personal and private decisions. Where one lives, how one
travels, which school one's children are to attend are not for the individual
to decide. Until recently, the state specified with whom one could have sex
and marry and prosecuted those who fell foul of the law. In this chapter,
William Munro examines state intervention in organized sports, an aspect of
civil life dear to South Africans, although no less so than in other societies.
Until the late 1960s, he writes, the state strictly segregated private and public
sports in the interest of white supremacy but began to experience the negative consequences of international boycotts. In order to satisfy international
demands, sports went through one transmogrification after another, from
multinational to multiracial to deracialized sports. The world had to be lulled
into believing that sports were becoming integrated and free of state intervention, so that South Africa could send and receive athletes without harassment. But domestic sports remained segregated by law and in practice. The
world was not easily fooled, however, and as the momentum of sanctions
grew, policymakers intervened more thoroughly in segregated sports. The
result, Munro notes, is a system partially integrated, largely segregated, and
without a state presence either to uphold segregation or integration.

W. G. J.

A central theme in this book is that the current crisis of apartheid is in
part a crisis of the state. Previous chapters have analyzed various ways in
which the state has sought to shift its political and ideological ground in
order to maintain political control. This has brought into relief the question

117

of what the legitimate and proper role of the state should be in the regulation of the social order in a market society. Indeed, as the political order of apartheid has come increasingly under siege, the need to restructure the "ethicopolitical relations" of the polity has been recognized within the state. At this level, the changing face of apartheid entails an attempt to reorder the relationship between the public and the private realm, to privatize social and economic life, to depoliticize the social order, and to "move from a racial-statist to a fragmentary market-oriented ideology."[1]

Since the late 1970s, there has been an increasingly determined attempt by the government to dismantle the exclusive ideology of the 1960s apartheid upon which a pervasive statism was constructed and to redefine the public conception of the role of the state. Specifically, the government has attempted to discredit notions of group partiality within the state and to foster a shift from a view of the state as clearly racial, monolithic, and interventionist, to a more neutral view of the state as defender of law and order. The rhetoric of the 1960s—that apartheid would bring about separate freedoms—could no longer be taken seriously. At the same time, the government, under consistent attack from both left- and right-wing opposition, has been unable and indeed unwilling to relinquish the language of apartheid. The dilemma for government ideologists has thus been to dissociate government from that rhetoric in such a way that it could manage its political crisis and maintain its hegemony and power within the white community. In this situation, the state has attempted to disperse and diffuse its political control without in any way relinquishing or diminishing it. This required a major process of ideological maneuvering within that community. One vehicle for this process has been state policy on sports.

The development of sports policy shows two related processes whereby this ideological task is carried out. On the one hand, it involves a redefinition of the values of the group and its attitudes to other groups in order to accommodate changes in the political world; on the other hand, it involves a withdrawal of the state from overt intervention in particular areas of civil society and, to that extent, a depoliticization of the social order. The first process entails moving from an exclusive to a more incorporative ideology. Thus, the notion of *volk* (ethnic nation) as a distinct and exclusive cultural entity has been gradually broken down and the principles of merit, free association, and personal choice given prominence. This is clearly depicted in sports policy but can also be traced in the political weakening of conservative Afrikaans cultural organizations such as the South African Bureau for Racial Affairs (SABRA) and the Federation of Afrikaans Cultural Associations (FAK), and, most recently, in the abolition of the Mixed Marriages Act and the Immorality Act.

The second part of this process entails the political deregulation by the state of areas of social activity and intercourse that it had previously controlled directly or overtly. As the case of sports shows, ideological control now rests primarily with two distinct mechanisms. The first is an entrenched sense of individual racism already inculcated by history and consolidated under the apartheid state, which is capable of being sustained by the social fabric itself. The willingness of the government to devolve control to local authorities and club owners indicates that this mechanism is not only compatible with the principles of personal choice, autonomy, and nonintervention, but indeed relies upon them. This mechanism is of course powerfully supported by a growing sense of physical insecurity. The second mechanism arises out of the requirements, not of the racial-interventionist state, but of the law-and-order state. These requirements are that the state should maintain healthy conditions for the promotion of growth, stability, and prosperity, while impinging as little as possible on the social order. Thus, state intervention is justified on the basis of the defense of law and order, as in the case of numerous multiracial sporting events, and in the government's attitudes to the nonracial movement led by the South African Council on Sport (SACOS).

This chapter sets out to show, by a discussion of sports policy during the past twenty years, how the language of policy and the context of political control have articulated, shifted, and evolved in the government's attempt to meet the demands of hegemony in a changing political situation.

The Context of Control

The encompassing penetration of civil society by the state and the draconian system of white power structures—specifically state power structures—and control demanded by the basic principles of apartheid have been extensively documented. However, it is noteworthy that fully integrated sports clubs are no longer disallowed in terms of sports legislation, and participation in mixed sporting events never has been.[2] Nevertheless, significant political and legislative constraints, both formal and informal, act upon individuals and provide the political milieu for the debate about sports. There are two major forms of control that pertain to sports, in which the role of the state is crucial.

Perhaps the most obvious impact of the state is in the differential allocation of public funds and amenities for the different race groups (as defined). This disparity has been regularly noted and commented upon by opposition Members of Parliament. Financing for African sports has been provided by public funds, the SA Bantu Trust, and the Bantu Sport and Recreation Fund, which is floated on money provided by major companies. This aid all goes to the racial sports associations and ignores the organizations allied with the nonracial movement (that is, the sports organizations that favor nonracial sports). By contrast, the entire budget allocated to white sports has come from public funds. This has meant that while funding for white sport is rationally allocated by one department, funding for black sport has been determined on a very ad hoc basis.[3] Overall funding for sports among the different race groups has also been consistently unequal.[4] Similarly, the provision of sporting facilities allowing people to develop sporting proficiency has been heavily skewed in favor of whites.[5] The construction and maintenance of sports facilities in the townships have been financed largely from income generated by local authorities through liquor sales in the beer halls.[6] Unsurprisingly, the government has been more anxious to provide for sports stadiums in the homelands. Thus, the state is able to control and regulate particular forms of social intercourse, even where those forms are generally regarded as falling outside the realm of direct state intervention.

The second form of control is provided by the legislative framework of apartheid. Although mixed sporting clubs and mixed sports contacts are not directly prohibited by legislation, there has been a plethora of surrounding legislation that impedes such contacts. Of these the Group Areas Act, the Reservation of Separate Amenities Act, the Blacks (Urban Areas) Consolidation Act, and the Liquor Act have been the most central. Moreover, sports remain segregated at the school level. The Group Areas Act stresses occupation, and until the 1980s, the government pressed this point by designating intermittent forms of occupation, such as visiting a theater, restaurant, or sporting club, as subject to the act.[7] In 1965, the Group Areas Act was also extended by Proclamation R26 (amended by Proclamation R228 of 1973) to empower the administration to ban multiracial sports contests played on private land in the presence of spectators.

The liquor act has required that clubs with liquor licenses, in order to serve liquor to persons of all races, acquire a further license for "international status." In 1980, the requirement under the act that licenses for international status be renewed every year was withdrawn, but the provision that an international liquor license cost twice as much as an ordinary license was retained. This has the effect, as Vause Raw pointed out in Parliament, of penalizing the holder for serving blacks and might make him or her think twice about the value of such a license.[8] Moreover, conditions attached to a license for international status with regard to sports clubs held that

> liquor, refreshments and meals may only be sold to a black person who is a competitor taking part in any match or practice on the grounds of the club, is an official accompanying competitors taking party in any match, or is a guest of a club member. When, by virtue of the authority, liquor, refreshments or meals are supplied to any person or any person is admitted as a guest to the licencee's premises, no dancing shall take place in that part of the premises in which such a person is present. The Minister of Justice, or any person acting under his direction, may in a particular case suspend any of these conditions and restrictions.[9]

These measures have had the effect of inhibiting or controlling contacts between athletes of different races by making it difficult and unattractive for athletes to compete, by making it difficult and unattractive for sports organizers and club owners to make their facilities available, or by creating uncertainty about the legal status of club activities or club-organized events. Although it might be pointed out that the opportunities are nevertheless there for those who have sufficient motivation, and moreover that where there are facilities for the separate use of the different race groups, these constraints are minimal and do not apply, a further major constraint is provided by the Reservation of Separate Amenities Act (1953). This act overthrows a 1934 appellate division ruling that provision of separate facilities for the use of different races on the basis of equality is reasonable and allows any person in control of public premises to reserve separate and substantially unequal facilities for different races.[10] As a result, the provision of unequal facilities for different race groups has persisted in the most everyday spheres of public life—public transportation, parks, restaurants, sports facilities, and so on. Not only have the facilities available to black people remained poorer, but in numerous cases local authorities have acted to prevent multi- or nonracial sporting events from taking place within their area of jurisdiction on the grounds that adequate separate facilities were not available. In this way, a remarkable pincer works to control sporting contacts. On the one hand, the state imposes itself on social choice by insisting that contacts between people of different races be regulated by the provision of separate facilities; on the other hand, it declines to impose itself on social choice by refusing to require that such facilities be provided. This puts the state in a position to both allow and disallow contacts simultaneously.

It should be noted further that the system of education also acts as a major mechanism of control. Under the 1984 constitution, the educational system has acquired greater prominence in the control of sports. The differential system of education is partly responsible for the disparity in number and quality of athletes across the racial groups. The breakdown of the independent and mission school network by the government in 1955 affected both the quality of education and the quality of facilities, training, and opportunities. The maintenance of separate school sports also of course has a major ideological impact. The importance now given to this less-politically direct method of control provides some indication of the success of the government's ideological strategies.

The Evolution of Sports Policy Since 1965

The evolution of sports policy since 1965 falls into two fairly distinct phases. Until the late 1970s, sports policy was geared toward protecting the racial order and was based on a conception of group membership as the primary determinant of individual social identity. Since 1977, however, there has been a rapid and rather dramatic shift toward trying to change the policy's representation, as exemplified in a new emphasis on individual choice. The central concern of sports policy shifted from reinforcing a conceptual gap between domestic sports and sports played on the international level to a more penetrating reevaluation and restructuring of the views and organization of domestic sporting contacts. This shift reflects the changing demands of political hegemony.

In 1965, state policy with regard to sports was rigid and clear-cut. Sports were to be racially separationist at all levels. This principle was set out clearly by Prime Minister Hendrik Verwoerd in September 1965 when he refused to allow a New Zealand national rugby team that contained Maori players to tour South Africa. It was starkly and unequivocally supported in an editorial of *Die Transvaler,* the popular mouthpiece of the National party, on 5 September 1965: "In South Africa the races do not mix on the sports field. If they mix first on the sports field, then the road to other forms of social mixing is wide open. . . . With an eye to upholding the white race and its civilization not one single compromise can be entered now."[11]

Within National party ranks and within the wider Afrikaner leadership, the ideology of separation and racial exclusivity remained monolithic throughout the 1960s. In sporting circles, however, it elicited a growing storm of international disapprobation, which was to ensure that the next five years were traumatic for South Africans as they increasingly were cut off from world sporting events.

During the Verwoerd administration, the philosophical tenets of apartheid became an entrenched part of the social consciousness of the white, and particularly the Afrikaner, community. This was achieved by the passage of a plethora of racial legislation embodying stringently racist values that sought to regulate questions of personal morality. The Immorality Act and the Mixed Marriages Act provide the best examples of such legislation. The aim, and the effect, of this legislation was to inculcate a "proper" sense of color. Accordingly, the rhetoric of the 1960s was racial in character. John Vorster, who succeeded Verwoerd in 1966, emphasized that each color group's sports were to be practiced and administered separately: "[F]rom South Africa's point of view no mixed sport between Whites and non-Whites will be practised locally, irrespective of the standards of proficiency of the participants. . . . [I]n respect of this principle we are not prepared to compromise, we are not prepared to negotiate and we are not prepared to make any concessions."[12] On the international level, however, Vorster was prepared to be slightly more flexible. In 1967, again in the context of a proposed New Zealand rugby tour, he agreed to allow mixed international teams to tour South Africa.

There are, however, two important points to be noted about this decision. First, it applied only to teams from countries that had "traditional" sporting links with South Africa. Thus, although the decision was a gesture to the immense popularity of rugby, especially among the Afrikaner community, the same concessions were not likely to apply to less mainstream sports. Second, this position was still very far from the conventional wisdom of the inner circles of the National party, or indeed of the Broederbond.[13] A deep sensitivity on matters of race was again demonstrated the following year in the famous D'Oliviera affair. Basil D'Oliviera, a colored cricketer who had left South Africa because he would never have been able to represent the country on the cricket field, had been included in the MCC (English) cricket team scheduled to tour South Africa. Vorster, however, called D'Oliviera's selection political and therefore unacceptable to the South African government. The result was that the MCC immediately canceled the tour and declared that there would be no further test matches between England and South Africa until South African cricket was played multiracially and teams were selected on merit.

The inconsistencies in Vorster's treatment of the New Zealand rugby team and the D'Oliviera issue suggest strongly that the concessions Vorster was willing to make were simply a response to the political effects of international pressure and did not, nor were they intended to, indicate any movement or concession on the racial principle of sports organization. Vorster also at this time was trying to get South Africa readmitted to the Olympic Games in time for the 1968 Olympiad. Moreover, he was under considerable pressure within the Afrikaner leadership to make no deviation from what was regarded as Verwoerd's sacred and steadfast policy.[14] The sacrifice of South African cricket on the altar of apartheid ideology through the D'Oliviera affair was undoubtedly a deeply damaging blow to South Africa's standing and political integrity in international sporting circles. However, the incident indicates the strength with which the Verwoerdian conception of apartheid as a political philosophy still permeated the Afrikaner leadership. As a concession to the right wing within the leadership, the predominantly English cricket was a much more acceptable sacrifice than was rugby. In other words, the language of apartheid remained nonnegotiable for the government's political constituency. The incident also illustrates the bluntness of the political tactics required to maintain the ideology of apartheid. The need to rely on such tactics has persisted in all aspects of apartheid policy and has provided one of the severest obstacles in transforming the ideology and overcoming the political crisis of the state.

It was immediately clear that such blunt regulation and intervention in sports, and in particular the overtly racial character of this intervention, would not be acceptable to the outside world. This was highlighted by the disastrous Springbok rugby tour to Britain in 1969–1970, which was brought to the headlines by the vociferous, and sometimes violent, large-scale demonstrations organized by Peter Hain's Halt All Racist Tours (HART). It is true that the tour did not have a major negative ideological impact among white South Africans, due largely to vigorous media campaigns proclaiming the fact that many of the demonstrators had been paid for their services and many did not have a very clear knowledge of South Africa or its peoples and policies. The political innocence of the athletes was loudly proclaimed—an argument that still enjoys wide popularity both within and outside South Africa.[15] Thus, the impression was fostered in white South Africa that demonstrations, intimidation, and boycotts against athletes constituted a morally undesirable infringement on the individual rights and liberties of the athletes. The government was able to stress that it was not South Africa but others who were determined to bring politics into sports. Nevertheless, South Africa's worsening position in the international sporting arena was spotlighted. By 1970, South African athletes were almost entirely isolated in most of the world's major sports, and this did have at least potential domestic repercussions. It was becoming increasingly difficult for ambitious young white athletes to win their "green and gold" Springbok blazer. The prospect of sporting stagnation began to loom. Moreover, the Broederbond, ever sensitive to issues that might affect the *volk*, began to receive signals from its huge network of branches and contacts that the social and political implications of such stagnation might be vast and deleterious.[16]

Against this background, a new sports policy was formulated in 1971. The state could not afford total sports isolation. Nor could it afford (indeed, it did not wish) to fly in the face of the principle of separateness. The determination of the state to regulate and control social relations remained unchanged. Its ability to reformulate sports policy, however, was facilitated by two factors. First, tensions within the Nationalist leadership finally had erupted in 1969 and had led the hard core, right wing of the leadership to leave the NP and form the Herstigte Nasionale Party (HNP). In the 1970 general election, the HNP had been comprehensively routed despite the heavy emphasis it had laid in its election appeals on the fatal drift toward racial integration of sports that was contained in the government's policy. Vorster could therefore feel that his policy still enjoyed sufficient grass-roots support. Second, the 1970 touring New Zealand rugby team had included Maoris, and the tour had been a resounding success. Nevertheless, the new policy did not contain any major sporting or political concessions. It aimed simply to effect a shift in the language in which organization of and participation in sports were henceforth to be understood and to change thereby the moral tenor of the principle of exclusivity the new policy embodied.

The language of the new sports policy was designed to deracialize but not depoliticize sports. By taking race out of policy rhetoric, South Africa could now be called a multinational rather than a multiracial society. Thus, the thrust of the new policy of multinational sports was to defuse the notion of racial discrimination by promulgating an image of South Africa as a collection of different "nations," an image that would accord well with the doctrine of national integrity and group self-determination. It is, therefore, in the changing language that the real significance of the new sports policy can be traced.

The policy of multinationalism held that in international and domestic sports different nations (as defined by the South African state) would compete separately, thereby shifting the burden from multiracialism whereby South Africa could still be conceived as a single nation comprising a number of races. Under multinationalism, mixed sports were excluded on the domestic level, whether club, provincial, or national. There was only one exception to this, namely, that in certain "open" international events, African, colored, Indian, and white athletes would be able to compete against each other. They would do so, however, not as members of any South African or national team, but only as individuals. These open internationals were moreover to be distinguished from ordinary internationals in which South Africa's national teams would remain uniracial, and the Springbok emblem would remain reserved for whites only. On the other hand, visiting international teams could be multiracial, but they would compete against separate teams representing the white, African, Indian, and colored "nations." Only in four specific cases would South Africa send multiracial teams overseas: the Olympic Games, Canada Cup golf, and Federation and Davis Cup tennis. But even in these cases, no mixed trials would be held to select the teams. Selection would be based on an "open international" held in South Africa.

The intended effect of this policy was that nothing would change. Government control remained as stringent as ever. For example, the Federation Cup tennis tournament was held in Johannesburg in March 1972 following mixed trials held at a private venue from which all but the tennis players themselves and the officials were excluded. This procedure was immediately prohibited by the prime minister in a statement to the effect that racially mixed trials were not permissible and that open internationals would serve the purpose.[17] Thus, the principles of strict separation remained sacrosanct. This understanding was strengthened by the agreement of black racially defined sports organizations to affiliate with the white sporting bodies and to cooperate in the implementation of the policy of multinationalism in sports. The South African African Rugby Board (the African body) and the South African Rugby Football Federation (the colored body) both fielded sides against the touring English team in May 1971, and the federation sent a team called the Proteas to visit England at the end of 1971. This had an important legitimating effect for the policy, especially among the white community. The white federations tended to regard these associations as the legitimate representatives of black sports and therefore negotiated only with them.

This practice did not, however, go unchallenged. These racial unions were opposed by nonracial unions, mostly under the rubric of SACOS, such as the South African Rugby Union, the SA Lawn Tennis Union, and the SA Amateur Athletics and Cycling Board, which refused to cooperate with white national controlling bodies on the grounds that this would amount to the acceptance of subservient status.[18] These organizations tended, and still tend, to be overwhelmingly black and were usually excluded from participation in selection meetings. Thus, official sports remained easily controlled politically and conformed readily to the requirements of multinationalism, while placing the onus on individual black athletes to exclude themselves from pursuing the highest goals of sporting achievement. The nonracial unions, however, gained steadily in political power, their position in the evolution of sports policy being a paradoxical one. They acted as a spur to sports policy and by that very action excluded themselves from it.

The 1971 sports policy had two aims. It aimed to return South Africa to the international fold without compromising the government's racial policy; and the policy aimed to play its role in legitimating the entire political edifice of National party apartheid, especially within the white community. Thus, the government set out to legitimate racially separate sports, especially within the white community to whom it was politically accountable and where large-scale organized sports were most highly prized. It is in terms of this ideological function that the convolutions of sports policy must be viewed. For instance, despite the policy that multiracial teams from countries with which South Africa had traditional sporting relations would be allowed to compete in South Africa—although only to play against separate racially selected teams at segregated venues—the Department of Sport refused permission for a women's softball team from John F. Kennedy College in Nebraska to tour South Africa in 1971 on the grounds that the team included black players. Such action in a minor sport was not likely to create a major furor but would nevertheless serve to demonstrate the determination of the government's stand. The new policy was, indeed, full of inconsistencies, to the point of administrative and organizational—although not political—incoherence. But the central, implacable point of the policy was unmistakable—within South Africa, racial separation in sports was nonnegotiable. The government's strategy was to create a separation between the way that people thought about sports on the international level and the way they thought about sports on the national level and to confine the area of contention and confrontation to the former level. Thereby the government could maintain a commitment to the principle of group identity and group integrity that was a crucial link with its political base and at the same time declare to the outside world its openness within historical constraints.

The outcome of this strategy was a web of political doubletalk. For instance, while South Africa was quite happy to entertain Maori sportsmen,

Danie Craven, the powerful president of the (white) South African Rugby Board, stated in May 1972 that there was "no chance whatever" of mixed trials taking place for the selection of the 1973 rugby Springboks. South Africa, he said, was "not going to be prescribed to by anybody as to what we have to do in this country . . . only by what we think is right."[19] Meanwhile, black sports bodies that were prepared to cooperate with the policy of multinationalism were encouraged with promises of international tours. Thus, the administration and organization of sports became a tangled mess of open internationals, multiracial touring teams, white Springboks, and racially defined representative teams. In the background the Broederbond launched an extensive campaign to infiltrate and control white sporting bodies. Broeders were advised by the executive of the Bond to use the term *multinational* rather than *mixed* sports. A survey conducted among Broederbond members in 1974 showed that 97.4 percent of the members thought that the establishment of national sporting bodies for every separate nation and their affiliation with world sporting organizations ought to be expedited.[20]

This policy provided the framework for the organization and administration of sports in South Africa up to the late 1970s. It was a clear statement that the statist ideology of apartheid, through a deep penetration of the state into all areas of civil society, was sacred. But although *Die Vaderland* optimistically suggested that the new policy might herald an important international breakthrough for South Africa,[21] it was soon clear that this policy had channeled itself into a political and ideological impasse. First, the policy had totally failed to appease international opinion. This was vividly demonstrated by the Springbok rugby tour of Australia in 1971, where match venues resembled battlefields and were "guarded by miles of barbed wire and hundreds of police," where hotels denied the players accommodation, and the railways refused to carry the team.[22] Second, there was the growing strength of the nonracial sporting bodies who refused to cooperate with the policy of multinationalism or with the white sports bodies that required their support in working within the framework of government policy; the nonracial organizations were intransigent in their stand for nonracial sports from club level upward. At the same time, top white athletes were displaying increasing willingness to participate in multiracial sport. Thus, the government faced the problem of dealing with these issues without threatening its own ideological underpinnings.

The strategy of driving a wedge between international and national competition does, however, appear to have been fairly successful. Indeed, this strategy must be seen as an attempt to solve the impasse. Because of its high visibility and emotional importance within the white community, the sports policy of the government has always been primarily directed toward the maintenance of ideological and political control. The difficulties of international competition provided the almost exclusive focus of concern for the white bodies, which were in any case the most powerful and the ones that the government was most concerned about. The nonracial movement, lacking access to facilities and facing a daunting array of political obstacles, did not pose a major threat. But clearly, given the publicity attendant on international sports, the government's policy remained a source of vulnerability. Indeed, a communication from the executive of the Broederbond to its members in 1975 noted that the Bond had received confidential information convincing it "that international ties, especially in rugby and cricket, have serious implications at this critical stage for our country, regarding international trade, national trade, military relationships and armaments, and strategic industrial development."[23] Clearly, this was cause for some political concern.

By the mid-1970s, then, the contradictions embodied in sports policy had taken clear shape. The state ideology of apartheid was not to be touched, but at the same time, the political implications of the ideology were becoming so severe that they could not be left unresolved. In this sense, sports policy reflected one aspect of the general escalation of apartheid's crisis of coherence. The solution again was sought in a convoluted and incoherent policy. In 1976, Piet Koornhof, acknowledged master of political doubletalk and sleight of hand and also known as one of the most *verlig* (enlightened) of the National party inner circle, was appointed minister of sport and recreation.[24] In September of that year, government policy with regard to multiracial sport was slightly amended to give the impression of relaxation and also to contain the ambiguities of the government's position. On the one hand, it was stipulated that sports clubs should remain strictly separated along racial lines, each group controlling, arranging, and managing its own sporting fixtures. The new policy, however, stressed the facilitation of competition between groups. Thus, while the organizations of each racial group would arrange and administer their own leagues and programs, it was suggested that "wherever possible, practical, or desirable, the committees or councils of the different race groups should consult together or have such contact as would advance the interests of the sport concerned," and "where mutually agreed, councils or committees may, in consultation with the Minister, arrange leagues or matches enabling teams from different racial groups to compete."[25] Notably, intergroup competition with respect to sports involving individual participation—such as athletics, boxing, cycling—would be allowed at all levels (should the controlling bodies so decide), but team sports—such as rugby, cricket, soccer—should be arranged by the councils or committees of each racial group in leagues or programs within each racial group. This was a clear signal to its supporters that the government would not shirk its responsibility of racial control at all levels. The government also reemphasized that "each racial group should arrange its own sporting relationships with other countries or sporting bodies in accordance with its own wishes, and each should award its own badges and colours." But at the international level, Koornhof was careful not to close the door too tightly: "If and when invited or agreed, teams comprising players from all racial groups can represent South Africa, and can be awarded colours which, if so desired, can incorporate the national flag or its colours."[26]

Indeed, at the end of that year, Koornhof was reported in the press as having stated that the next South African rugby team to tour New Zealand would be a merit-selected, integrated team; and in November, he was again reported as saying that all South African teams taking part in international sporting events would be selected on merit, on the basis of racially mixed trials. On the other hand, when eight white rugby players participated with black players in Port Elizabeth in early October, Koornhof declared that the match had been contrary to sports policy, which did not provide for mixed teams, and was also illegal because the white players had not had permits to play on public grounds in a black area.[27] Interracial sports on the domestic level, then, were one thing; mixed sports were another thing altogether.

The apparent incoherence in this policy demonstrates that the state was holding firm in its attempt to keep domestic and international sports two different concerns in the minds of the public. Thus, Koornhof's statement of the new policy on 23 September 1976 needed to convey two not altogether compatible messages. The government's grassroots support had to be reassured that the government had not lost touch with the requirements of racial integrity and separation and that it was not reneging on its commitment to preserve and promote Afrikaner identity. On the other hand, the message for the international sporting community was that South Africa, while sensitive to its historical racial difficulties, was moving gingerly and intelligently toward a normalization of relations. Thus, the policy was intended to acknowledge both group exclusivity and social integration. This required, inevitably, a tricky political juggling act, sustained by such mechanisms as the continued disparity in funding and provision of facilities for the different race groups, which would keep intergroup competition at a low level; as the consistent refusal of passports to the leaders of SACOS and the South African Non-Racial Olympic Committee (SANROC) in order to deny them access as far as possible to the international sporting ear; and, of course, as the continued large-scale political intervention of the state into all aspects and levels of sporting administration, especially by control of permits. The apparent ambiguities and inconsistencies in sports policy meant that sports administrators and athletes were often confused about what was allowed and what was not allowed and (which was not always or altogether the same thing) what was acceptable under policy and what, indeed, policy was. Mixed clubs were neither clearly forbidden nor clearly authorized. The effect of this confusion was that before any positive action could be undertaken, the Department of Sport generally had to be consulted and its sanction sought. It seems probable that policy was actually formulated at this stage of negotiation. More informally, the efforts of the Broederbond were deployed to cushion the effects of the concessions made at the international level and to soothe frayed public nerves at the local level. For instance, sporting heroes such as rugby Springbok Naas Botha (one-time Dallas Cowboys trialist) and his brother Darius, were recruited into the Ruiterwag, a junior wing of the Broederbond.[28]

It was, of course, a profoundly contradictory and ultimately impossible position to sustain. However, it provides an insight into the increasingly contradictory nature of the ideological and political requirements of apartheid, contradictions that lay a great deal deeper than the need to create a dual illusion of the domestic organization of sports as exclusive and the international organization of sports as inclusive. Indeed, the increasing pressure of these internal contradictions and the concomitant threat to the political and economic order pressed the government into a concerted attempt to restructure conceptions of the role of the state in regulating the social order.

This shift can be readily traced in the development of sports policy. The spirit of the process, and the dynamic behind it, was admirably captured by Pen Kotze, minister of community development, when he introduced the Group Areas Amendment Act in 1982 and said that the government still believed that sports "could best be engaged in within an ethnic and group context, but we simply do not make laws in this connection."[29] Thus, the moral dimension of sports was brought closer to home. This indicates the determination of the government to engage its own political constituency more directly in the process of ideological change. A different ideological device—that is, "total onslaught," the government's term for the alleged communist assault on South Africa—was used to approach international sports relations. The government also found it expedient to include the SACOS axis in the "total onslaught" bracket, thereby defining SACOS out of legitimate discussion of sports policy.[30]

The thrust of the government's new strategy was to demonstrate its withdrawal from intervention and control in the sphere of civil society, including the organization of sports, by declaring its commitment to a depoliticization of the social order and a greater dependence for social coherence and cohesion on the choices and decisions of individuals, social groups, and local authorities. Indeed, during this time, government policy was repeatedly referred to in public statements in terms of the deracialization and depoliticization of sports.[31] Thus, this rhetoric aimed to demonstrate to the world at large that the organization and administration of sports in South Africa were neither racially nor politically regulated by the state, without in any real sense relinquishing or diminishing the capacity of the government to regulate sports in these very ways. The first step in this process was to emphasize that there was no legal impediment to any athlete joining or using the facilities of any sporting club. This would establish the principle of individual choice on the part of the individual athlete and the club. This point was emphatically made by the minister of sport in a letter to a delegation from the International Tennis Federation that visited South Africa in February 1978, and again in an address to the Associated Clubs of South Africa in October.[32] The second step was to bring all sports under the administration of one department, the Department of Sport and Recreation, which would therefore become a service department for all races outside of the homelands and thereby end the racial division of government sports administration. Proposed in 1977, this administrative centralization was finally achieved in 1979.[33]

The effect of these developments on the administration of sports was to foster profound confusion, which favored government strategy. A plethora of controlling mechanisms remained, any of which could be invoked in order to ensure that sporting contacts between races remained controlled, orderly, and suitable. First, there was a system of permits. Koornhof's announcement that no legal permission or permit was required by any player to use sporting facilities or to join any club did not go unqualified. An annual clearance still had to be obtained by national and provincial bodies for the attendance of mixed spectators at sports events. The government's pledge that applications for whites to watch sports in black areas would be viewed favorably remained just that; so, too, did the pledge that there would be no restriction on mixed seating and the use of facilities.[34] As experience was repeatedly to show, such pledges were not to be relied upon, especially when application had to be made to more than one authority. Moreover, permit requirements included application to the clubs as well as to the city councils and administration boards for the use of the facilities under their control. This meant that multiracial sporting events were at the mercy of the goodwill not only of the central government and the Department of Sport, but also of local authorities, and in a number of cases local authorities simply refused to make their facilities available for multiracial sports. This was a useful mechanism for control because it allowed the government to remain uninvolved; for instance, when, in August 1978, the Pretoria City Council prohibited the use of its grounds by any blacks at all, Koornhof declared himself unable to intercede.[35] At the same time, the government defended the continued application of the Separate Amenities Act, the Group Areas Act, and the Liquor Act, all of which had direct application to racially mixed events and which required sports authorities to obtain permits for any event involving participants of more than one race, on the grounds that these laws did not apply specifically to sports but were intended to defuse potential conflict in South Africa and maintain law and order.[36] Thus, government policy sought to cast the role of the state in an essentially negative light, as the mere defender of social stability.

The state was not of course limited to this role. Two white members of a nonracial rugby team in Port Elizabeth were convicted and cautioned on charges of contravening the Urban Areas Consolidation Act for playing rugby in the New Brighton township, and another claimed that he was being harassed by police because of his club membership.[37] More than ever, however, political control of multiracial sporting contacts lay in the widespread confusion engendered in the administration and organization of multi- and nonracial sport by the policy itself. As the system and the policy were not always consonant, the government had considerable flexibility in making pronouncements and taking actions and could test the political wind before doing so. Thus, assurances given one day, or by one authority, could be refuted the next, perhaps by another authority altogether. Facilities made available one day, or for a particular occasion, might be refused the next, or for another occasion. Decisions made at the local level could be either overthrown or overlooked by a higher authority.[38]

This flexibility was politically necessary if the government were to demonstrate its withdrawal from active regulation of social relations without alarming its electorate unduly. By the end of 1979, the key term of sports policy was "autonomy." The government continued to invoke the 1976 policy as the official position, but it now argued that these guidelines should not be enforced by means of legislation. Autonomy of sports bodies was recognized so long as order was maintained and the laws of the country upheld; and the autonomy of the owners of the facilities with regard to making them available also was recognized.[39] On the other hand, the consolidation of a single Department of Sport was justified as rationalization on the grounds of technical efficiency, elimination of duplication, and greater uniformity.[40] Thus, the government could argue that there was no major change in policy. In May 1979, the minister of sport was still protesting to National party meetings that the government did not support integration, that government policy held that different racial groups should not be members of the same club, and that there should be separate leagues.[41]

Use of these strategies involved intricate ideological shifts on the part of the government. While it sought to show its commitment to the principles of individual choice and state nonintervention, it needed to show its supporters, especially in the face of a sustained rhetorical onslaught from the HNP, that it remained committed to their interests and to its chosen course in solving the political problems of the country. By emphasizing both the technical necessity for restructuring and a commitment to the policies of 1976, the government was able to present itself as a kind of honest broker, thereby dissociating itself from the charge of undue government intervention in the institutions of civil society and from the charge of neglecting the maintenance of social relations advantageous to its support base and allowing potential racial conflict and lawlessness to prevail. It is notable that the first public hint by a member of the cabinet that South Africa had adopted a policy of integration in sports came from the minister of police, Louis le Grange, a man not known to be liberal.[42]

This announcement, in August 1979, heralded a period of deepened political self-confidence on the part of the government, in which it showed itself willing to press policy developments and consolidate a shift in ideological ground. The Botha government seems to have believed that its new political-moral language could be secured without irreparable damage to the party. Indeed, the political-moral language of sports policy in 1980 would have been unthinkable in 1971. For instance, when the right-wing minister of public works, Andries Treurnicht, sought to prevent the participation of colored schoolboys in the Craven Week schools' rugby tournament, the prime minister countered with the argument that he interpreted South African law as being unconcerned with the organization of sports competitions unless to ensure the maintenance of law and order. Thus, he argued that the nonracial rugby week had broken no law; the involvement of whites and coloreds was up to the individuals themselves and their parents, and it was not the place of the government to interfere.[43] In 1983, Danie Craven was able to demonstrate the fundamental break with the old ideology in an article bemoaning South Africa's isolation as "our own fault," and arguing that the 1965 government ban on Maori players together with the 1968 prohibition of Basil D'Oliviera had "heralded the doom" of South African sports. Craven concluded that "we are now reaping the fruit that we ourselves sowed."[44] This points to the acceptance in influential circles of the obsolescence of the old statist ideology of apartheid. It represents what Giliomee has referred to as "a distinct but not yet decisive shift away from an identity that rests on exclusivity and privilege towards an orientation in which culture, merit and free association are preferred to race as a basic ordering principle of society."[45]

Perhaps the clearest indication of the government's determination to carry this ideological shift through can be traced in its willingness to use sports policy to modify some of the legislative and philosophical bastions of apartheid, features that had defined the very character of the system, and to force the breakaway of the right wing of the party under Treurnicht to form the Conservative party (CP). By the end of 1979, the anomalies in sports policy organization and administration had left sports in complete disarray. As Dave Dalling, the sports spokesman of the Progressive Federal party (PFP), pointed out in Parliament, while the government proclaimed a policy of sports autonomy, it still adhered to the policy outlined in 1976, with the result that the practice of sports bore no resemblance to government policies. The discriminating laws affecting sports were still on the statute books but were circumvented by administrative instruction.[46] Indeed, the government was under severe pressure, from both its own right wing and the opposition, to clarify and rationalize its stand on the legal status of sports autonomy.

In the early 1980s, the government gingerly began to ease legislative controls that applied to multiracial sport. In February 1980, a committee of the Human Sciences Research Council (HSRC)—a body technically autonomous of the government yet clearly sympathetic to it—was set up to investigate legislation hampering sports relations in South Africa. The initial report of this committee, submitted in September 1980, found that discriminating legislation was unacceptable in principle in the field of sports and that the principle of sports autonomy should be maintained and promoted. Sports autonomy, as the committee understood it, entailed the right of sports organizations to decide their own membership, enforce their own disciplinary measures, appoint their own officials, and arrange their own competitions. But it also included the right of these bodies to differentiate (differentiation being distinguished from discrimination) on the basis of race, culture, religion, language, and so on. Thus, according to the committee, there should be neither legally enforced segregation nor enforced integration, and sports should not be used as a political instrument by the authorities.[47] More substantively, the report recommended the amendment of the relevant sections of the Group Areas Act (and Proclamation R228), the Liquor Act (1977), the Reservation of Separate Amenities Act (1953), and the Black (Urban Areas) Consolidation Act. In its final report, released in September 1982, the HSRC laid down clear principles to govern sports in South Africa. These held that

1. people must have "freedom of association and choice in sport"—the right to take part, to administer sport as they think fit, and to watch the sport of their choice and have free access to amenities;
2. there must be equality of opportunities in sport, regardless of race, color, creed, sex, and age;
3. sport must be depoliticized as far as possible, and various undesirable and humbling pieces of legislation should be amended;
4. the final decision for open school sports should be left to the local bodies controlling schools;
5. there should be equal financing of sports facilities.

Notably, the report blamed most of the chaos and lack of facilities in South African sport on the "fragmented, inefficient" system of sports administration.[48]

These reports fell directly in line with the government's political and ideological interests, and the government moved rapidly to show its acceptance of the new principles. In 1981, the Liquor Act was amended to exempt holders of club liquor licenses from racial restrictions on the serving of liquor, thereby enabling sports (and other) clubs that catered wholly or mainly to whites to offer liquor to black members or visitors if the club committee so decided.[49] In 1982, the Group Areas Act was amended to nullify the provisions of the act regarding any person attending, as a member or a guest, a bona fide sports meeting or club for which a club liquor license had been granted.[50] The government also declared its intention to amend the Black (Urban Areas) Consolidation Act (1945) "to repeal its applicability to *bona fide* sports occasions."[51]

Both the PFP and the CP greeted the Group Areas Amendment Act as a departure from grand apartheid, as in one sense it of course was. But this by no means meant that the CP's oft and loudly expressed fear that concessions made on the integration of sports would make it difficult to maintain separation in schools and residential areas (one of the major issues in the breakaway of the CP in 1982) was on the way to being realized. On the contrary, the change in law in fact demonstrates an ideological and political victory on the part of the National party leaders. The arguments of both sides of the opposition had, in an important sense, been subverted, and the ideological goals of the government in this respect appear to have been advanced in a significant measure.

First, the loss of control feared by the CP had not occurred. When the minister of sport, Punt Jansen, declared in 1980 that municipalities could themselves decide whether or not to open sports facilities under their control to people of all races, it was made clear that this devolution of control and responsibility was not to go unpatrolled. It was subsequently stressed by the minister of community development that although the government was eager to create a "much more relaxed atmosphere" in South Africa with regard to the use of sports facilities, it also had an obligation to consider public safety and good order. The Liquor Laws Amendment Act, for instance, did not come into effect immediately, owing to the government's need to iron out "certain administrative difficulties."[52] In fact, it was only at the height of the state of emergency in February 1986 that the racial provisions of the Liquor Act were finally removed. Experience had shown, it was argued, that it was not possible to remove all controls as there had been many instances of "severe confrontation and danger to persons and property" at uncontrolled sporting events. Consequently, the government made clear that the statement of the minister of sport had referred only to organized sports under the control of a recognized sporting body.[53] Ultimately, the amendment of the Group Areas Act simply removed the statutory restrictions imposed by that act. The question of government or local sanction of multiracial sports meetings remained. This explains the extreme reluctance of the government to take any steps to amend the Reservation of Separate Amenities Act (1953), which would mean partial or full desegregation of public amenities. It would certainly be politically dangerous to introduce legislation to compel owners of sports facilities, and particularly municipalities or city councils, to admit athletes of all races despite the continuing occurrence of "racial incidents." On the whole, the government had been able to (and does) rely on local authorities to act "responsibly" with regard to multiracial and nonracial sports.

Consequently, the notion of sports autonomy emerged from the debate fairly unscathed and politically safe for the government. It did not cause undue alarm within the electorate. Indeed, in one way the notion of sports autonomy was strengthened because the government, acting in accordance with the argument that sports should be depoliticized and left in the hands of sports administrators, abolished the Department of Sport in 1983 and brought sports under the umbrella of the Department of National Education. Thus, sports do continue to be directly controlled by the government at the most fundamental social level, namely, in schools. In this respect, the policy holds that ordinary school sports are part of the educational program (indeed, of the school curriculum) and as such should remain racially segregated. Schools that wish to hold interracial competition could do so with the approval of the parent-teachers association, the principal, and the Department of National Education.[54]

Although this ambiguous situation exists, it is very unlikely that any radical integration in sports will result from the amendment of this legislation. Indeed, as Pen Kotze argued in introducing the amendment, it would allow athletes and administrators to "fight isolation in the field of sport with greater confidence and a clear conscience and we are neutralising a very strong weapon that SANROC and our other enemies ... used against us in the past."[55] The government has been at pains to reassert its commitment to the principle of separate development, institutions, and amenities outside of the sports arenas. However, as subsequent political developments have testified, the ambiguity of government policy—an ambiguity that is not superficial but goes to the very core of the dilemma of apartheid—has paralyzed the government at a crucial moment.

The strength of the government's position vis-à-vis its political foes is its insistence on restricting debate about sports inequality to the mere ending of discriminatory policies and spending. The government's commitment is essentially negative—that is, it countenances the withdrawal of the state from the organization of sports rather than seeking to positively redress the injustices and anomalies inherent in the system. On the level of state withdrawal and nondiscriminatory spending, the government is entirely willing to concede. The PFP has consistently during the past two decades based much of its criticism of the government's policy on discrimination in provision of sports facilities.[56] But the government now recognizes the backlog in the provision of sports and recreational facilities for black people and states, regretfully and somewhat disingenuously, that although it is eager to redress the problem, a major constraint is the lack of finance. The private sector is therefore called upon to provide a significant amount of the money needed to close the gap. Much of the money thus far raised comes from business interests headed by Afrikaners such as Anton Rupert and Louis Luyt,[57] and how these funds are spent is significantly controlled by these business interests. Thus, most funds go to the organization of tours, tournaments, and competitions; less are invested in infrastructural development. The implication of this pattern of funding is that the process of privatization is largely undertaken and funded by the private sector itself. Moreover, the government deploys much of its investment money on large-scale prestige schemes such as the construction of international sporting arenas and stadiums, which are not optimal projects for the development or improvement of sports in general. The government is able to fall back on the dictum that "Rome wasn't built in a day" [Apartheid wasn't dismantled in a day?]. In this way, the government succeeds in deflecting much of the moral force of the PFP's argument while manipulating the PFP into an essentially political argument, where the government is on strong ground. Indeed, in the matter of SACOS, there has been considerable agreement between the PFP and the government, both of which are hostile to that organization. This is an indication of the sustained political and ideological strength of the government within the white community.

The ability of the government to effect these shifts successfully has several important political ramifications. Not only have its party political opponents been disarmed, but a marked shift among government supporters regarding the accepted role of the state in regulating social life can be discerned. A poll conducted among white voters in 1970 by the newspaper *Dagbreek* showed a firm majority of respondents against competition between whites and nonwhites at athletic meetings within South Africa (58.2 percent against; 26.6 percent for).[58] However, an attitude survey taken in 1982 found that although whites were more inclined to favor multiracial sports on a national rather than on a school or club level, a large majority (84.7 percent) believed that clubs themselves should decide whom to accept as members.[59] Thus, the government has been able to maintain a secure popular affiliation that allows it room to maneuver in other politically sensitive areas.

A further political ramification of government strategy is that the nonracial movement, headed by SACOS and SANROC, has been moved beyond the boundaries of legitimate political dialogue on sports. Just as the government, through the late 1970s and early 1980s, sought deliberately to exclude the state from the language of sports policy and from the organization and administration of sports, so the nonracial movement sought deliberately to make that language a political language. Just as the government created, established, and progressively entrenched the principle of sports autonomy and individual choice, so the nonracial movement increasingly called for a political commitment from its membership. Ideologically, the government turned the tables in the debate. The government now can (and does) point the accusing finger of political interference and manipulation of individual choice at the nonracial movement, while positing its own role as that of defender of the integrity of citizens from such impositions upon their powers of choice.[60]

On the domestic front, this situation brought about a polarization between the two groups of sports organizations. In "legitimate" sports circles, backed by the powerful media, the nonracial movement has often been cast as the villain of the piece and classed with South Africa's other (legion) enemies as a part of the "total onslaught."[61]

On the international front, South Africa's position became more precarious because the nonracial movement has much more political influence in this sphere. This influence accounts for the government's reluctance to provide the leaders of the movement with passports. The force of international disapprobation has been dammed fairly effectively, however, and a spirit of defiance fostered by the ability of South African sports organizations to bring "rebel" cricket, rugby, and soccer teams (that is, teams that visit South Africa despite the objections of their government and ruling sports organizations) to South Africa.[62] But the success of the government's maneuvers was perhaps most neatly captured by Rudolph Opperman, president of the South African Olympics and National Games Association, when he declared that, despite the belief of cynics, South African sportspeople not only intend, but have, removed all forms of discrimination in sports.

> We are prepared to make pledges relating to non-discrimination, autonomy of sport, non-interference by government, merit selection at all levels, open club membership, democratic elections in sport, and such other requirements which might be agreed between my committee and the International Olympic Committee.[63]

The poignancy of the statement lies in the fact that it is made in the sincere belief that this position is reconcilable with the fabric of apartheid. Thus, it becomes clear how the new political-moral language fits into and supports the rhetoric of "total onslaught"; the conception of the state not as the creator and maintainer of a racially exclusive social, political, and moral fabric, but as the defender and protector of group and individual rights in the face of particular historical constraints and a (now largely externalized) political enemy is promoted.

This view continues to be vigorously fostered, as evidenced by the considerable success of "rebel" tours—notably of West Indian and Australian cricket teams—despite their enormous expense and occasional financial failure. (Many West Indian cricketers have remained in South Africa during the season to play for local clubs.) The government has maintained that it has no part in the organization or funding of these tours. In the same vein, in March 1985, the umbrella organizations of South African sports issued a declaration committing them to nonracial sport at every level and pledging to use sports as "a channel of mobility and achievement for people to improve their opportunities for advancement and their quality of life."[64] On 4 April 1986, in the throes of the state's severest political crisis, the South African Games, touted as the country's "biggest sports festival," were opened with a "glittering opening extravaganza" that was likened to the opening ceremony of the 1984 Los Angeles Olympics.[65] There can be, perhaps, no more dramatic demonstration of the attempt to separate the political order and the social order in the public view and the reality of their inextricability.

Conclusion

The ideological impetus behind this restructuring process, at least in the sphere of sports, has evolved from the intransigence of the 1960s, through acceptance of the HSRC report, to the pledge of the umbrella sporting organizations and the South African Games of 1986. Nevertheless, the ultimate political failure of this process is today pressingly obvious in everyday South African social life. The stress on political realities that informs the political-moral language of the impartial law-and-order state does not directly address the philosophical antinomies of South African political thought (or the political antinomies of South African society). As was shown in the case of sports policy, such thought allows for repeated subversion in practice of its own principles. The ideological shift that current political thought represents is not, and cannot be, far-reaching enough, and it in fact serves only to obfuscate the philosophical tensions that it is intended to address. This would suggest that there is a fundamental dichotomy between political reality and the language of political-moral discourse—one that is perhaps widening daily. In a game in which the government has sought to cast itself as the referee, the play has clearly escaped its control, and South Africa has moved in a dramatic, and certainly tragic, way, into injury time.

Notes

1. Stanley B. Greenberg, "Ideological Struggles in the South African State" (Paper presented at Yale University, South African Research Program Workshop, 4 December 1984), 5.
2. This was established in a test case before the Durban Supreme Court in 1962–1963; see Robert Archer and Antoine Bouillon, *The South African Game: Sport and Racism* (London: Zed Press, 1982), 188.
3. *Hansard, Questions and Replies* (Cape Town: Government Printers, 1978), cols. 5175–5176. Thus, for instance, in 1974/75, only R 1,200 was made available from public funds to further sports among the Indian population—paid in grants-in-aid to

the only two sports organizations that had applied for assistance. On the other hand, R 32,640 was paid from public funds and R 431,677 from SA Bantu Trust funds for the furtherance of African sports. R 333,792 was paid from public funds for the promotion of colored sports. See South African Institute of Race Relations (SAIRR), *Annual Survey of Race Relations* (Johannesburg: SAIRR, 1976), 396–397.

4. In the 1975/76 fiscal year, the following amounts were granted by government departments to promote sports among the different race groups: African sports—R 422,139 (18.28 percent); Indian sports—R 20,300 (0.87 percent); colored sports—R 449,112 (19.44 percent); white sports—R 1,417,609 (61.39 percent). See SAIRR, *Annual Survey of Race Relations* (Johannesburg: SAIRR, 1977), 561; also see *Hansard, Questions and Replies* (Cape Town: Government Printers, 1980), col. 381. In 1983, a PFP spokesman noted in Parliament that the government was spending twenty-four-hundred times as much for furthering sports participation on each white child as it was for each African child. R 9.9 million was spent on 1 million white pupils and only R 4,700 on 3.6 million African pupils. See *Hansard, Questions and Replies* (Cape Town: Government Printers, 1983), col. 6122. Ken Andrew (PFP) gave the per capita expenditure on sports as R 9.84 per white child and 0.41 cents per black child.

5. In May 1983, the Cape Provincial Council was informed by Molly Blackburn of the PFP that 49,000 African pupils in Port Elizabeth had seven rugby fields, one cricket ground, and no hockey fields or tennis courts, while 26,078 white pupils had 84 rugby and 35 hockey fields and 176 tennis courts. In the same year the *SA Swimmer,* the mouthpiece of the (nonracial) Amateur Swimming Association of South Africa, said that it was not possible to have genuine mixed swimming in South Africa because blacks were not allowed to use pools set aside for the use of whites, which comprised at least 99 percent of the pools in South Africa. See SAIRR, *Annual Survey of Race Relations* (Johannesburg: SAIRR, 1983), 221. Some authorities, including the naval base at Simonstown, have made their pools available for the use of black people on particular (separate) days.

6. Archer, *The South African Game,* 168–169.

7. See John Dugard, *Human Rights and the South African Legal Order* (Princeton, N.J.: Princeton University Press, 1978), 81.

8. SAIRR, *Annual Survey of Race Relations* (Johannesburg: SAIRR, 1980), 368–369.

9. Ibid., 368.

10. Dugard, *Human Rights,* 64.

11. Quoted in Archer, *The South African Game,* 194.

12. *Hansard, Questions and Replies* (Cape Town: Government Printers, 1967), cols. 3960–3961.

13. *Broederbond* can be broadly translated as "Brotherhood"; it is an extremely powerful and largely secret Afrikaner political and cultural organization from which the Afrikaner political leadership is drawn.

14. Hans Strydom and Ivor Wilkins, *The Broederbond* (New York: Paddington Press, 1980), 240–241.

15. See, for instance, SAIRR, *Annual Survey of Race Relations* (Johannesburg: SAIRR, 1982), 589–590.

16. Strydom, *The Broederbond,* 241.

17. John Kane-Berman, "Sport: Multi-Nationalism Versus Non-Racialism,"

(SAIRR Research Paper, June 1972).
  18. Ibid., 2.
  19. Quoted in ibid., 4.
  20. Strydom, *The Broederbond,* 247–249.
  21. SAIRR, *Annual Survey of Race Relations* (Johannesburg: SAIRR, 1971), 314.
  22. Ibid., 321.
  23. Quoted in Strydom, *The Broederbond,* 250.
  24. One opposition MP referred to Koornhof, in a sporting analogy, as "probably the most slippery wing I have ever had to face, a man with very fancy footsteps." See *Hansard, Questions and Replies* (Cape Town: Government Printers, 1979), col. 6908.
  25. Quoted in SAIRR, *Annual Survey of Race Relations* (Johannesburg: SAIRR, 1976), 394.
  26. Ibid.
  27. Ibid., 395–396.
  28. *Sunday Times,* 3 February 1985.
  29. See *Hansard, Questions and Replies* (Cape Town: Government Printers, 1982), col. 3511. Also see SAIRR, *Annual Survey of Race Relations* (Johannesburg: SAIRR, 1982), 585.
  30. See, for instance, Pen Kotze's speech on the Group Areas Amendment Act, 1982 in *Hansard,* 1982, col. 3034.
  31. There are two dimensions to the notion of depoliticization. Political intervention in sports on the international level had been loudly abhorred by South African politicians since the early 1960s. What was new in the late 1970s was the government's avowed intention to eschew a formal, coherent sports policy.
  32. *Hansard,* 1978, col. 5175; *Hansard,* 1979, col. 6944; and SAIRR, *Annual Survey of Race Relations* (Johannesburg: SAIRR, 1978), 487–488.
  33. *Hansard,* 1979, col. 6909.
  34. *Hansard,* 1978, col. 5175.
  35. SAIRR, *Annual Survey of Race Relations,* 1978, 489.
  36. *Hansard,* 1978, col. 6988.
  37. *Hansard,* 1979, cols. 6944–6945; and SAIRR, *Annual Survey of Race Relations,* 1978, 489.
  38. See SAIRR, *Annual Survey of Race Relations,* 1979, 583–584.
  39. *Hansard,* 1979, cols, 6900–6902.
  40. *Hansard,* 1979, col. 6906.
  41. SAIRR, *Annual Survey of Race Relations,* 1979, 583.
  42. This statement was made in August 1979 at a (rowdy) public meeting in Potchefstroom, ibid.
  43. SAIRR, *Annual Survey of Race Relations,* 1980, 586–587.
  44. SAIRR, *Annual Survey of Race Relations,* 1983, 640.
  45. Heribert Adam and Hermann Giliomee, *Ethnic Power Mobilized; Can South Africa Change?* (New Haven, Conn.: Yale University Press, 1978), 126.
  46. *Hansard,* 1979, cols. 6909, 6916; and *Hansard,* 1980, cols. 6948–6950.
  47. SAIRR, *Annual Survey of Race Relations,* 1980, 587. The recommendation about the use of sports as a political weapon was also aimed at the nonracial movement.
  48. SAIRR, *Annual Survey of Race Relations,* 1982, 586.

49. Act 117, 1981. This act did not, however, come into effect immediately.

50. Group Areas Amendment Act, no. 62 of 1982; and *Hansard,* 1982, cols. 3034, 3180.

51. *Hansard,* 1982, col. 462.

52. Ibid., col. 45.

53. SAIRR, *Annual Survey of Race Relations,* 1980, 378.

54. *Hansard,* 1983, cols. 6144–6145.

55. *Hansard,* 1982, col. 3590.

56. This discrimination, at the school level, was confirmed by the HSRC report: 72 percent of all sports facilities were in white schools; 23 percent of the schools investigated had no sports facilities, while only 40 percent had athletic tracks (it is notable that athletics was one of the few fully integrated sports). Whites owned 73 percent of all athletic tracks, 93 percent of all swimming pools, and 82 percent of rugby fields. These facilities were also of a better quality than the facilities in the black areas.

57. *Hansard,* 1978, cols. 5203–5205.

58. See Archer, *The South African Game,* 215–218.

59. SAIRR, *Annual Survey of Race Relations,* 1982, 586.

60. See, for instance, Pen Kotze's statement in Parliament that "we are striking a blow for sport in South Africa. Sport is being depoliticized to the benefit of everyone involved. In future we shall be able to fight political interference in sport with greater confidence and with a clear conscience." See *Hansard,* 1982, col. 3510.

61. *Hansard,* 1980, col. 6945; *Hansard,* 1982, col. 3182; and *Hansard,* 1983, cols. 6152–6153.

62. The rebel teams comprise overseas athletes who are willing to defy the rulings of their own national sporting bodies to accept very lucrative contracts to tour South Africa as alternative national teams.

63. Quoted in SAIRR, *Annual Survey of Race Relations,* 1983, 641.

64. *Sunday Times,* 16 March 1985.

65. *Sunday Times,* 30 March 1986; and NBC Nightly News, 5 April 1986.

ANNETTE SEEGERS

Apartheid's Military:
Its Origins and Development

In this chapter Annette Seegers examines the history, traditions, and role of the military apparatus in southern African politics. Her primary concern is to explain and detail the rise of the ideology and practice of "total onslaught," an anticommunist strategy that underlies the military's destabilization of its neighbors and that seeks to check the progress and effectiveness of the national liberation movements, especially the African National Congress. Her argument is that the military has become more central to national decisionmaking, that its interests—principally, the security of the white minority regime—are more paramount in the state, and that its links with the social structures of white society on the one hand, and with the private sector on the other, ally the military with the goals of an apartheid-led capitalist development. The military is not a neutral, nonracial institution; it is seen by blacks as a defender of white interests. For blacks, this is most clearly manifested in the role of the military in township disorders, where it serves more as an occupation force than as a defender of public interests. Seegers notes that the military is not primarily interested in pacifying the townships, but neither is it particularly opposed to doing so. In the end, military personnel view themselves as the only force capable of restoring law and order and maintaining the present racial boundaries within which the reformist program of the Botha government is carried out.

W. G. J.

The South African military is hardly a neglected subject within and beyond the halls of academia. South Africa has a thriving tradition of military scholarship, but, whereas this tradition was and remains primarily inter-ested in the study of battles, campaigns, and wars, the preoccupation of this chapter is with the military in its political and social roles. The twin strands of scholarship—military history and social science—usually present ex-treme images of the military in general. The former views the military as an apolitical entity operating within the borders of society but divorced from it, while social scientists presently tend to equate the military with govern-ment, see the military as a self-conscious political agent, or depict society as militarized.[1]

Perhaps the most valuable contribution of the more recent scholarship is the redefinition of what is meant by the military in South Africa. Rather than speaking of the South African Defence Force (SADF), scholars prefer the terms *security establishment* or *defense community,* which include the following: the SADF and the noncivilian Department of Defense; the various intelligence services, consisting of Military Intelligence, the National Intelli-gence Service, and the Security Police; the armaments and related indus-tries, including the Armaments Corporation of South Africa (Armscor), the Atomic Energy Commission and its subordinate agencies, the South African Transport Services (SATS), the Council for Scientific and Industrial Research (CSIR) and the petroleum firm SASOL; the South African Police (SAP); cer-tain individuals and segments within universities and "think-tank" institu-tions; and the State Security Council (SSC). This definition is wide and re-flects the post-1960 changes in South Africa's security machine, but in using the term *the military* I do not always rely on this comprehensive meaning. The SAP, for example, is mentioned, but no systematic discussion of it is at-tempted, as is true with several industrial institutions such as the CSIR.

In developing arguments about the societal role of the military in South Africa, social scientists often do strange battle. When the emphasis is on the role of the military in national decisionmaking, the difficulty in formulating an argument resides in the absence of hard information. With little to go on except personal interviews and statutory legislation, the hypotheses ad-vanced to date have been suggestive yet highly speculative and conjectural. Even if hard information were to become available, it is debatable whether an exclusive focus on superstructure is appropriate in this case or whether the superstructure needs to be systematically related to the substructural levels of society. Scholars who elaborate the concept of militarization—that military and social institutions are organized along analogous lines—en-counter different problems, although similar to those of analysts elsewhere who avail themselves of the same concept. Militarization implies "more than enough," but then the problem of defining "enough" presents itself. If all societies have a right to self-protection and hence military establishments, when do we say the military oversteps limits and on what grounds do we base our judgment? The solution to this problem has often been found in comparisons across time, but South African scholars tend to see the present "rise" of the military as contained within the confines of the 1960s and especially the 1970s, and they give little or no attention to what went before.

This chapter approaches the military's role in South Africa with the assumptions, concepts, and other theorizing of the civil-military relations body of scholarship. This scholarship has reached staggering proportions, and its central features and disputes cannot be adequately discussed here. It is necessary, however, to summarize (and, unfortunately, also to simplify) at least some of these assumptions and features as they ground the discussion that follows. First, analysts do not view the military as an "apolitical" or necessarily politically subservient institution; they presume instead a civil-military interpenetration or, in principle, fluid and informal boundaries between what is civil and what military. The precise degree to which these presumptions hold in a particular country is a matter of empirical investigation and requires extensive knowledge of nonmilitary processes and structures of society as well as of the regional patterns of such societal processes and structures.[2] Second, regional studies have revealed a difference between militaries that temporarily act beyond their usual boundaries in order to achieve limited goals of direct interest to the military (conjectural intervention) and militaries that seek a more permanent political role in society by, for example, replacing civilian rulers or by extending their role to include civil functions (structural intervention). The latter type of intervention is typical of many so-called Third World militaries, where they are at times known as "armed bureaucrats," or simply as managers and technocrats in uniform.[3] Third, there are, broadly speaking, three explanations for the political rise of the military in society. When the military, conceived of as a class or as a technocratic organization, outperforms less cohesive and less technocratic or otherwise "weaker" social institutions, it then challenges and/or replaces these institutions (the "military-as-modernizers" theme)[4]; when the ruling (capitalist) class finds its interests threatened, it relies more on instruments of coercion, and then the influence of the military as obedient agent of the ruling class tends to increase[5]; and when social conditions and contradictions prevent classes from enforcing their interests, an executive or state power (which includes the military) may develop, which then may rely on increasing military instruments to sustain itself (the "autonomy-of-the-state" thesis).[6]

Given this oversimplification of complex issues, the following discussion focuses on the present role of the military in South Africa, with attention given to the military before 1960, the roots of "total strategy," and the role of the military after 1970.

The Rise of the Military in South Africa

Any discussion of the present role of the military in South Africa must begin with history, and, despite the absence of a comprehensive single study that discusses the role of the military in the evolution of South African society, we have available the information supplied by many studies of South African military history.[7] This literature usually deals with campaigns and wars; ironically, we seem to know more about the political uses of force and the military's political significance through studies of the Zulu and other precolonial societies than we do about military institutions in later societies of the Dutch and British periods.[8]

There is no tradition in South Africa of large standing armies. Some use of this type of army occurred in the regular units of the British in the Cape and Natal colonies, but these units were always complemented by volunteers and commandos. In the Orange Free State and the Transvaal, there was even less reliance on regular units; here the commando system dating back to the initial Dutch settlement in the Cape was the prevailing mode. Indeed, men seemed unwilling to adjust to the basic military discipline—a problem that also plagued the commando system, where absenteeism and indiscipline were punished with fines.[9] With the creation of the Union Defence Force (UDF) in 1912, South Africa's military became more exposed to the British military tradition, but the UDF still incorporated older Afrikaans-Dutch traditions: The Permanent Force (PF) consisted of regulars organized into four mounted regiments, an Active Citizen Force (ACF) incorporated volunteers organized in regiments, and the Defence Rifle Associations (or *skietkommandos*) reflected the commando system. All these units were organized for land warfare, with a fledgling air force and navy being created shortly thereafter. The UDF was supposed to meet any external threats, but it assisted the police when shortages of manpower occurred (as in the suppression of the Boer Rebellion of 1914 and the administration of South West Africa (SWA) between 1915 and 1920).[10]

Given that the British military tradition ideally held that the military is an apolitical entity or, rather, an entity subservient to civilian-political direction, South African authorities were acutely sensitive to the problems that could arise from the political use of the UDF. A major reason for this sensitivity was the (feared) accusation of nationalistically minded whites that the UDF was being used to fight Britain's wars. The standard military employment contract thus stipulated that no member of the UDF could be forced to participate in military actions outside of South Africa's borders, and so volunteers made up the units that fought in the SWA campaign of 1915, in German East Africa, and in Europe during World War I. The units that participated in World War II again were composed of volunteers.[11]

Another sensitive issue was the use of nonwhite soldiers in the UDF.

Since 1906, a Cape Corps of Coloreds had existed, and in the SWA campaign, 35,000 Africans, coloreds, and Indians served in a mainly supporting capacity, that is, as drivers, messengers, orderlies, or personal assistants. But authorities were reluctant to encourage recruitment of these race groups on the grounds that recruitment could arm and otherwise inculcate military skills in a preferably subservient population.[12]

The period between 1945 and 1960 saw very little growth in the UDF.[13] The PF initially benefited from the returning war veterans, but the ACF declined, particularly during the term of office of Nationalist defense minister F. C. Erasmus. The probable reason for the Nationalists' opposition to the volunteer dimension of the UDF was that it had strong regimental traditions in the British fashion and hence attracted English-speakers.[14] As far as combat experiences was concerned, post-1945 experiences were confined to the South African Air Force (SAAF) participation in the Berlin Airlift and participation in the Commonwealth contingent during the Korean War. Participation in these activities continued to be voluntary. The Defense Act of 1957 (that replaced the act of 1912) preserved the contractual clause that no member of the UDF could be forced to participate in (Britain's) foreign wars. Interestingly, the parliamentary debate on the act of 1957 revealed at least two traditional views. The classical tradition's spokesmen argued that, as civil servants, members of the UDF could not defy political instructions, while other spokesmen held that a citizen army had to be consulted before being sent abroad.[15] These differences, moreover, were not an exercise in hypothetical conditions: Since the turn of the century, successive South African governments (including Nationalist ones) saw South Africa's military as part of the Western defense system, a view strengthened in the 1950s by the Simonstown Agreement of 1955 and South Africa's links with the Commonwealth.[16]

By 1960, the UDF reflected the consequences of neglect. The number of military personnel had declined, the Citizen Force and *skietkommando* units were in disarray, and despite links with the Western defense system, South Africa "remained outside of the mainstream."[17] In what was to become a familiar theme, the West's failure to take South Africa seriously as part of the Western defense system was described by Minister Erasmus as "tragic."[18] Regardless of who was to blame for this failure, however, South Africa by 1961 possessed a modestly sized military[19]; in size the PF consisted of 11,500 troops, with 56,500 ACF and commando part-timers and volunteers, and 10,000 national servicemen.[20] Black recruitment was discouraged, and the Cape Corps and Indian Battalion (created in 1942) fell into official disuse. Clearly, the UDF was supposed to be "white," and after 1945, there were indications that the SADF was becoming more representative of some whites than others. After the formation of a National party government in 1948, there were accusations that the government was, by various means (for

example, pressures for early retirement and bilingual language requirements) discouraging English-speakers from joining or remaining in the
UDF.[21] Although it is unclear whether this was the case even before 1945, it is
clear that the UDF by the 1960s and later was an Afrikanerized institution. In
1974, for example, 85 percent of the army PF was Afrikaans speaking, compared to 75 percent in the air force and 50 percent in the navy.[22]

To summarize: In the period prior to 1960, South Africa developed traditions reflecting different views of the nature and political role of the military, including the citizen-volunteer soldier of the citizen force or commando
tradition and the small, ideally apolitical, regular army that characterized the
British tradition. Although soldiers drawn from other race groups made a
significant contribution to the military, it was regarded as a politically
"white" institution and more particularly after 1945.

The Structures of White Security

The current expansion of the military's roles is rooted in institutional structures and processes that came into being before the 1960s. These structures
and processes were a consequence of the regime's search for the internal
dispensation that could best protect whites' security as well as deal with perceived threats to racial domination.

Since the term of office of Prime Minister H. F. Verwoerd, an institutional-
structural framework of state organization known as separate development
has been the point of departure of state action. What is important for the
purposes of this chapter is not, however, why these separate development
structures came into being, but the size and shape they assumed after 1945.

In some cases, the state bureaucracy is organized along functional lines,
such as foreign or energy affairs, but in other cases, the organization of the
state bureaucracy is clientele based—that is, state organizations are dupli-
cated in order to administer separate race groups. By the end of the 1960s, it
was clear that "in its structure and functions the machinery of government
was showing dangerous signs of heavy strain."[23] The principal reason for this
strain was that the state lacked the finances and personnel to staff the extending network of institutions, a network given added impetus by the bureau-
cratization of homeland government starting with the Bantu Authorities Act
of 1951, the Bantu Education Act of 1953, the Promotion of Bantu Self-
government Act of 1959, and the Transkei Constitution Act of 1963.[24] The
growth of this network far exceeded demands made by a growing population. Between 1947 and 1966, the permanent establishment of public services increased 128 percent, while the white population and total population
grew by only 47 percent and 88 percent respectively. State departments as
such increased from thirty in 1950 to forty-one by 1969.[25]

Simultaneous with the signs of serious strain in the state bureaucratic network, several other difficulties were encountered. The first difficulty arose out of increasing international hostility to South Africa's racial policies, a hostility most often expressed by newly independent African states through the Organization of African Unity (OAU) and the United Nations. As the 1960s wore on, it became clear that the African states (individually and collectively) posed no direct military threat to South Africa—they were more interested in achieving unity by means of mutual and rhetorically exaggerated verbal attacks on South Africa. Internal divisions in the OAU precluded any military activity. However, these states described the South African regime as illegitimate, encouraged other states to do likewise, and attempted to isolate South Africa from international contact. South Africa's major ally, Britain, had already expressed criticism of domestic racial policies and the use of British-supplied equipment in quelling racial disturbances. In response to Commonwealth hostility and criticism of the way in which the South African regime dealt with internal disturbances, South Africa refused to reapply for Commonwealth membership, and a period of estrangement began. The second difficulty arose within the context of the United Nations, where the Security Council in 1963 and 1964 called for a voluntary arms embargo, which was followed by Britain's decision in 1964 to end arms sales to South Africa. Arms from various sources did continue to reach South Africa after 1964, but henceforth there was to be no guarantee of a stable arms supply. Consequently, the regime in 1964 created an armaments board responsible for obtaining arms supplies from local and overseas sources and an armaments development and production corporation empowered to launch or coordinate research.[26] On another level, the regime consistently criticized the West for ignoring South Africa's strategic importance. South Africa was a prized pawn in the communist attempt to deprive the West of strategic minerals, so the argument went, and from a South African base Communists could interfere with the West's shipping traffic along the Cape route.[27]

Within South Africa, the 1960s began with the declaration of a state of emergency following the Sharpeville massacres and indications of a more militant posture by the African National Congress (ANC) and the Pan African Congress (PAC), to which the regime responded with a combination of legal and police measures. The ANC and PAC were outlawed, new security legislation gave the police discretionary power to arrest or detain opponents of the regime, and a number of treason and other security-related trials led to executions and lengthy terms of imprisonment.[28] This response, together with difficulties within the opposition movements, made for a state of relative domestic quiet until the end of the 1960s.[29] The regime also responded with a combination of legal and police measures when violence broke out in South West Africa/Namibia.[30] In the neighboring territories of Angola,

Mozambique, and Rhodesia, guerrilla struggles also had replaced earlier types of opposition, but these struggles did not appear to make any consistent progress until late 1969. The nature of these struggles did, however, have an effect on the South African regime, which recognized that struggle in the region would assume an unconventional or guerrilla form connected, presumably, with the communist attempt to conquer the world through revolution.[31]

By 1970, the regime's confidence reached an unprecedented level for the threat to its interests appeared to have been nullified with the "disappearance" of the ANC, the lack of progress made by the various guerrilla movements in adjacent territories, the government's ability to acquire military supplies, and its capacity to sustain economic growth while defending white interests. But the institutions, perceptions, and processes that were to become central to the extension of the military's role were already in place. The regime's policy of separate development required the extension of the state bureaucracy, the regime saw self-reliance (especially in military procurement) as a necessary part of defense, and the regime's estrangement from the West's conventional defense posture coupled with guerrilla struggles in the region produced a threat perception and a defense posture premised on communist-backed unconventional warfare.

From the Politics of Security to Total Strategy

The change in South Africa's constitutional ties with Britain (which removed Britain's security umbrella) and the change in the threat perception produced by the experiences of the 1960s forced the regime to reconsider its defense structure and the way security-related decisions were made. In the courses at the Defence College and Military Academy, the writings of André Beaufre and Basil Liddell-Hart on indirect strategy—that is, the pursuit of objectives by means primarily nonmilitary in nature (of which guerrilla or unconventional warfare is a type)—were already appreciated, but attention now turned to the organization of a national security system and the means by which a guerrilla movement could be defeated. Specifically, attention turned to the British experience in Malaysia, where the role of Gerald Templar and the so-called Briggs Plan revealed the value of clear-cut and functionally defined goals, bureaucratic-military coordination, and centralized command in defeating a guerrilla movement.[32]

Except for some wartime adjustments, South Africa's external security concerns were traditionally handled by the cabinet; this remained the case after 1960, although Prime Minister John Vorster was advised by a so-called State Security Advisory Board. Several suggestions were put forward during the 1960s that the cabinet should have a subsidiary body for the definition of goals and the coordination of activities, which led to the appointment of a commission to investigate the matter. In 1969, the Potgieter Commission recommended the creation of a State Security Council (SSC), which was followed in 1972 by legislation that established the SSC.[33] The SSC, however, initially lacked personnel of its own (a staff or secretariat) and met only infrequently.[34] These problems prompted, in 1973, the Commission for Administration (then the Public Service Commission) to embark on an investigation of the shortcomings of the state's national security machinery, published in September 1975 as the *Report on the National Security Situation*. This report outlined the weaknesses of the SSC and made several recommendations, among them the need for "an active national security management system" that operated at various levels, the coordination of activities, and the strengthening of the SSC by providing it with a secretariat.[35]

According to theoretical policy guidelines, "total" strategy is formulated at the cabinet or executive level because at this level the formulation and coordination of the country's means of coercion take place. Total strategy in this sense is closely identified with the concepts of grand or national strategy, with general strategy (the specified means of coercion, such as a naval strategy) and operational strategy (the execution of general strategy) taking place at other levels.[36] The reorganization of the South African national security apparatus partly reflected Beaufre's guidelines; the intent behind the reorganization was to coordinate policy at the highest level and to distribute the burden of defense among various departments so that national security could not simply be equated with defense policy. More precisely, defense policy was to provide a firm base for the execution of foreign and internal policies; at the same time, these latter policies were also the basis of defense policy.[37]

During 1971, developments in SWA/Namibia indicated that the regime's strategy of legal and police measures could not contain hostilities, and the SADF in 1972 was called in to assist the police. In the years since the assumption of an active role, the SADF has demonstrated what it considers the optimum strategy for containing or repelling counterinsurgency warfare (or COIN, as it is known in SADF parlance). First, legal and police action is extended and intensified. Chief among the legal actions are the retroactive application of the Terrorism Act of 1967, the extension to SWA/Namibia of the Riotous Assembly Act of 1956, and the application to SWA/Namibia (in 1966) of the Suppression of Communism Act of 1950 (later the Internal Security Act of 1976). In addition to these laws, the SADF and SAP regularly rely on other coercive measures, such as curfews, prohibitions on travel, and restrictions on entry into certain areas. With regard to police action, the regime created two local paramilitary forces—the Home Guards to protect tribal leaders and the Special Constables as well as the special counterinsurgency police unit operating under the name of Koevoet (Crowbar). In composition, these units are predominantly non-white (although they are led by whites), and in most cases, they are recruited from the operational area of the unit. In general, COIN training at a center near Groblersdal has become a prominent part of police training. Second, in addition to control of the population gained through legal measures and police action, the SADF attempts to prevent aid to the South West Africa People's Organisation (SWAPO), which is a national liberation organization waging war against South Africa, or harassment of villagers by SWAPO by means of fortified or protected villages—that is, compounds, hamlets, or villages are enclosed by fences, sandbagged and/or guarded by sentries in watchtowers. These protected villagers also may house people uprooted by the war and the clearing of no-go, free-fire zones. Third, given the linking of SWAPO's activity with communist backers, the SADF since 1974 has seized the opportunities provided by the Angolan civil war to attempt destroying SWAPO's support structures in southern Angola by raids.[38] Apart from the SAP, the SADF's activities are complemented by the SWA Territorial Force, which was created in the mid-1970s to eventually become SWA/Namibia's defense force.[39]

The SADF's final strategy is political action undertaken to undercut SWAPO's support. On the one hand, there is an effort to create a "political alternative" to SWAPO, and, on the other hand, there are the civic action programs designed to "win hearts and minds." Whether the civic action is in fact an attempt to win support (the war being labelled 80 percent "political" and 20 percent "military") or whether the action was forced by the collapse of infrastructure in the northern areas especially is by no means clear, but what is certain is that a substantial number of SADF personnel, especially national servicemen, play civil-political rather than military roles in SWA/Namibia. These include roles as doctors and other medical personnel, agricultural advisors, technical advisers, teachers, social workers, psychologists, and transportation and food services workers. The SADF does very little to conceal this civil-political activity; on the contrary, it points to its role as the "army of development" with pride.[40]

The SADF's experience in SWA/Namibia is important not only for what it reveals of SADF counterinsurgency doctrine and the expansion of the military's role, but also because SWAPO's actions led to the perception that the status quo in South Africa was under attack. The perception of an assault was facilitated by the collapse of the Portuguese empire in southern Africa and the intensification of the war in Rhodesia, which left the interests of racial domination geopolitically more exposed to threats from outside. Simultaneous with the crumbling of the "white bastion" came the recognition that South Africa could not in any meaningful sense rely on the support of Western states. South Africa's intervention in Angola (in pursuit of SWAPO insurgents) during Operations Savannah was ostensibly undertaken, if not with the encouragement, then at least with the blessing of the United States and, when the intervention was internationally opposed, the United States remained aloof. Even worse, South Africa's actions in Angola and Zambia were mentioned in the U.N. Security Council mandatory arms embargo of 1977—an action that all the Western powers declined to veto. During 1977, Western nations also played a conspicuous role in U.N. conferences in Mozambique and Nigeria that sought to increase the regime's isolation.

Although most of these activities were purely rhetorical, a very real indication of South Africa's isolation was its inability to attract or retain long-term Western investments. These events seemed finally to end the regime's effort to seek a role in the Western defense system, as official announcements during 1979 declared a more neutral role in foreign affairs.[41] To make matters worse from the regime's point of view, the first widespread black assertiveness and collective action since the early 1960s occurred in 1976. The student rebellions in Soweto in 1976 hardly constituted a countrywide revolt, but

> because the white elite in South Africa (was) accustomed to an absolute monopoly of political power, relative shifts of political initiative and the growth of black consciousness with its capacity to stimulate black self-consciousness (was) taken to represent a fundamental challenge . . . the effect of which (was) to sensitize the elite to the need for preventative action in the face of impending racial conflict.[42]

The worsening security situation or, more accurately, the increasing threats to racial domination as perceived by the regime, came to be expressed as "total onslaught," which was described as "the overthrow of the present constitutional order and its replacement by a subject, communist-oriented Black government." The enemy, to whom the Western states made themselves available as handymen, was "applying the whole range of measures it possesses—coercive and persuasive or inventive—in an integrated fashion. Apart from the use of military means, there is action in the political diplomatic, religious, psychological, cultural/social and sports spheres."[43]

Total Onslaught and Military Power Seeking

Certainly the (perceived) existence of total onslaught required a change in the style of governing. The tenure of Prime Minister Vorster had culminated in the information scandal, which exposed not a rational oligarchy but rather a regime prone to cliquishness, nepotism, self-indulgence, and a host of ineffective, wasteful practices. Not only did the successor government of P. W. Botha promise "clean" government, but it also introduced a more rationalistic brand of government. The number of civil service departments was reduced from forty-two to eighteen, several departments were reor-

ganized internally, and the office of the prime minister was strengthened
and reorganized, with Vorster's twenty ad hoc committees replaced by five
functionally based permanent cabinet committees: the State Security Council, Constitutional Affairs, Economic Affairs, Social Affairs, and Urban Black
Affairs.[44]

As the SSC is the only statutory body among these committees, its membership necessarily includes the prime minister—changed in 1984 to state
president—as chairman, the senior minister in cabinet ranking, and the ministers of defense, foreign affairs, justice, and law and order. Those that the
prime minister may wish to coopt onto the SSC include the director of the
National Intelligence Service, the commandant-general of the SADF, the sec-
retaries of foreign affairs and justice, the commissioner of the SAP, or heads
of other departments. The SSC has its own working committee and a secretariat (a full-time staff organization). The secretariat has four branches:
strategy, national intelligence interpretation, strategic communications (engaged in psychological warfare or "cultural action"), and administration.
The national intelligence interpretation branch does not generate its own
intelligence but interprets information provided by the National Intelligence Service, the Department of Military Intelligence of the SADF, the SAP
Security Branch, and the Department of Foreign Affairs and Information. Finally, there are the interdepartmental committees, which ensure implementation of strategy at civil service level, and the joint management centers,
which ensure implementation at local and regional levels.[45]

The role of the SSC in executive-level decisionmaking has aroused considerable interest and disagreement. Observers usually agree that the
bureaucratic and cabinet-level reorganization has deepened the trend toward administrative or executive government in South Africa and that this
trend is further accentuated by the personal style of P. W. Botha. Much of this
controversy centers around the charges that the SSC is a "kind of inner
cabinet" led by Botha[46] and that because the SSC largely consists of men
from the security establishment, military men stand at the hub of the regime's decisionmaking structure. The implication of this arrangement is that
the military is engaged in a self-conscious search for political power. Other
analysts point to the equally important role of coopted experts from the private sector and universities,[47] while still others make a case for the powerful
role of senior cabinet members.[48] At present, this debate seems stalemated
because more information on who influences or makes decisions is unlikely
to become available; thus, the debate has shifted to the role of the military as
reflected in what kinds of policies are made (this presumably reflects the
decisionmakers themselves) and in the militarization of society.

Military and Economic Development

Although it is important to provide facts and figures when speaking of the military's role in economic development, it is not always possible to do so. In addition to the data being subject to diverse interpretations, in South Africa defense spending is distributed among various civil service departments. The construction of military bases or camps, for example, is under the aegis of the Department of Public Works; national service and conscientious objectors report to the Department of Manpower; and funding for intelligence is provided by the Department of Treasury. Also, the annual defense budget is usually supplemented with funds allocated by the Part Appropriation Bill (or minibudget) of the following year, and at the same time, inflation makes it difficult to determine real increases in spending.

The SADF budget has increased in quantum leaps. The first leap took place in the early 1960s, followed by a period of minor increases between 1964 and 1973, which in turn gave way to sharp escalations. In 1969, defense spending was between R 40 and R 44 million, compared to R 472 million in 1973, but by 1976 the amount rose to R 1,257 million, in 1979 to R 2,136 million, in 1981/82 to R 2,465 million, to R 3,093 million in 1983, and then to R 3,754 million in 1984. Approximately 33 percent of the present budget is allocated for "area defense" against an insurgency threat (R 1,005 million), while conventional defense receives R 481 million, air defense receives R 179 million, and the remaining R 153 million goes to maritime defense. It is unclear how much the war in SWA/Namibia absorbs of area defense funds, although the figure is reportedly as high as R 1.5 million per day.[49]

Converted to percentages, the defense spending reveals the following: Between 1972 and 1982 defense spending rose by approximately 860 percent; as a portion of the Gross National Product (GNP) for the same period, it rose from 2.2 percent to 5.1 percent; and as a portion of state expenditure, it rose from about 13 percent in 1973 to more than 20 percent at present. When one adjusts for inflation, however, a slightly different picture emerges. Unadjusted, the 1982/83 defense budget, for example, showed an increase of 15.9 percent above the previous year, but when adjusted for inflation, the budget increased by only 1 percent and as a proportion of the GDP by even less (by 0.5 percent). Does this latter figure then suggest that in real terms South Africa is only a fair to moderate military spender?

As pointed out earlier, the formal SADF budget is only a small part of the picture, but regardless of how much funds the SADF has available, there is evidence of irregular and unauthorized expenditure, thefts, unreliable stocktaking, and weak internal control, especially as regards the special defense account. There is also the issue of the military's role in economic development.

First, as a larger portion of the state's expenditures is allocated to the military, less funds are available for other functional areas, for example, black housing and education, in dire need of state funds. This bureaucratic distribution of funds is heavily influenced by the annual *bedreigingsdokument* (threat document) produced by the various intelligence services that outlines the "state of the threat" and consequently influences the process whereby state funds are distributed to various civil service departments. The threat document also describes or lists the likely targets and regions of enemy attack. Likely targets are covered by the National Key Points Act, which empowers the minister of defense to order necessary security precautions for owners, while the concept of area defense covers regions most likely to witness enemy attacks. The construction and location of military bases and other facilities have long been pivotal to the economic rejuvenation of towns and surrounding areas, prominent examples of which are the effects of national servicemen camps near Bethlehem, Phalaborwa, Pietersburg, and Oudtshoorn. Area defense now influences not only towns and their immediate vicinity, but the distribution of state funds to entire regions, such as northern Natal and northern and eastern Transvaal, where ANC guerrillas are considered most likely to become active and hence where various forms of nonmilitary readiness are required.[50] Thus, the defense establishment influences the distribution of state funds to various bureaucratic departments and to different regions within the country.

Second, state expenditures and their distributive consequences are again only part of the story. The Botha regime has repeatedly stated that the state will not assume all the financial responsibility for national security. Historically, the linkages between capital, private industry, and the SADF resided in the defense production office,[51] but an investigation prior to the establishment of a local arms industry in 1964 held that such an industry could be better operated outside the public sector.[52] Presently, seven of the ten-member board of directors of Armscor are from the private sector, and it is common practice to rotate top personnel between subsidiaries, contractors, and Armscor's head office.[53]

Although the interests of capital and racial domination are viewed as "interpenetrated, mutually reinforced," the relationship between the SADF and the private sector has, since 1960, produced tensions.[54] Perhaps the most important of these was the manpower issue. People in the private sector complained that a two year, full-time national service, followed by call-ups, was draining manpower resources. The SADF complained about losses to the private sector; the SADF said, for example, in 1975 that "the officers strength [was] moving toward a potential danger point" and that "personnel losses in the other rank categories have already, since 1969, exceeded the gains." This situation, a 1975 white paper on defense and armament production stated, forced the military to employ women and to consider using people from race groups other than the coloreds already employed.

A complete discussion of the state-capital nexus is beyond the scope of this chapter, but the role of Armscor in that nexus is worth discussing. In the period since its creation, Armscor has become one of the largest financial or industrial undertakings in South Africa; presently, it employs between twenty-three and twenty-nine thousand people and has nine affiliated industries or subsidiaries.[55] Armscor's assets exceed R 1,500 million (up from R 200 million in 1974), with an annual cash flow of about R 1,800 million.[56] Besides creating at least one hundred thirty-two thousand job opportunities in the private sector, Armscor's subcontracts to the private sector for military hard- and software amount to between twelve and nineteen hundred[57], at least four hundred of these subcontracting companies are unable to exist without defense contracts.[58] Indeed, between 70 and 80 percent of Armscor's deliveries to the SADF are produced by the private sector.[59] Since 1980 when the SADF's needs were largely met,[60] the defense establishment has acted to protect the interests of capital in the private sector by launching an aggressive international marketing campaign and by marketing products locally. In the former instance, Armscor participated in international arms conventions, in Piraeus (Greece) during 1982 and in Santiago (Chile) during 1984.[61] In editions of the *International Defence Review* and *Jane's Defence Weekly,* Armscor advertises a "tested-under-fire" range of weapons.[62] Exports will, it is hoped, increase from R 10 million to R 150 million annually.[63] In the latter instance, Armscor wishes to sell its products on the local market, although not under the same name or appearance.

It is, in short, hard to determine where the interests of the military stop and those of capital start. When the influence of the military in the functional and regional distribution of state funds is added to this nexus, it makes for a highly significant role of the military in economic development.

Structural Vulnerability and the Military

Although the rhetoric about it has shifted, the regime has, since the 1950s, regarded separate development as the best framework for the protection of white interests. The dynamics and logic of separate development have had two important structural consequences: the growth of the state and the differentiation of the ruled population. In both of these dimensions, the SADF has extended its role beyond military duties.

Structures of the state here refer to the hierarchical range of government institutions, which consists of the central bureaucracy (or civil service departments) and its local components, the local state bureaucracy (for example, courts), and the administrative structures of the homelands that are variably integrated with the central state. As argued previously, racial differentiation requires the growth by duplication of the state, and although separate development may have been intended to rid the central state of part of its burden, the practice of separate development has further extended the state. Yet the civil sector of white society lacks the personnel and financial resources to maintain this structure. It lacks, for example, the resources to simultaneously manage influx control (with 269,000 pass-law offenders in 1974), provide sufficient income for administration boards, provide staff for the black education system, run hospitals, provide agricultural services in rural areas (including the homelands), and otherwise provide services for the white and black populations.[64] Indeed, the regime has acknowledged that the homelands and the local state are financially dependent on the resources of the central state.[65] The resulting situation is a vast network of state structures variably integrated and dependent on the resources of the center. The central state, having available a pool of national servicemen that includes skilled personnel, has used the military to prop up the state bureaucracy. It is in this sense that the military's role expands, for military personnel are armed bureaucrats as well as soldiers, and they simultaneously perform military and nonmilitary roles.

In SWA/Namibia, the role of SADF personnel as "armed bureaucrats" is vast. An official publication of the SADF describes this role as "dynamic" and supplies evidence of an increasing number of military personnel who serve as teachers, veterinarians, agricultural advisors and technicals, dentists, doctors, psychiatrists, nature conservationists, and social workers.[66] Within South Africa, the same process takes place, with the "army of development" or "Bantustan bureaucrats" especially active in northern Natal and northern and eastern Transvaal, but also in urban areas such as Soweto.[67] The military in this regard, moreover, provides "more than just services" for which it has a "calling," but also plays a key role in the development of "healthy human and race relations."[68] The military's intention is "to project an image of the soldier as a man of action who is nonetheless a friend of the Black man and who is prepared to defend him. We want the national serviceman to teach the Black man whilst his rifle is standing in the corner of a classroom."[69]

It is because of this "hearts-and-minds" rhetoric that the military's actions have often been explained with reference to ideology and/or counterinsurgency. However, the use of the military in positions hardly worthy of a "hearts-and-minds" treatment—as accountants in the Department of the Treasury, as tax collectors for the Receiver of Revenue, as customs and excise agents, as prosecutors in the Department of Justice,[70] as doctors in urban and rural hospitals[71] without whose services the medical profession would be in dire straits,[72] and essentially as police[73]—suggests that overextension of the state is the more fundamental reason for military activities.

The use of the SADF in quelling township unrest since October 1984 can also be explained by the overextension of the state. Indeed, the minister of law and order and the chief of the army have made this explicit by stating in interviews that SADF personnel had to be used because there were too few police, an explanation strengthened by statements by a prominent SADF officer (Major-General G. L. Meiring) to the effect that the nature of unrest determined how the SADF was to be used.

The nature of the societal need or problem determines how and why the military assumes civic responsibilities—a situation that suggests the absence or weakness of moral and other notions inhibiting the military's expansion of its civil roles.[74] The legal framework provided by the Defense Amendment Bill of 1984 makes it possible for the military to be used in this way, for it states that the SADF is to be used for defense against external attack, the prevention and suppression of terrorism and internal disorder, and, significantly, the preservation of life, health, and property and the maintenance of essential services. Clearly, the military can legally be used in a host of nonmilitary state activities, and the military, for reasons of self-interest (a better image, information, and so forth), looks upon this involvement with favor, although it is not caused by the military's political ambitions, but rather by the financial, personnel, and other deficiencies of the overextended state structure.[75]

There are also other areas in society where the military more deliberately, although less openly, seeks to "win hearts and minds." The motives for this involvement are to create a sympathetic attitude to the military and particularly to military service and to provide services and goods because "a population whose basic needs are provided for is less vulnerable to enemy propaganda."[76] Not much detailed information is available about the urban variety of civic action, largely because the SADF's involvement is not always overt, and since the national directorate of the SADF's civic action was disbanded in 1980 and civic action responsibilities subsequently devolved upon regional commands, news about SADF activities is usually confined to regional newspapers and official military publications.

This type of civic action assumes various forms and includes tours of military bases by African school children, holiday camps for handicapped colored youths, youth camps for colored youths, play groups or *kom speel saam* (let's play together) programs in Western Cape communities, hiking trips to the Jock of the Bushveld trail and the Timbavati Nature Reserve, "adventure" and "leadership" camps for colored youths, and the provision of other educational, health, and recreational services to black African but mostly colored and Indian communities. The military men who are usually involved in these activities are the civic action sections of the regional commands (the Natal and Northwestern Commands, for example), the Cape Corps, and especially the recently created First Battalion of the South African Cape Corps (SACC), but they also include instructors and members of local commando units. It is not the military alone that is involved; also involved are the departments of Foreign Affairs, Information, Internal Affairs, and National Education, city councils such as that of Cape Town, childcare organizations, and members of community councils.[77]

The urban variety of civic action seems to concentrate on the colored communities, especially in the southwestern Cape area. SADF urban involvement is connected with the SADF's personnel deficiencies and efforts to encourage recruitment, the new constitutional dispensation (the tricameral Parliament), and, in general, with the regime's belief that the colored and Indian communities could be the nucleus of a moderate middle class capable of buttressing the regime against its opposition.[78] Yet, why is the military so thoroughly involved in an area that is the terrain of the Department of Internal Affairs? Time and again the reports indicated that the military can provide facilities, food, personnel, and transportation lacking in other civil service departments. Although there is little doubt that the military intends to inculcate discipline, patriotism, anticommunism and antiterrorism, and youth preparedness in general while presenting itself as "neutral" (that is, not an instrument of racial domination), the extension of the military's role is a function of the resources the military alone commands.[79]

Military Growth and the White Community

Since 1960, the SADF has grown dramatically in size. Compared to the 10,000 national servicemen in 1960, there presently are in excess of 65,250 national servicemen in the army, air force, and navy; compared to the 11,500 PF force of 1960, the 1981 PF of the army amounted to 11,000 troops while the air force had a PF of 6,300, and the navy had a PF of 3,500. ACF and commando strength in 1960 was at 56,500 troops; in 1981, ACF strength was at 155,000 and the commandos at 110,000.[80] But, apart from sheer size, how has the SADF changed since 1960, and how do these changes affect the SADF's relationship with the white community?

First, the SADF has become a vastly more differentiated, technologized, and specialized entity, encompassing more than three thousand suborganizations, apart from linkages to and organizations contained within the defense establishment outlined earlier. There are four service arms: the army, air force, navy, and medical service. In addition to these service arms, there are staff components (or the Department of Defense). These consist of the chiefs of staff for personnel, intelligence, logistics, finance, the quartermaster-general, and the chaplain-general, who are all headed by the minister of defense. The army (with headquarters in Pretoria) is divided into territorial commands and draws on PF, ACF, commando and National Service personnel organized into units of armor, artillery, infantry, logistic support, and maintenance and service. The air force and navy, likewise, are organized along geographical and functional lines. Most of the personnel incorporated in the PF component of the SADF are not amateurs or dabblers but are well-trained men responsible for the operation and maintenance of sophisticated equipment. As regards the national servicemen, their service presently includes a two-year, full-time service, followed by fourteen years of part-time service (not exceeding ninety days per year) in the ACF and commandos, followed by five years in the reserve of the ACF, and then service in the commandos of twelve days annually up to the age of fifty-five. Those between the ages of fifty-five and sixty-five are part of the National Reserve.

Second, the officer corps of the PF is increasingly drawn from the white middle class in urban areas, although this change may have more to do with the changing social character of the white community and particularly the Afrikaans-speaking portion of that community than with recruitment policies. The SADF nevertheless retains internal control of the training, education, and upward mobility of the officer corps. The training and promotion of officers remains primarily a matter of staff courses offered by the South African Defence College; indeed, only 16.3 percent of the officer corps in 1981 were university graduates.[81] Since 1963, no SADF officers have attended military schools abroad. Also, in contrast to their earlier experience, the SADF's permanent staff members today regularly have combat experience, and this experience is primarily of the counterinsurgent kind. Combat (or operational area) experience creates its own mechanisms of career mobility, and it is increasingly likely that higher echelon officers will have previously occupied top command positions in the different operational areas.

Third, the SADF today cautiously welcomes the participation of nonwhite people in its activities and structure. This willingness has two expressions, one of which is to encourage service in the PF by coloreds and Indians, although the SADF does have a training base for Africans at Lenz (21 Battalion), after which troops are incorporated into the South African Support Services Corps. The other is the SADF's willingness to train homeland armies, such as those of Bophuthatswana, Ciskei, Transkei, and Venda.[82]

Although the changes discussed here do not support the claim that the SADF presently is a nonracialistic, mass, or technocratic entity in the fashion of, say, the U.S. military, these qualitative and quantitative changes have influenced the organizational style of the SADF. Increased differentiation and specialization have required, among other things, the development of bureaucratic and managerial skills, and the influx of previously civilian national servicemen and, later, part-time military service creates problems of morale and readiness that cannot be solved by domination but require manipulation and persuasion.

The influx of civilians into the military raises another question, that of the relationship between the SADF and the white community. Three issues are relevant in this regard: the effect of national service, the links between the SADF and the secondary school system, and the SADF and partisan white politics.

As was discussed earlier, the SADF after 1945 was or became an Afrikanerized institution. But, at least since 1970, the SADF (and the regime) has been aware of the dangers of having a military alienated from its social constituency. Public relations campaigns have subsequently been aimed at English-speakers, accompanied by the cultivation of an image of the military as an institution valuing merit, technical skills, and patriotism and eminently worthy of consideration as a career choice.[83] Little is known about the effectiveness of these efforts; yet the most important link between the SADF and the white community is not contrived by means of public relations campaigns, but by the nature and consequences of national service. Originally, national servicemen were volunteers or were randomly selected, but service has subsequently become compulsory, with lengthy full- and part-time terms.[84]

The important effect of national service is that it provides virtually the only social arena where whites regardless of socioeconomic standing, linguistic group, political affiliation, religion, or any other social cleavage are compelled to mix. Combined with the effects of combat and other experiences in the operational areas and the notion of a common enemy, national service constitutes a very important mechanism for the maintenance of racial solidarity. Whether the cultivation of white cohesion is a matter of official SADF policy is beside the point. By its very nature, national service moderates intrawhite cleavages, creates bonds that override social and other distinctions, and circumvents the problem of self-selection among volunteers.

National service is not the only area where whites are exposed to military life. Exposure starts much earlier with various types of paramilitary training in white primary and secondary schools, including adventure camps, leadership courses, veldschools, youth preparedness, and the cadet system for boys. It is here that the imitation of military life is most conspicuous. Uniforms, salutes, survival training, parades, and marches are part of common practice. In some areas (Cape Town, for example), the best cadets actually attend an annual camp run by the SADF, which also provides camps for white school teachers. Indeed, the SADF (through its Directorate of Education) cooperates closely with the Department of Education because, in addition to inculcating patriotism, loyalty, and so forth, paramilitary service in schools blunts later exposure to military life and, importantly, lessens the likelihood of national service evasion. Many men certainly do not meet all their national service obligations, but conscientious objection in South Africa is still limited and primarily based on religious—not political—grounds.[85]

Finally, there is the issue of white partisan politics in which, as discussed earlier, the SADF and security issues used to be a highly divisive concern.

Since 1960, there have been occasions where the SADF used divisive tactics such as emphasizing external danger during elections (accusing the opposition of being "soft on defense") or undermining the opposition in other, more subtle, ways. Yet, under P. W. Botha, the regime has also sought to elevate the military beyond the scope of partisan criticism or to carefully circumscribe the limits of criticism, both in parliamentary debates and by trips to operational areas for members of the parliamentary opposition.[86] That such trips have dividends is evidenced in the opposition's support for lengthy national service, as published in an official SADF publication.[87]

Since 1960, the enlarged and qualitatively changed SADF has developed strong links with all sectors of the white population through paramilitary training, national service, and the encouragement of a bipartisan political approach to the military's activities. The military is crucial to the maintenance of white racial solidarity. The institutional arena the military provides and the bonds that national service creates further racial cohesion among whites. Certainly, there are few indications that whites will publicly criticize the military's activities by opposing either the effectiveness and wisdom of counterinsurgency in SWA/Namibia or the national service.

South Africa and Its Neighbors: The Basis for Peace

Before 1974, analysts and politicians typically argued that the southern African region was a white bastion characterized by ideological affinity for white minority rule in whatever guise and by regional integration with dependence on South Africa's economy and infrastructure. It was in South Africa's interest to have other states located between it and the rest of hostile Africa that could bear the brunt of the liberation offensive, and, even if these states were to succumb to the liberation offensive, South Africa could, through the exploitation of economic dependence, weaken the pressures against it. Dependence, in other words, could provide the mechanisms for punishments and rewards necessary to maintain white domination.

Since 1974, South Africa's policy of punishments and rewards has become known as "destabilization." South Africa has meted out punishments in the form of support for opposition groups in Angola, Lesotho, Mozambique, and, reportedly, Zimbabwe, the de facto occupation by the SADF of southern Angola and frequent military action in the area, violations of neighboring countries' airspace, economic disruption and manipulation, and by the reward of financial and other aid. This policy has been dealt with extensively by analysts who all suggest that South Africa derives material and symbolic benefit—chiefly the "neutralization" of the ANC—from action against numerous "targets of opportunity" offered by the dislocations and disunity in the newly independent states and that this action in turn worsens these problems.[88] Analysts also point to the fact that military action often masks a great deal of manipulative subtlety in South Africa's regional policy, as, for example, in Mozambique, where support of the Mozambique National Resistance movement in the northern provinces is accompanied by a more placatory role in the south (where agents for South African mines recruit labor) and the offer of aid formalized by the Nkomati Accord.[89] As South Africa's neighbors cannot withstand the pressure and are forced into signing formal agreements (such as Nkomati) and otherwise to develop an understanding with the South African regime about support of the ANC, the old dependence based on ideological affinity and regional economic and technical integration has been replaced by a dependence based on instability.[90]

What is important about the policy of destabilization is that because South Africa is militarily dominant in the region and does not hesitate to exploit its dominance, the regime has presented itself to the world (and particularly to the United States) as the key to peace in the region.[91] Whereas earlier arguments attempted to demonstrate South Africa's value to the West on the grounds of its geopolitical position and mineral wealth, the current argument is that South Africa is the regional kingpin of peace. In addition, the military has come to exercise a considerable degree of influence, with consequent tensions between the more "dovish" Department of Foreign Affairs minister R. F. Botha and the "hawkish," "tough and uncompromising" military. More to the point, military participation and success in regional affairs more than anything else have legitimated the military's role in national policymaking.[92] This does not mean that the military actually determines all regional policies, but when it does participate in policymaking, it does so with a legitimate and powerful voice. Finally and perhaps most importantly, the policy of destabilization has provided proof for policymakers that much can be achieved by aggressive, combative behavior. In short, destabilization "works," or, as General Magnus Malan has stated:

> Forceful military action by the South African Security Forces during the last decade or more has provided sufficient time to allow Africa to experience the dangers of Russian involvement in their countries, as well as the suffering and retrogression that follows upon the revolutionary formula. . . . [Military action] is a basis for peace.[93]

The military's role in regional affairs thus is taken as proof of the power of the South African military (and by implication the regime itself), legitimates the military's role in policymaking, and has given it a reputation for efficiency. It remains to be seen whether the regime can indefinitely sustain a policy of destabilization or whether it will not revert to the exploitation of the older type of dependence, but the reputation the military acquired as a result of destabilization will, in all likelihood, long outlast the policy as such.

Conclusion

The body of scholarship that served as point of departure for this chapter stresses empirical investigation of civil military relations from various theoretical perspectives; this approach denies the validity of definitional truths of the military as an apolitical entity. What, therefore, is the nature of civil-military relations in South Africa, and what factors explain them?

Civil-military interpenetration in South Africa is of the structural—not conjectural—kind; the structures of society lend themselves to permanent and institutionalized civil roles for the military. In national policymaking, the military's participation is regarded as legitimate. The military is viewed as an efficient organization, and although it may not actually decide what policy should be, on the basis of security concerns, it can veto policy proposals by other bureaucratic entities. Also, the military is in the position to powerfully influence the functional and regional distribution of state funds. This role in the executive level of government has not been presented as resulting from the military's self-conscious political ambitions. Perhaps it is more accurate to say that the military has been coopted by the civilian executive, although the military (in view of its growth and ability to accrue resources) can hardly find this cooptation objectionable.

On another level, the military penetrates civil society by the extension of its roles. While the rise of the military as a corporate actor in the executive operates along a vertical axis, military role extension occurs on a horizontal axis, with the military simultaneously functioning in nonmilitary and military roles. The first major object of this role extension was SWA/Namibia, but subsequently South Africa itself, the homelands, the colored, Indian, and also African communities, and the civil service departments came under the aegis of this extension. Again, this activity is held to be in the military's self-interest. It allows the military to satisfy personnel demands, seek a better image, and loosen any close association with only one sector of society.

The corporate rise of the military and its role extension are often taken to be products of the regime's recognition in the late 1960s and the 1970s that "its mechanisms of domination [were] being tested to the limits" by threats from within and without.[94] This recognition then led to the total onslaught strategy, which is an idealized and internal application of the concept of national security. Indeed, the total onslaught strategy is the regime's rationalization of its worsening position as well as its efforts to maintain the status quo with some modification. But, as this chapter has argued, the roots of the increasing civil-military interpenetration lie much deeper in South African politics and society. The very functioning of structures that were supposed to protect white racial domination has produced an overextended state structure that cannot continue to function without the systematic assistance of armed bureaucrats. No doubt the rise of the military is also called for by assaults on structures—for example, the riots of 1976 and international pressures—but the more fundamental impetus to increasing military influence originates from within—not beyond—an overextended state.

The rise of the South African military does not readily fit any theoretical mold. The military certainly is not the only bureaucratically and organizationally developed institution in South African society; if it cannot outperform other societal institutions on the basis of its internal characteristics, it does command resources (personnel and money, especially) on the basis of which it bests or fills the vacuum left by other public/state institutions that have less resources. Certainly, the military's recruitment or its social constituency and its organizational style are middle class and modernistic, but judging from the military's self-interest regarding personnel problems, it is unclear whether the military will even support efforts to more extend democratic rights and privileges.

That the military seeks to present itself as "neutral" and "not as an instrument of racial domination" to the ruled cannot be taken as evidence that the military in fact is an autonomous institution. Even if this were the case in the past, the effect of the total onslaught strategy has been to forge more thorough links between the military and all sectors of the white population (in a sociological and political sense) and between the military and capital and the private sector. Likewise, the military's position in the bureaucratic-executive domain has been strengthened. Since the end of World War II, capitalist-racial domination has been closely linked with state power, and the stresses and strains within that state have required an increasing bureaucratic-civil role for the military in South Africa.

Notes

Acknowledgements

In writing this chapter I have benefited enormously from conversations with Philip Frankel of the University of the Witwatersrand and with former colleagues in the Department of Political Sciences of the University of South Africa. I also wish to gratefully acknowledge the assistance of Dorothy Rowse of the University of South Africa.

1. As regards military history, see (for example) most of the articles in the journal *Militaria*. Recent social science perspectives on the political role of South Africa's military can be found in Philip Frankel, *Pretoria's Praetorians* (Cambridge: Cambridge University Press, 1984); and Kenneth Grundy, *Soldiers Without Politics* (Berkeley: University of California Press, 1983); as well as in numerous book chapters, journal articles, and monographs mentioned in the following notes. Because of its length and scope, Frankel's *Pretoria's Praetorians* is the centerpiece of this literature, but the work is unfortunately marred by the unsystematic use of theoretical

concepts and the advancement of claims that lack persuasive evidence.

2. For an introduction to the literature on civil-military relations, see Kurt Lang, *Military Institutions and the Sociology of War* (Beverly Hills, Calif.: Sage, 1972); Charles Moskos, Jr., "The Military," *Annual Review of Sociology* 2 (1972):55–77; Henry Bienen, "Civil-Military Relations in the Third World," *International Political Science Review* 2 (1981):363–370; and Henry Bienan, "Military Rule and the Political Process," *Comparative Politics* 10 (1978):205–225.

3. Morris Janowitz, *Military Institutions and Coercion in Developing Nations* (Chicago: Chicago University Press, 1977); Morris Janowitz, *The Military in the Development of New Nations* (Chicago: University of Chicago Press, 1964); and Alexandre de S. C. Barros and Edmund C. Coelho, "Military Intervention and Withdrawal in South America," *International Political Science Review* 2 (1981):341–349.

4. The work of Bienen and Janowitz are representative of this thesis. Also see Manfred Halpern, *The Politics of Social Change in the Middle East and North Africa* (Princeton, N.J.: Princeton University Press, 1963); and John J. Johnson, ed., *The Military and Society in Latin America* (Stanford, Calif.: Stanford University Press, 1964).

5. Many orthodox Marxist scholars support this view.

6. One of the best expositions of this view is found in Karl Marx, *The Eighteenth Brumaire of Louis Bonaparte* (New York: International Publishers, 1970); also see Samuel Decalo, *Coups and Army Rule in Africa* (New Haven, Conn.: Yale University Press, 1976), 239; E. De L. Figueiredo, "The Military and the State in Latin America, with Special Reference to the Brazilian Case, 1930–1980" (Paper read at the Twentieth Annual Conference of the Interuniversity Seminar on Armed Forces and Society, University of Chicago, October 1980); Edward Feit, *The Armed Bureaucrats* (Boston: Houghton Mifflin, 1973); and Amos Perlmutter, *The Military and Politics in Modern Times: On Professionals, Praetorians and Revolutionary Soldiers* (New Haven, Conn.: Yale University Press, 1977), 100–102.

7. Philip Frankel, "Book Review," *International Affairs Bulletin* 7 (1983):59.

8. E. A. Ritter, *Shaka Zulu* (London: Longmans and Eugene V. Walter, 1985); and E. A. Ritter, *Terror and Resistance* (London: Oxford University Press, 1969).

9. E. M. Meyers, "Die Suid-Afrikaanse Soldaat: 'n Historiese Profiel" ("The South African Soldier: A Historical Profile"), *Militaria*, (5 February 1984):35.

10. Richard Dale, "The Armed Forces as an Instrument of South African Policy in Namibia," *Journal of Modern African Studies* (18 January 1980); and J. van Wyk, "Die Unie Verdedigingsmagte op die Voorand van die Tweede Wereldoorlog (1934–1939)," *Militaria*, (6 April 1976):35.

11. South African units distinguished themselves in action in Europe (especially Italy and Poland), North Africa, the Mediterranean theater, and Madagascar. See Neil Orpen and H. J. Martin, *South African Forces in World War II* (Johannesburg: Purnell, 1968, 1971, 1975, 1977, 1979, and 1981/1982).

12. Grundy, *Soldiers Without Politics*; Kenneth W. Grundy, *Defense Legislation and Communal Politics: The Evolution of a White South African Nation as Reflected in the Controversy Over the Assignment of Armed Forces Abroad, 1912–1976,* Papers in International Studies, African Series, 33 (Athens: Ohio University, Center for International Studies, 1978); and Meyers, "Die Suid-Afrikaanse Soldaat," 39.

13. There are some exceptions to this rule. The Pretoria Regiment, for example, has long attracted Afrikaans-speaking men.

14. The wartime production of rather sophisticated equipment (armored cars, for example) in the workshops of companies such as AE&CI, the mining industry, ISCOR, and the South African Railways and Harbours came to a standstill. See R. J. Bouch, "The Railways and the War Effort, 1939–1945," *Militaria,* (5 February 1975):66–75; and Richard Cornwell, "South African Armoured Car Production in World War II," *Militaria,* (7 March 1977):30–41.

15. Grundy, *Defense Legislation,* 38.

16. G. G. Lawrie, *South African Defence and the Commonwealth* (Johannesburg: South African Institute of International Affairs, 1961).

17. Deon Geldenhuys, *South Africa's Search for Security Since the Second World War* (Johannesburg: South African Institute of International Affairs, 1978), 5.

18. James Barber, *South Africa's Foreign Policy* (London: Oxford University Press, 1973), 86.

19. Geldenhuys, *South Africa's Search,* 5.

20. Kenneth W. Grundy, *The Rise of the South African Security Establishment: An Essay in the Changing Locus of State Power* (Johannesburg: South African Institute of International Affairs, 1983), 6.

21. Grundy, *Defense Legislation,* 34–36.

22. Cynthia Enloe, *Police, Military and Ethnicity: Foundations of State Power* (London: Transaction Books, 1980), 56. Also see Frankel, *Pretoria's Praetorians,* 36–40; and Stanley Trapido, "Political Institutions and Afrikaner Social Structures in the Republic of South Africa," *American Political Science Review* 57 (1963):75–87.

23. Ben Roux, "The Central Administration, Provincial and Local Authorities, and the Judiciary," in Denis Warrall, ed., *South Africa: Government and Politics* (Pretoria: Van Schaik, 1971), 129.

24. See Muriel Horrel, *The African Reserves of South Africa* (Johannesburg: SAIRR, 1969).

25. Ben Roux, "The Central Administration," 82, 187.

26. In 1976, these organizations were amalgamated as Armscor.

27. See Michael Hough, *The Strategic Importance of South and Southern Africa: The Pretoria View* (Pretoria: University of Pretoria Institute for Strategic Studies, 1981); and J. E. Spence, *The Strategic Significance of South Africa* (London: Royal United Services Institution, 1970).

28. Edward Feit, *Urban Revolt in South Africa* (Evanston, Ill.: Northwestern University Press, 1971); and Newell M. Stultz, "The Politics of Security: South Africa Under Verwoerd, 1961–1966," *Journal of Modern African Studies* 7 (1969):1–20.

29. Tom Lodge, *Black Politics in South Africa Since 1945* (Johannesburg: Ravan Press, 1984), 180–260.

30. Dale, "The Armed Forces," 57–71.

31. Barber, *South Africa's Foreign Policy,"* 196–197; and Spence, *The Strategic Significance,* 28–30.

32. Andre Beaufre, *An Introduction to Strategy* (London: Faber and Faber, 1945); Basil Liddell-Hart, *Strategy—The Indirect Approach* (London: Faber and Faber, 1967); J. L. McCuen, *The Art of Counterrevolutionary War* (London: Faber and Faber, 1966); Peter Paret, *French Revolutionary Warfare* (New York: Praeger, 1964); and Robert Thompson, *Defeating Communist Insurgency: The Lessons of Malaya and Vietnam* (New York: Praeger, 1967).

33. Act no. 64, Security Intelligence and State Security Council Act of 1972 stipulated two major functions for the SSC: to advise the government (at its request) on the formulation and implementation of national security policies and the ways in which the government can defend itself against threats and to determine intelligence priorities.

34. Deon Geldenhuys and Hennie Kotze, "Aspects of Political Decision-making in South Africa," *Politikon* (October 1983):35.

35. Andre J. van Deventer, *Statement to the Press* (Pretoria: 21 September 1983).

36. Beaufre, *An Introduction to Strategy.*

37. Van Deventer, *Statement to the Press*, 2. Also see South Africa, *White Paper on Defence and Armament Production* (Pretoria: Government Printers, especially 1973, 1975, and 1977).

38. Some of the important raids include the following operations: Savannah (in 1975–1976), Reindeer (May 1978), Rekstok and Safraan (aimed at Zambia in retaliation for the shelling of Katima Mulilo), Smokeshell (June 1980), and Klipklop (July 1980). In 1981, three operations (Carnation, Daisy, and Protea) established a de facto SADF presence in Southern Angola. Since 1981, there have been Operations Super (an airborne raid during 1982), Meebos (August 1982), and, most recently, Askari in December 1983 (*The Pretoria News*, 9 February 1984, 21).

39. Paul L. Moorcraft, *Africa's Superpower* (Johannesburg: Sygma/Collins, 1981), 42–49; S. Sonderling, *Bushwar* (Windhoek: Eyes Publishing, 1980); and Willem Steenkamp, *Borderstrike* (Durban: Butterworths, 1983).

40. Moorcraft, *Africa's Superpower*, 43; and Paul Moorcraft, "The SADF in SWA," *Militaria*, (14 January 1984):37–41.

41. On these economic and other developments, see Robert H. Davies and Dan O'Meara, "The State of Analysis of the South African Strategy," *Review of African Political Economy* 29 (1984):64–76; Colin Legum, *The Western Crisis Over South Africa* (New York: Africana, 1980); Colin Legum, "The Great Evasion," *The Economist* (21 June 1980):3–30; and John Seiler, ed., *South Africa Since the Portuguese Coup* (Boulder, Colo.: Westview Press, 1980).

42. Philip H. Frankel, "Race and Counter-Revolution: South Africa's 'Total Strategy,'" *Journal of Commonwealth and Comparative Politics* 18 (1980):274.

43. Deon Geldenhuys, *The Diplomacy of Isolation* (Johannesburg: Macmillan for the South African Institute of International Affairs, 1984), 209. In the same fashion as the organizational restructuring of the national security machinery reflected Beaufre's ideal guidelines, so threat perception was described in idealized strategic terms. Witness the stress on "coordination," "applying the whole range of measures," and direction given by communist states.

44. James Roherty, *The Security Management System in South Africa's 'Total National Strategy'* (Newport, R.I.: Naval War College, 1984), 5–15.

45. For more details, see Geldenhuys, "Aspects of Political Decision-making," 34–45; and Roherty, *The Security Management System*, 21–22.

46. Geldenhuys, ibid., 42.

47. Kenneth W. Grundy, "South Africa's Domestic Strategy," *Current History* 82 (1983):110–114, 132–133.

48. Roherty, *The Security Management System*, 21–22.

49. The figures are derived from several sources—see Geldenhuys, *The Diplo-*

macy of Isolation, 124; R. Jaster, *South Africa's Narrowing Security Options,* Adelphi Papers, no. 159 (London: International Institute for Strategic Studies, 1980), 16; Willem Steenkamp, "The SA Defence Force," *Leadership SA* 2 (1982):51–71; Stockholm International Peace Research Institute (SIPRI), *World Armaments and Disarmament SIPRI Yearbook 1980* (London: Taylor and Francis, 1980); and the annual *Military Balance* published by the International Institute of Strategic Studies.

50. Paul Rich, "Insurgency, Terrorism and the Apartheid System in South Africa," *Political Studies* 32 (1984):68–85.

51. The office was established in 1951.

52. *This is ARMSCOR?* (unknown place of publication, undated), 2.

53. *Salvo* (September 1984):2. Another example of capital-military interpenetration is the men from prominent companies (Anglo-American, Barlow Rand, South African Breweries, and Tongaat) who serve on the Defense Advisory Council.

54. Frankel, "Race and Counter-revolution," 277. The interests of international capital/transnational companies can be included in this interpenetrated condition. See Raimo Vayrynen, "The Role of Transnational Corporations in the Military Sector of South Africa," *Journal of Southern African Affairs* (5 February 1980):199–255.

55. These subsidiaries are the Atlas Aircraft Corporation and Telcast in Kempton Park, Infoplan in Pretoria (computer services), Kentron Electro in Pretoria and Kempton Park (guided weapons and optical equipment), Lyttelton Engineering Works in Verwoerdburg (small arms and guns), Musgrave Manufacturers and Distributors in Bloemfontein (guns and rifles), Naschem in Lenz and Potchefstroom (heavy ammunition), Somchem in Somerset West and Wellington (rocket components), and Swartklip Products (ammunition) on the Cape Flats. See *This is ARMSCOR?* 7.

56. Steenkamp, "The SA Defence Force," 53.

57. South African Research Service, *Work in Progress* 24 (1982):19.

58. NUSAS, *In Whose Defence? Conscription and the SADF* (Athlone Industria: Esquire Press, 1984), 34.

59. *Salvo* (June 1984):12.

60. *Salvo* (July 1983):5.

61. *Rand Daily Mail,* 11 April 1984, 6.

62. *The Star,* 15 September 1984, 6.

63. Peter L. Bunce, "The Growth of South Africa's Defence Industry and Its Israeli Connection," *RUSI* 129 (1984):48.

64. Pauline H. Baker, "South Africa's Strategic Vulnerabilities: The 'Citadel Assumption' Reconsidered," *African Studies Review* 20 (1977):97.

65. See the Browne Report (1982), the Yeld Report (1978), and the publications of the Croeser Working Group, which consist of representatives of provincial and municipal authorities, state departments and administration.

66. "Die SAW in SWA" ("The SADF in SWA"), *Militaria,* (14 January 1984): 38–41.

67. See the following editions of *Paratus:* (April 1980):36–37; (July 1980):14–15; (October 1980):25; (March 1981):16–17; (April 1981):26; (June 1982):47; and (August 1982):24–25. Also see Moorcraft, *Africa's Superpower,* 43; and Bruce Meier, "Militarisation in Education," *Militarisation in Focus: Speeches* (Cape Town: University of Cape Town Representative Council, 1982, 16–20.

68. This is a translation of a speech delivered by the surgeon-general (Lieutenant-

General Nichol Nieuwoudt) as reported by *Die Beeld,* 9 September 1984, 7. Also see the speech of Major-General J. J. van Zyl on the SADF as a "service-oriented" institution reported in *Die Vaderland,* 9 April 1984, 5; and the speech of Brigadier Joffel van der Westhuizen about the SADF striving for stability in various areas of civil life as reported in *Die Oosterlig,* 22 September 1983), 3.

69. Michael Evans, "Total War in South Africa," *Militarisation in Focus,* 7. In addition to creating "healthy human and race relations," the military also seeks to gather information. This was revealed by their actions in the Ingwavuma district where arms-bearing military men questioned villagers about the Inkatha movement while reminding villagers of the help given them during a recent cholera epidemic. The chief of the SADF apologized for the incident. See the *Daily News,* 14 December 1982, 1; and *The Star,* 15 December 1982, 2.

70. Grundy, "South Africa's Domestic Strategy," 112.

71. *Rand Daily Mail,* 29 July 1983, 3.

72. *Daily Dispatch,* 26 April 1983, 5.

73. *Natal Witness,* 6 April 1983, 4.

74. Hermann Giliomee, "Onderhoud met Minister Louis le Grange, 16 April 1985: 'n Onrussituasie Is Nie Sitkamerspeletjies Nie" ("An Interview with Minister Louis le Grange, 16 April 1985: An Unrest Situation Is Not Household Games") and "In Gesprek met Genl. Jannie Geldenhuys" ("A Conversation with General Jannie Geldenhuys") *Die Suid-Afrikaan* (The South African) 3 (Autumn 1985):15–17; and Simon Baynham, "South Africa, Namibia and Angola," *Southern African Record* 40 (October 1985):3.

75. Also see the following articles in a SADF publication that deal very positively with the military's civic role: F. C. de Beer, "Die Weermag as Ontwikkelingsinstrument in die Derde Wereld" ("The Army as an Instrument in Third World Development"), *Militaria* 82 (1978):1–11; and A. D. Shaw, "The Military as a Contributor to National Development," *Militaria* 9 (1979):28–45.

76. Geldenhuys, *The Diplomacy of Isolation,* 143.

77. See the following issues of *Paratus:* (June 1981):23; (October 1981):66; (August 1981):24; (May 1984):24–25; (February 1980):30–32; (May 1980):45; and (August 1980):23. Also see *The Argus,* 2 September 1983, 2; *Cape Herald,* 7 April 1984, 10; *The Objector* (April 1984):3; and Janet Cherry, "A Feather in the Cap? The South African Coloured Corps, Ruling Class Ideology and Community Opposition," in L. Cooper and D. Kaplan, eds., *Reform and Response: Selected Research Papers on Aspects of Contemporary South Africa* (Cape Town: University of Cape Town, 1983), 121. Communities affected by the military's provision of social services include Eersterus, Elsies River, Genadendal, Guguleto, Hanover Park, Langa, Mamre, Malmesbury, Mitchell's Plain, Paarl, Steenberg, Stellenbosch, Westridge, and Wrenchville.

78. The middle-class strategy of the regime has been the subject of many analyses, but for a good critical account, see Davies and O'Meara, "The State of Analysis." For a sympathetic although unfortunately shallow account, see Calvin Woodward, *Understanding Revolution in South Africa* (Cape Town: Juta, 1983), 64–76.

79. Jonathan Kapstein, "Armed Confrontation Builds in South Africa," *PROCEEDINGS, United States Naval Institute,* 107.12.946. (1981):37.

80. These figures are drawn from Grundy, "The Rise of the South Africans," who

uses data from the annual *Military Balance* published by the International Institute for Strategic Studies. The SADF does not publicize its own force levels.

81. Geldenhuys, *The Diplomacy of Isolation,* 141. Many of these officers were trained within the military at the Military Academy at Saldanha Bay, which also doubles as the faculty of military science of the University of Stellenbosch. See Normon L. Dodd, "'Discendo Armemus,' The Military Academy of the South African Defence Force," *RUSI* 29 (1984):50–52.

82. Grundy, *Soldiers Without Politics,* 197–248.

83. Cynthia Enloe, *Police, Military and Ethnicity,* 55–56.

84. There have been suggestions that women be included in national service, but these have encountered opposition, some of which originate from highly conservative political sources. Women in the SADF usually occupy managerial or service positions. See Margaret Nash, "Women Behind the War," *Militarisation in Focus,* 11–15.

85. Several observers have also pointed to the militarization of whites' cultural life. The examination of cultural life falls beyond the scope of this chapter, but see Ampie Coetzee, *Rhetoric and Ideology: Modern Afrikaans Prose and Militarization* (Johannesburg: University of the Witwatersrand, unpublished, 1985); Elsa Joubert, "Die Nuwe Afrikaanse Oorlogsliteratuur" ("The New Afrikaans Military Literature"), *Die Suid-Afrikaan* 3 (Autumn 1985):46–48; and Keyan Tomaselli, "'Adapt or Die': Militarization and the South African Media, 1976–1982," *Reality* (January 1984):8–13.

86. On the SADF's pressure on the opposition, see *The Eastern Province Herald,* 25 March 1980; 1. Also see *Die Transvaler,* 25 March 1980, 1; and *Rand Daily Mail,* 8 March 1984, 6.

87. "Why We Support National Service," *Paratus* (March 1980):20–23.

88. See Christopher Coker, "South Africa: A New Military Role in Southern Africa 1969–1982," *Survival* 25 (1983):59–67; Geldenhuys, *The Diplomacy of Isolation;* Simon Jenkins, "Destabilization in Southern Africa," *The Economist* (16 July 1983):15–28; T. B. Millar, *South Africa and Regional Security,* Bradlow Series, 3 (Johannesburg: South African Institute of International Relations, 1985); and Vale, "Pretoria and Southern Africa: From Manipulation to Intervention," in SARS, *South African Review I* (Johannesburg: Ravan Press, 1983), 7–22.

89. Ibid., 14.

90. Jenkins, "Destabilization," 28.

91. Coker, "South Africa," 62–63.

92. Geldenhuys, *The Diplomacy of Isolation,* 145.

93. *Rand Daily Mail,* 12 April 1984, 1.

94. Frankel, "Race and Counter-Revolution," 274.

HERIBERT ADAM
KOGILA MOODLEY

9

Interstate Relations Under
South African Dominance

In this chapter, Heribert Adam and Kogila Moodley present eight theses about South Africa's external political environment: (1) The peace accord between South Africa and Mozambique in March 1984, the partial withdrawal of South African troops from Angola, and the prospect of an internationally acceptable settlement of Namibia amount to a neocolonization of hostile frontline states by South Africa. (2) The Mozambican state ideology amounts to a rhetorical socialism that can pragmatically accommodate the new relationship. (3) The accord not only legitimized the South African regime but implicitly redefines the conflict from liberation to civil rights reform. (4) An internationally recognized settlement in Namibia remains the key to a long-term accommodation between South Africa and its black neighbors. (5) Greater Western economic and political involvement in the region hinges on more genuine internal South African reform. (6) Neocolonization has eroded the expectation of external liberation and forces South African blacks to focus more realistically on internal means of political change. (7) The likely fragmentation of the antiapartheid opposition in the wake of detente could backfire when Pretoria needs a cohesive negotiating partner. (8) Pretoria and the African National Congress (ANC) now have a clear reason to begin a dialogue for the first time, albeit this indaba is sought for quite different reasons and with different agendas on both sides.

W. G. J.

South Africa has never been more isolated internationally than in the late 1980s. Previous decades of merely rhetorical condemnation have been followed by a slow withdrawal of international capital, more widespread international sanctions, and a rapid decline of the country's currency due to an official declaration of bankruptcy in 1985. This economic crisis has its main root in the unresolved political question of the exclusion of blacks from the state. Continuous township resistance together with the inability of the state to enact meaningful reform elevated the country into a risk area.

Yet only a few years earlier the international position of the minority regime had dramatically altered in its favor. The peace accord between South Africa and Mozambique in March 1984, the partial withdrawal of South African troops from Angola, and the prospect of an internationally acceptable settlement of Namibia heralded a new constellation in the region and amounted to a neocolonization of hostile frontline states (FLS) by South Africa. This trend compared in importance with the political decolonization after the coup in Lisbon ten years earlier. Our analysis traces the decline of the apartheid order by exploring Pretoria's earlier international advances. These were ultimately eroded by domestic policy failures and unprecedented black resistance. The interaction between developments in the frontline states of Mozambique and Angola and their changing relationship with South Africa forms the focus of this analysis.

The Dynamics of Neocolonization

Why have implacable socialist governments suddenly agreed to enter into deals with an outcast apartheid regime? Why did South Africa suddenly show itself willing to modify its aggressive and belligerent policy toward its black neighbors after it had engaged in economic and military destabilization for years?

Commonly accepted answers to the first question have stressed the debilitating effects of South Africa's pressures, the three years of severe drought, the depressed world market for most commodity exports in a global recession, and the administrative disintegration of Mozambique and Angola as a consequence. Indeed, hopelessly underdeveloped by the most negligent colonial power from the start, Angola, and even more so, Mozambique, never had the chance to recover after most of the non-African entrepreneurial and professional intelligentsia left the strife-torn area. Eastern bloc assistance proved no substitute. Tied in to the South African economy by manifold historical links (electricity supplies, railway and harbor connections, migrant labor remittances), Mozambique was worn out when it decided in favor of pragmatic survival rather than ideological martyrdom. Internal peace, accompanied by South African trade and tourists will, so it hoped, fill the empty shops with food and the bankrupt state coffers with hard currency.

For South Africa, the long-term benefits of a Southern African Economic Market promised to be considerable. First, formal economic hegemony is far cheaper than costly military dominance. There are clear limits to the aggressiveness that an inflation-ridden economy with a severe shortage of skilled labor can sustain without eroding the affluence of the ruling minority. To replace coercion with development assistance amounts to much more elegant and efficient control.

Second, formalized economic collaboration with Mozambique and other hostile frontline states reestablishes the lost *cordon sanitaire*. Although the importance of this buffer zone for strategic purposes generally has been overrated, it constitutes nevertheless a severe setback for the military activity of the ANC.

Third, the Nkomati Accord, together with the partial withdrawal from Angola and the establishment of a joint Popular Movement for the Liberation of Angola (MPLA)/South African monitoring force, cast Pretoria in the role of regional peacemaker. The accompanying renewed international legitimacy of the South African government was a much needed ideological boost to counter black militant sentiments at home.

Fourth, the economic incorporation of frontline states into the South African orbit inhibits potential sanctions. Insofar as the frontline economies become dependent on South Africa, any damage to the republic will have a ripple effect on its clients. The South Africans, therefore, rightly can argue that punitive actions against them will be counterproductive. Moreover, the frontline governments now have a vested interest in stalling sanctions.

Fifth, the detente between these two extreme ideological adversaries (South Africa and Mozambique) has exposed the failure of socialist development economics and demonstrated the weakness of the Eastern bloc, which could not or would not come to the assistance of its allies. This de-Marxification would not be lost on black opinion inside South Africa. Pragmatic stances rather than ideological postures on the question of linkages with multinationals and free-market recipes to economic exigencies would carry the day, the neocolonials hoped.

Sixth, the rapprochement between Mozambique and South Africa runs counter to the goals of the Southern African Development Coordination Conference (SADCC). Set up in 1980 by nine southern African black governments and assisted by Western aid, its main purpose is to lessen the dependence of the black economies upon the republic. The bloc represents an economic response to a political problem. Yet only a political reconciliation can be the answer to the economic disparity. The Nkomati Accord amounts to a recognition of this contradiction. On the other hand, the accord merely ratifies what had taken place anyway in the form of increased incorporation of the frontline economies into the South African orbit. For example, Zimbabwe's trade with its SADCC partners has fallen since the organization's inception in 1980, and the intention of pruning long-established economic linkages with the South African powerhouse for political reasons was doomed from the start. The turmoil in Mozambique has particularly increased the dependence of frontline states on South African transport links. Indeed, SADCC would mostly benefit from South African membership, provided no political strings were attached. However, South Africa's domestic policies so far have precluded this.

In pursuing detente rather than destabilization, Pretoria banks on the governments in Maputo and Luanda loving power more than they detest apartheid, as Simon Jenkins aptly pointed out.[1] They have been forced into this predicament by what South Africans cynically refer to as "destructive stabilization" or "behavior modification." It does not represent a victory of the antiapartheid forces in the region, although they call it a triumph for internal reasons. Faced with the option of steady collapse or pragmatic capitulation to save the core, the choice for the Front for the Liberation of Mozambique (Frelimo) was survival. Might, though not right, could impose its terms.

This reversal of historic trends has hardly been comprehended in the propaganda war. Instead of the predicted demise of the last colonial outpost, the relic itself begins to recolonize. Jenkins, who dismissed the idea of a southward-rolling revolution, suggested the very opposite: "If there is any revolutionary danger, it is of South African counter-revolution rolling northwards."[2]

Despite the public pronouncement of friendship, the uneven relationship between South Africa and Mozambique rests on a barely concealed contempt by South Africa. From the paternalistic view of South Africa, the socialist failures at its doorstep demonstrate not only the superiority of capitalism but, more importantly, the expected chaos of majority rule at home. For most South African tourists or journalists in Mozambique or Zimbabwe, the lessons of these failures are all too obvious. Herein lies the tragic failure of strife-ridden and undemocratic frontline states to make their mark on the solution of the South African conflict. When even a relatively blessed country, such as Zimbabwe, slides into large-scale minority repression and civil rights violations without redress, how can the liberal/socialist alternative sustain a credible promise in South Africa?

Mozambique's unexpected rapprochement with South Africa proved correct Marx's assumption that true socialism cannot be built on hungry stomachs. The full stages of capitalist development, so Marx always implied, were a precondition for its genuine socialist transformation. Freedom from burdensome basic necessities depends on technological development and concomitant material affluence. In its absence, Leninist terror perverts the vision of liberation. But Mozambique not only lacked basic development but also sufficient means of terror to discipline the peasants into acquiescent labor, as Lenin's party achieved with the Russian kulaks in the 1920s. Administrative disintegration followed an ideological urban mobilization that could not incorporate its vast underdeveloped hinterland. The banditry of the Mozambique National Resistance Movement (Renamo or MNR), even with massive South African support, could not have been as paralyzing without the tacit apathy of large sections of Mozambique's rural poor.

Renamo was initially created by the former Rhodesian Central Intelligence Organization in the early 1970s to keep a check on Frelimo and its Zimbabwean allies rather than rely on inadequate Portuguese information. The deliberately small group of less than five hundred men, almost all black, had its own clandestine radio station, the "Voice of Free Africa," in Umtali. It attracted mainly disenchanted Frelimo fighters. The organization also received financial support from Jorge Jardim, one of Mozambique's wealthiest men and one-time personal business representative of Antonio Salazar. Jardim's aide, Orlando Cristina (assassinated under mysterious circumstances in South Africa in 1983), became its political spokesman and Alfonso Dhlakama, a former Frelimo soldier, its military commander.

When Rhodesia became Zimbabwe in 1980, the operation was taken over by South African military intelligence, expanded, trained, and coordinated to cripple the fledgling Mozambican economy. Together with other South African moves (decrease of migrant workers and Maputo harbor use), the MNR campaign is said to have cost the country several billions in direct damage. However, the movement never developed its own ideology or articulated a political alternative to the Marxist government it wanted to overthrow.[3] It is therefore doubtful whether the so-called leaders of the MNR who signed ceasefire agreements in Pretoria in August 1984 have effective control of the guerrillas in the bush. Supporters of Dhlakama already see the Nkomati Accord as a sellout.

Frelimo, on the other hand, underestimated popular discontent. It fed the well-organized resistance as much as South African arms did. What is now criticized as "excessive formalism" and "commandism" in Mozambique resulted in a widespread alienation so "that for the first time Mozambicans expressed the idea that the state was no longer 'theirs,'" as a sympathetic left analysis put it.[4] Public flogging for minor economic crimes, the attempt to remove all "unproductives" from urban areas in a period of worsening rural starvation, the earlier policy of state farms at the expense of peasant family production in an atmosphere of orchestrated campaigns from above by a secretive Central Committee—all added to a fertile ground for disenchantment and skepticism toward government mobilization. In his 1984 end-of-year speech, Mozambique's president, Samora Machel, attacked "the indiscipline, apathy, passivity and disrespect for the people" that is still evident in "certain sectors of the state apparatus." This showed that "we still have enemies in our midst who clearly intend to sabotage our revolution and stir up general discontent."

This state of affairs reduced Frelimo's (and many other African) versions of freedom ideology to rhetorical socialism. With an undereducated, underfed, and disillusioned constituency, socialist slogans are bandied by the urban elite but do not strike a chord with underprivileged peasants. The rhetoric placates sponsors and creates an internationally progressive image but is hardly taken seriously by its proponents. In a crunch, the elite therefore adjusts ideological interpretations as arbitrarily as it adopted them. No ideological conversion is involved, as is frequently assumed, because a collective ideological commitment hardly existed in the first place. Opportunistic socialism is filled with practical capitalism under a new formula that turns defeat into victory. Instead of explaining the predicament to the people, Mozambican propaganda presented the Nkomati agreement as a heroic victory by the people to whose determination the South African enemy finally had to yield. The irony of a smiling Machel, the victim, in a London-tailored marshall's uniform and a dour Botha, the destabilizer, in a rumpled civilian suit could have hardly been lost on a more sophisticated TV audience. Each side could believe it had upstaged the other.

The Frelimo leadership need not fear an ideological rebellion against the change of course as long as it can deliver the new goods. With a government-controlled media, the leadership can manipulate domestic opinion to a great degree and need only be concerned with success. This means that Frelimo cannot be merely a reluctant party to the treaty, as the ANC had hoped. The party will have to identify with the new reality because its own fate is bound to the treaty's success. As a result, the "socialist" clients of South Africa inevitably must develop a vested interest in peace and stability in the republic. An ANC that relies on armed struggle to achieve a South African transformation becomes an objective adversary of progress and development in neighboring states. These diverging interests are likely to lead to a further deterioration of the former ideological unity between frontline states and the ANC. Once locked into increased economic ties with South Africa, the FLS become more dependent on the bond and can hardly afford to cut it at will. The policy, therefore, does not amount to a tactical retreat the signers can ultimately control. The notion that Mozambique can judiciously "use capitalism against itself" remains an illusion. As the dependent and weaker party to the deal, Maputo is not in a position to dictate the terms for business involvement. The vision of a "controlled tourism," for example, will soon fade in light of Sol Kerzner's investment conditions and the lucrative terms of casino hotels. (Kerzner is president of Southern Suns Hotels, a major tourist/entertainment empire in southern Africa.)

Yet it would be wrong to perceive the frontline states as extended Bantustans. They are not South African creations but sovereign entities whose populations, unlike that of the Bantustans, identify with the political leadership. Their greater maneuverability, therefore, cannot be compared with the total dependence on Pretoria of the Matanzimas and Sebes. It is for this reason that, contrary to accusations, an overthrow of Frelimo was not in Pretoria's interest. Likewise, it is wrong to assume that South Africa would benefit from replacing (if it were possible) the MPLA in Luanda with a National Union for the Total Liberation of Angola (UNITA) regime. Were such designs carried through, South Africa would have to prop up another unpopular government. Dealing with several Namibian situations exceeds Pretoria's financial and military capacities. In short, South Africa proves to be a regional power bloc of considerable influence, but it cannot afford political and military colonization beyond economic hegemony.

In this respect, the anti–South African lobby abroad has shown little grasp of the contradictions of South African aggressiveness. For example, Basil Davidson, the noted British Africanist and vice president of the Anti-apartheid Movement hailed the "gains" of the anti–South African forces because Pretoria has "failed to overthrow the independent regimes and governments of Mozambique and of Angola." According to Davidson, South Africa's plan was not only "to destabilize and undermine and eventually overthrow" these governments but "to install a racist South African hegemony over all the countries of the subcontinent."[5] Such ascriptions, however, vastly overestimate Pretoria's capacities and aggressive calculations. Pretoria cannot afford the Bantustanization of its periphery. It wants to shed administrative responsibility rather than acquire it. South Africa even cedes black territory to neighboring states as the failed Ingwavuma deal with Swaziland has shown. The adventurism of some military meglomaniacs notwithstanding, Afrikaner nationalism is a defensive not an expansionist one. John Vorster and his general Hendrik van den Bergh, it must be remembered, were reluctant to become involved in Angolan affairs in the first place in 1975. U.S. encouragement initially entangled the military under P. W. Botha in the Angolan civil war as Washington's proxy. However, unlike fascism, Afrikanerdom never perceived its problem to be a *Volk ohne Raum* (people without space). To be sure, South Africa aims at "stemming the tide" as far as possible away from the Transvaal by surrounding itself with dependent hostage states. But, apart from propaganda purposes, Pretoria is little concerned about the rhetorical ideology of its neighbors, as long as they do not provide bases for ANC guerrillas. If friendly contact and trading relationships can be secured with "exotic Marxists" (Samora Machel, Robert Mugabe) or black dictators (Hastings Banda), Afrikaner technocrats would be the last ones to object to grabbing the opportunity.

At the same time, South Africa has no qualms about using auxiliaries to pressure neighbors to fall in line. By supporting UNITA, Pretoria hopes to force the MPLA to control the South West Africa People's Organization (SWAPO). Dissident groups in Lesotho and Zimbabwe also received South

African support. This allows Pretoria to set itself up as arbitrator, peacemaker, or enforcer, according to its purpose. In the case of Renamo, however, the counterforce created could not be turned off at will. It took on a life of its own for the time being, independent of the control of its masters. This may lead the South Africans to become the Cubans of Mozambique: an outside force invited by the host government to stabilize it against its own unpopularity.

However, so far South Africa has insisted that it will not heed Frelimo's invitation to send troops (beyond a few military advisors) into the country to protect the Cahora Bassa power lines or other areas. Pretoria seems to have a clear understanding that it cannot afford a Vietnam at its doorstep. The South African Defence Force (SADF) learned its lesson in Rhodesia where the demands for South African assistance in both equipment and personnel simply escalated. Renamo continues therefore to operate across a wide area of Mozambique and even in close vicinity to the capital.

The Nkomati Accord itself does not oblige the contracting parties to assist each other militarily. It merely states the mutual intention not to engage in hostile acts. For once, the state-controlled South African Broadcasting Corporation is correct in stressing that South Africa has a very real interest in ensuring that the accord works and is properly implemented: "It would appear to be the height of foolishness for South Africa to assist Renamo in any effort to continue guerrilla activity in Mozambique."[6] Despite these intentions, Pretoria's full control of the activities of its opponents in its own security establishment is still in question. The *Financial Mail* reported "a surprising statement" by a senior SA military intelligence officer, Major-General H. Roux, as "a possible indication, that not everybody in the SADF is happy with SA's peace moves in Mozambique and Angola." The general insisted that the MNR has at least 60–80 percent popular support in Mozambique. "We are not just saying this—we're very sure of our facts. Whatever they are called, they are a factor. I can't tell you that they are angels, but war is war. In the propaganda they may be called bandits, but that is not correct."[7] The general also confirmed that the MNR had been able to increase its confrontations with the Frelimo government after the Nkomati Accord, with 30 percent of all incidents taking place in the Maputo province. The South African extreme right considers the pact a communist trap and sellout to an ideological enemy whose removal by any means possible remains a worthy goal despite opportunistic deals.

When the Gorongosa headquarters of Renamo were overrun by Zimbabwean forces in 1985, evidence suggested that the South African military had flagrantly violated the Nkomati Accord by continuous support of Renamo. In a bizarre dispute between the Department of Foreign Affairs and the then retiring chief of staff it was disclosed that Deputy Minister Louis Nel had secretly flown to Renamo airstrips, allegedly without the knowledge of

Foreign Minister R. F. Botha. The South Africans justified their Renamo contacts with the need to act as brokers of peace and exert influence on Renamo while the Mozambican government considers Pik Botha a helpless ally in a conflict with an independent military.

The Lisbon-based MNR does not only have a South African father who wavers on his alimonies but a Portuguese mother who continues to nourish the unacknowledged offspring. This situation not only includes privately arranged supplies by embittered former residents of Mozambique within the large and generally conservative Portuguese community in South Africa. According to reports, some influential industrialists (Manuel Bulhose) and cabinet ministers (Mota Pinto, Almeida Santos) in Portugal hope for an MNR success that would restore their confiscated property rights.[8] Because Prime Minister Mario Soares needed their support, Portugal did not act against the MNR, despite the damage done to Portuguese interests in Mozambique by the banditry. Gillian Gunn describes the calculations of this support group: "Rather than move forward to a new economic relationship, they want to move back to an old one. They want to 'recolonize' rather than 'neocolonize.' They believe that the MNR is on the verge of military victory, and believe it is worth a considerable gamble to replace the South Africans as the bankroller of the movements operations."[9] While the South African government tried to intervene in this connection—it is rumored that South Africa sent supplies from Malawi, Saudia Arabia, and Morocco via the Comores Islands to the MNR—the new reactionary coalition may be well outside Pretoria's or even Lisbon's influence. U.S. ultraconservatives, for example, argue for an active support of Renamo while the Reagan administration provides moderate military assistance to Frelimo and the British government offers training assistance of Mozambican army units in Zimbabwe.[10]

The result of all this maneuvering has been that the MNR has become much more deeply entrenched, and Machel has turned out to be much weaker than anyone suspected. South African and Western intelligence have failed to anticipate that Renamo, to a considerable extent, has become uncontrollable. Speculations that the Frelimo government may have to return to the bush if forced from power are not too farfetched. Zimbabwe has limited its initial military support to the protection of the Beira-to-Mutave railroad and oil pipeline mainly because of fear that too close a contact with demoralized, badly fed, and rarely paid Frelimo troops will affect its own soldiers. Observers believe that the electricity supplies from the Cahora Bassa scheme have to be written off permanently after almost three hundred electrical pylons were destroyed. In the meantime, Machel inveighs against "ignorance, chauvinism, careerism and even extreme leftism," replacing "indifferent" veterans with more competent ministers.

There even has been speculation that Frelimo would be forced to include four members of Renamo in a government of "national unity" as a consequence of the worsening economic and security situation. Although such a grand coalition represents an obvious compromise in Angola where UNITA commands widespread loyalty as a cohesive movement, this is not the case in Mozambique with its scattered anarchy and ideologically unfocused dissent. At most, a general amnesty but no formal recognition of what has indeed developed into mere rebellious banditry can be expected from Frelimo. In the meantime, a protracted civil war will continue. The vital security for economic development and outside investment will be absent, except in some isolated sectors such as offshore oil drilling, harbor and transport upgrading, and, perhaps, pockets of well-protected tourist development. In David Rockefeller's assessment, "Mozambique has a long way to go before foreign investors are going to find it an attractive place to put their money or before bankers are going to make substantial loans."[11]

Above all, Rockefeller suggested a linkage of the Mozambican currency to the Rand as a precondition for large foreign investments, to which Maputo has agreed. Moreover, whether the underlying expectations of great benefits through closer economic ties with South Africa will materialize, as envisaged by Frelimo, remains doubtful. South Africa itself is in one of its deepest recessions. If South Africa is unable to turn its own homelands into showpieces, it is unlikely to turn a much larger and rudimentarily developed Mozambique into a success story. Apart from some trade agreements and South African outlays in tourism, agriculture, fishing, and harbor development, South Africa lacks the personnel and resources to take on vast underdevelopment in a high risk area. Even if South Africa accepts substantially more Mozambican mine workers, redirects freight through Maputo, and buys more electricity from the Cahora Bassa complex, this will hardly affect the overall poverty of the Mozambican population.

In the meantime, Mozambique also has joined the previously muchmaligned International Monetary Fund, which entitles the country to membership in the World Bank and International Finance Corporation. Rescheduling of its $1.3 billion debt has already taken place under stringent conditions. Membership in the Lomé convention resulted in more European Economic Community (EEC) aid. An investment code providing guarantees and incentives for foreign companies was introduced in 1984. The law excludes nationalization or expropriation. These "will only occur in exceptional circumstances" with the "guarantee of a just and equitable transfer in freely convertible currency." Generous tax exemptions for foreign investments and free transfer abroad of profits and reexportable capital may well attract some adventure capital from outside South Africa, if the security situation improves. On the whole, however, Mozambique will have to rely on foreign aid, particularly from the Scandinavian countries, for a considerable time. As a charity case and client state, Mozambique's political dependence on new donors will increase as long as East European sponsors are unwilling to pick up the tab.

Whatever combination of factors may have prompted the Mozambican changed stance, it also had to be justified in more than survival terms. It is in the ideological legitimation of the accord that the most fundamental change toward white South Africa can be found. Its key lies in the Mozambican definition of the South African conflict as "a civil rights struggle." This implies abandonment of revolutionary hope in favor of reformist expectations. Civil rights can be restored without altering the structure of domination. In other words, a civil rights perspective concedes that blacks can be incorporated into a nonracial capitalism. The possibility of such a reformed racial capitalism flies in the face of the Marxist assumption that apartheid and capitalism are inseparable in South Africa.

Simultaneously jettisoned was the cherished notion of liberation. Its clarion call derived from the definition of South Africa as a colonial situation. Although the legitimate residence rights of whites were always acknowledged, the ANC, in commenting on the accord, explicitly referred to the hitherto unanimously endorsed African challenge to defeat a colonial power structure of a minority settler regime. In contrast, Machel made explicit reference to the anticolonial struggles of the Afrikaners in the Boer war and welcomed Afrikaners as Africans. This refutation of temporary settler status in favor of permanent residence rights of fellow anti-colonialists by an African leader with the most impeccable anticolonial and socialist credentials constituted the most far-reaching legitimation of white South Africa. Although the much-ignored Lusaka Manifesto of 1968 conceded a similar legitimate status on Pretoria, provided it abandoned apartheid, the Machel recognition came without conditions. The Mozambican stance, of course, does not imply approval or indifference towards apartheid. However, it signals the realization that the frontline states neither feel in a position to force change on Pretoria, nor, more importantly, do they expect a major transformation of an historical enemy to come from within South Africa in the foreseeable future. Indeed, this realistic assessment for the first time marks a decisive departure from the sacred position of OAU and U.N. resolutions of three decades.

Although there is a substantive difference between the positions of Mozambique and Tanzania or even Zimbabwe, the potential disengagement of frontline states from the problems of apartheid is not confined to Mozambique. In an interview with Jim Hoagland, Angolan President dos Santos is reported to be prepared to live "in an atmosphere of tolerance" with South Africa, once Namibia is independent. Apartheid and white minority rule should be condemned by all nations, José Eduardo dos Santos said, but he suggested that they should be treated as internal problems when "South Africa, which is far away from Angola," returns to its borders.[12] Once more, the hope of South African blacks for liberation from outside has been dampened. Rhetoric notwithstanding, blacks in South Africa are on their own. In the words of Julius Nyerere: "However militant we may sound, we are not likely to go and fight on behalf of the people of South Africa."[13] Continuous township resistance seems to indicate that black South Africans have finally grasped this message.

The Namibian Question

When, after the November 1983 (re: the institution of a tricameral Parliament) referendum and the clear defeat of ultraright, technocratic considerations won out on the Namibian issue, Pretoria envisaged a different agenda from Washington's.

The ideologues within the Reagan administration have little interest in Namibian independence. They are even suspicious of any compromise solution worked out by intense State Department diplomatic activity in Angola. Indeed, a socialist SWAPO government in place of Pretoria's colonial control would be perceived as a defeat by neoconservatives. The only "victory" capable of being marketed to the U.S. electorate would be a Cuban departure from Angola. This, however, depends on the stability of the MPLA regime and on factional infighting within it. These factors are largely outside U.S. influence. The U.S. linkage between Cuban withdrawal and a Namibian settlement has thus proved paralyzing for any quick movement on the issue.

U.S. diplomacy does not normally cause change in Pretoria. Pressure from Washington is usually overestimated by Washington and by black South Africans. Afrikanerdom has rarely yielded to vague sticks but merely consumed the many carrots of "constructive engagement." But, contrary to leftist propaganda, Western governments became increasingly concerned about the potential instability in the region created by Pretoria's military aggression. Disintegration of Mozambique could have paved the way to a "Lebanization" of southern Africa. In a political vacuum, the various guerrilla armies would have operated outside governmental control and opened the avenue for Eastern bloc interference. A regional settlement would have reduced this potential instability and would have been in the interest of all three parties: South Africa, the frontline states, and Western governments. U.S. policy wanted to claim that it had given South African destabilization a purpose (nonaggression treaties), where before, destabilization was an end in itself.

In South Africa, the National party (NP) no longer had much to fear from right-wing critics of Namibian independence. It was the clear demise of the right-wing ideologues, as evidenced in the November 1983 constitutional referendum, that gave the ruling technocrats the confidence to pursue a pragmatic policy of neocolonization rather than military destabilization. As long as the present regime was threatened by its conservative ideologues, it could not entertain Namibian independence and controversial constitutional reforms simultaneously. A SWAPO red flag over Windhoek would have caused a backlash in the republic, fanned by returning Afrikaner civil servants in the same way as Rhodesian expatriates backed the conservative racist parties in South Africa. The unexpectedly high victory in the constitutional referendum in which 66 percent of white voters supported the government alleviated this fear, particularly because the NP could now count on approximately 30–40 percent support in the white English-speaking community. For a while, the Nkomati treaty served as a convincing model for dealing with a potentially hostile Namibian satellite on the Atlantic. In this sense, the highly developed self-confidence of South Africa's technocrats is not a "massive obstacle" to accommodation but its precondition.[14] Because the present ruling group has long overcome its earlier isolationist mentality and inferiority feeling, it now can make deals and venture into alternative policies that would have been taboo a few years ago.

However, Pretoria's decisionmaking machinery for setting regional policy is neither monolithic nor as streamlined as the newly introduced "scientific management charts" suggest. The academic debates about the role of the military and the State Security Council (SSC) obscure the simple fact that there is no master plan for southern Africa. Interbureaucratic rivalries and personality idiosyncrasies influence decisions, as do career and status considerations of the few dozen persons involved. Thus, only a few senior military officers support the efforts of an internationally sensitive Foreign Affairs Department to reach a neocolonial disengagement in Angola and Mozambique and an internationally acceptable settlement in Namibia. The Department of Military Intelligence (DMI), in contrast to the less-influential National Intelligence Service (NIS), views the presently practiced detente as premature. The police, on the other hand, support the Nkomati Accord because of its impact on the ANC. This situation provides a marked contrast to the view that upper military echelons are enlightened technocrats and the police are heavy handed traditionalists. In this respect, the role of the SA military in the administrative disunity of a government merely resembles military counterparts elsewhere. However, because a half dozen senior officers hold such informal influence that it amounts to a virtual veto power, Namibia negotiations and proposed talks with the ANC founder at present on military perceptions of how to subdue an enemy by covert and open force rather than by political incorporation.

Because there is such a diversity of opinion in Pretoria, the United States is able to exercise more informal influence over South Africa's policies than it would if there were a monolithic decisionmaking process. However, given the Reagan administration's limited leverage, the policy of "constructive engagement" has been oversold. It is not nearly as influential as Reagan's supporters and critics claim. It would be political suicide for any Afrikaner politician to be perceived as "in the American's pocket." The insistence on homespun solutions is proffered, not only for vote catching but to feed anti-Americanism. Unlike U.S. whites, South African whites cannot expect to keep political control through a universal franchise. The U.S. civil rights analogy overlooks the fact that U.S. whites never had to relinquish political control by granting blacks formal equal rights.

Generally speaking, there are three schools of thought in Pretoria about an Angolan-Namibian settlement now. One school (SADF) does not want a Namibian settlement that would lead to a SWAPO takeover in Windhoek at any price. Another school, which includes some SADF men and politicians, would accept a settlement if the terms were right. A third school, for a mixture of reasons, mainly costs and international legitimacy, has adopted a positive attitude toward a settlement and is pushing for one. The official policy of the Department of Foreign Affairs appears to be to delay Namibian independence until conditions are more favorable and, in the meantime, to support UNITA as far as possible. P. W. Botha and Pik Botha are believed to be prepared, eventually, to see SWAPO become the dominant party because they are confident that they could neutralize Namibia, if necessary.

However, the South Africans also face various dilemmas. Unlike the situation in Mozambique, Angola is too distant and too heavily supported to be throttled as easily. With no common border with South Africa, John Marcum has concluded, Angola has no "need to enter into close economic association" or even break off ties with the ANC.[15] Despite the overall success of the South Africans against SWAPO and Peoples Armed for the Liberation of Angola (FAPLA) forces, military considerations also impose limits on South African aggressiveness. Against the Angolans' MiG 23s and Mi 24 helicopter gunships, the SADF's 1960s aircrafts would be a poor match should fighting escalate. During their Askari operation in Angola, the South Africans were surprised by the resistance they encountered from FAPLA forces and by the sophistication of their Soviet weaponry. FAPLA forces were found to be well equipped and experienced, while SA draftees were mainly inexperienced. The South Africans were jolted by FAPLA's readiness to engage in direct combat and to spring surprises, such as night attacks and systematic mine laying. South Africa faces the prospect of ever-escalating levels of Soviet involvement in the provision of equipment and even of aircraft. The USSR has invested too heavily in support and prestige in Angola to allow an easy loss of face without a potentially dangerous escalation of hostilities through more outside involvement. The question also arises as to whether the SADF, with its limited professional army, could cope with widespread unrest in SA's black townships and at the same time slide into a neocolonial war in Angola. The war on "the border" is not popular with SA whites either, although most of their opposition is muted. Particularly during a deep recession, the optimal use of limited resources becomes imperative. The 1986 U.S. decision to support Jonas Savimbi (leader of UNITA) militarily was enthusiastically welcomed in Pretoria. Moreover, the move makes Washington a military ally of South Africa, paradoxically at the height of the disinvestment campaign and growing domestic protest. Few decisions have damaged the reputation of the U.S. government more in the eyes of apartheid opponents than its open support of South Africa's proxy, UNITA.

The Limitations of Neocolonization

The historic Botha tour of Western Europe in June 1984 has been variously portrayed as a breakthrough in South Africa's diplomatic isolation, a reward for Nkomati and the abandonment of destabilization policies, a concession on Namibian independence, and an attempt to gain international legitimacy for Pretoria's constitutional reforms. However, these suggestions of an unprecedented political rehabilitation miss the main purpose of South Africa's diplomatic quest. Pretoria alone cannot foot the bill for a successful neocolonization. In Botha's own words, the government is not in a position to "play Father Christmas." For the sake of domestic stability, the government's first priority lies in internal job creation in its own impoverished hinterland. The development capital of R 1,500 million that the republic has guaranteed to its own Development Bank of Southern Africa exhausts Pretoria's financial capabilities in the wake of recessionary trends and a depressed gold price. In short, serious domestic employment creation and simultaneous external development aid preclude each other.

On the other hand, South Africa would be the main beneficiary of an extended regional Common Market. With the underdeveloped purchasing power of the domestic market, South African capital is dependent on outlets abroad in order to utilize economies of scale. Ever since Vorster's ill-fated outward policy in the late 1960s, the main thrust of the newly developing government and private sector alliance had been to overcome the political (apartheid) barriers to the underdeveloped markets of black Africa.[16] Despite the rhetoric of isolation and boycotts, South African firms have gradually succeeded in gaining access to independent Africa, even though most times clandestinely.

What impedes accelerated private sector expansion now is the lack of infrastructure and security in countries such as Mozambique and political uncertainty, particularly in Namibia and Angola. Private investment needs both long-term commitments and predictability of risks. Therefore, it depends heavily on Western development aid as well as international legitimacy to create those stable trade and investment conditions. If, for example, West Germany were to adopt Namibia as a client in the same way it rescued a bankrupt Turkey for the Western alliance or in the way France looks after its west and central African territories, much of South Africa's costs could be cut, although the republic, as the direct neighbor, would remain the main beneficiary of such development aid. The same applies if U.S.-British interests were to concentrate on Mozambique in the Western division of neocolonial relations.

All these dreams were put on ice by the escalating domestic crisis in South Africa. The crude repression of dissent and the apparent inability of Pretoria to enter into real negotiations with its nationalist challengers made it impossible for Western interests to cooperate openly with a pariah state. Aroused public opinion in Europe and North America on South Africa for the first time had to be taken into account by bankers and politicians alike.

Even conservatives in the West now increasingly begin to question the wisdom of apartheid. Racist kith and kin sentiment takes a back seat to the new vision of exporting free enterprise to the Third World. In this combative zeal to confront socialist solutions with a superior capitalist performance, South Africa is an embarrassing ally that does not even allow its own blacks to make a profit according to market principles. The outspoken distancing and genuine moral reservations of the more sophisticated conservative opinionmakers toward South Africa is a new phenomenon. But beyond tactical political considerations, the cool receptions and public condemnations of apartheid by Botha's skeptical hosts in Europe indicate their reluctance to resume support for Pretoria's development role. Western states would rather see South Africa acting as their regional agent in a manner that does not require them to assume major financial responsibilities. South Africans, in their inflated image of their country's importance, often forget that they compete with other more attractive areas for the global cash flow.

Beyond the politics of imagery, there is also the lingering fear on the part of client states that any widespread unrest inside South Africa could spill over into client states and affect the growth potential of the entire region. Greater interdependence of the Western metropolis with peripheral trade and investment regions within the global economy undermines the ability of the periphery to ignore the political sentiments of the center.[17] Although the influence of Western governments on Pretoria has been generally overrated in the past, South Africa's newly sought after rehabilitation will have its price as well, a price that for the most part will be determined by political lobbies in Western capitals. Reforms will certainly exceed Sullivan codes (codes of conduct for U.S. corporations operating in South Africa) to incorporate some more credible forms of black political incorporation as well as some more symbolic scrapping of legal racial domination.

The most likely result of the unexpectedly strong boycott lobby in the United States will be an endorsement of the proposals to make continued investment in South Africa conditional on phasing out influx control and the migratory labor system by promoting housing near the workplace. Together with massive investment in black education and meaningful black political incorporation under more representative leadership (yet to be worked out), this could be used by the U.S. administration to demonstrate (finally) the "success of constructive engagement" and defuse protest against it. Especially if the inclusion of Gatsha Buthelezi's well-organized Inkatha movement into the central political process should result in a more legitimate system that is seriously negotiated rather than imposed (as was the case with earlier schemes), the black political landscape could change. The likely outcome of such cooptation attempts is a more intense intrablack conflict as the two strongest black forces, Inkatha and the ANC, clamor for legitimacy. The ensuing infighting will not relieve the government from also negotiating with the ANC, a precondition for a new stability in the increasingly ungovernable townships.

There can be little doubt that the ANC is justified in feeling "betrayed" by frontline states. The ANC was not consulted before the principles of the Nkomati treaty were elaborated, and the conditions of the ANC's future operation (and expulsion) from Mozambique proved rather "uncomradely," as one observer described it. The promised "moral, political and diplomatic support" of the ANC by Mozambique is restricted to a ten-member diplomatic office for which the organization had to submit names for approval. Of the suggested ten persons, six were rejected. Only four ANC members have been granted visa privileges to visit Mozambique at any time. It is clear that Frelimo would rather get rid of the vestiges of an embarrassing ally sooner than later. In Zimbabwe, Mugabe denies training facilities not only because he fears reprisals, but because the Moscow-linked ANC supported his rival Joshua Nkomo before Zimbabwean independence. With the ANC's Ho Chi Minh trails cut and the ANC officially expelled from Swaziland and Lesotho, the level of sabotage will be more difficult to sustain in the long run. This setback did not diminish levels of sabotage and did not erase the ANC from the South African map. After its diplomatic defeat, the ANC scored its biggest psychological victory in the internal revolt. The extent to which wishful thinking prevailed in official South Africa after Nkomati is expressed in a SABC comment: "The ANC now is probably a spent force in South African politics."[18]

The new strategic situation may well force the ANC to rethink its military preference. Under this strategy, the ANC attacked where the opponent was strongest and it was the weakest. A more political opposition, using unions and other legitimate organizations, might concentrate on areas where the apartheid defenses are weakest and the democratic opponents prove strongest. The journalistic focus on security considerations notwithstanding, so far Pretoria has been only moderately concerned about the occasional ANC incursions emanating from Maputo. In fact, South African propaganda exaggerated and utilized the ANC threat or the Cuban presence in Angola to mobilize white support at home. When the South African army bombed ANC shelters in Maputo or Lesotho, its prime motive was to placate domestic right-wing opinion. "Going soft" on the enemy would have undermined P. W. Botha's constituency where 80 percent of the white voters approved of an aggressive policy of retaliation.[19]

Both the ANC and the South African government are interested in exaggerating the impending threat to white rule. For Pretoria, the ANC bomb blasts lend themselves as timely reminders that the disintegrating *volk* (ethnic nation) better rally behind the wisdom of the government. Like the rockets fired by the authorities of Oceania on its own people in Orwell's *1984,* the rage against the enemy cannot be fueled by abstractions alone. The repetitious "adapt or die" admonitions are only credible if the dying is a demonstrated alternative, not merely a vague prophecy. When government leaders now plead for consensus, inveigh against confrontation, and warn of the costs of revolutionary turmoil, they repeat a theme on which the liberal opposition has based its apartheid condemnations for decades. But by coopting the reasoning of doom, the government at the same time implies that it has the foresight to avert disaster. It can lead the way out of the pending apocalypse if it has unquestioned support for racial reforms of a racist constituency.

The Nkomati Accord, on the other hand, undermined one of the propagated reasons for the reluctant reforms—the threat from an all pervasive outside enemy. It rendered obsolete the ideology of the "total onslaught" and similar myths, such as "the border," manufactured for domestic militarization. Anticommunism is still being peddled as a unifying menace but is increasingly difficult to sustain for the following reasons. The Soviet Union's ally in Southern Africa, Mozambique, in contrast to Angola, is not even considered a genuine Marxist state by Moscow itself, but merely "socialist oriented." The Soviet Union remains the major arms supplier for the ANC and SWAPO but has not acquired naval bases in the region, despite treaties of friendship and cooperation with Angola and Mozambique. Indeed, it is much more prudent for Moscow to let South Africa fester as the obvious racial sore of capitalism than seek an escalating confrontation with the West in this distant arena. With little costs in military hardware and diplomatic assistance, the Soviet Union reaps huge ideological benefits from a Western colonial racist association. For all these reasons, South Africa therefore ranks low in terms of Moscow's global priorities.[20] The Kremlin would be the last source to actively disturb the status quo in apartheidland. It is interesting that a government as obsessed with Soviet expansionism as is the Reagan administration, nevertheless, does not share the common South African perception of the Soviet Union as being intent to lay its hands on the subcontinent's treasures. "Southern Africa is, practically speaking, well outside the Soviet Union's zone of primary interest, indeed of its secondary interests.

We believe that Moscow is aware of this fact and, in reality, spends little time thinking abut the area," diagnoses Frank Wisner, the U.S. deputy assistant secretary for African affairs.[21]

If sanctions against South Africa are no longer in the interest of some frontline states that are participating now in ending the isolation of the apartheid state, then the international antiapartheid movement also will have to rethink its politics. The likely outcome, in the long run, is a split between those committed to military confrontation and those willing to participate in internal reform. What shape such a division will take and who will align themselves where depends on what channels of legitimate political participation are open to radical apartheid opponents.

The present tricameral system constitutes a dead end road as far as vital African political incorporation is concerned. The racist logic of the tricameral Parliament does not lend itself to an African inclusion; indeed, such inclusion would require that the entire constitution be scrapped. No internal ANC, if it were legalized, could participate in the system without committing political suicide. Even if the government were to release Nelson Mandela (which is likely), welcome back exiles committed to peace, and start to consult with the ANC/United Democratic Front about a new deal, there is nothing to negotiate about under the present terms. Despite all the admonitions about an internal peace accord, the government is at a loss about how to accommodate black demands for direct and meaningful political participation in central decisionmaking. This forces political activists to work clandestinely in legal bodies and to politicize unions, church, and student groups. Although authorities thus may succeed in prying away individuals from a specific historical resistance movement, the same people are then also no longer bound by the organizational discipline of a political movement. Such fragmentation of an opponent may be celebrated as a victory by the powerholders, but it can backfire at the same time. It takes only a few atomized and alienated individuals to cause havoc in an industrial society, as the terrorism of fringe groups in the capitals of the world proves almost daily. Lucky is the authority that can legitimately bind such attempts in cohesive organizations and institutions in which radical commitment finds a peaceful expression.

Despite the car bombs in South African cities, the ANC leadership, including its Communist party element, has so far successfully resisted pressure to resort to "terrorist" activities, that is, killing white civilians. This has been reiterated by the ANC's president Oliver Tambo and its secretary-general, Alfred Nzo. The deepening of the gap between external and internal militants, who are no longer under the control of a tight authoritarian organization, may well turn out to be a Pyrrhic victory. The strategic planners in the State Security Council may yet regret having achieved the weakening of a movement of great symbolic value for the mass of victims. They may yet long for the day when they could pinpoint a politically predictable and reliable opponent for negotiations, instead of having to deal with unmanageable anarchism.

Such difficulties do not arise in negotiations between states. It is, therefore, comparatively easier to conclude an external accord between two hostile but sovereign states than to achieve the same results between diverse domestic parties. A question for South Africa still remains—how can the pending peaceful coexistence between the states of the region be extended to encompass South Africa's more fundamental internal conflicts? A unified, cohesive movement that can legitimately represent and bargain for the underdog may indeed be in the interest of those who fear most for their security. On the other hand, a likely black pluralism of opposition groups with different ideologies and interests also could strengthen the chances of a democratic system.

Lasting stability of the core now depends more than ever on negotiations between Afrikaner nationalists and those who are constantly referred to as "the authentic leaders of the black masses." There is little doubt that among the many black leaders with a following, the ANC, with its hidden constituency in the UDF, ranks top among politicized urban blacks, although it is by no means the sole representative of black opinion. Pretoria seems remarkably unaware that collaborating blacks have been rejected by the more politicized segments they are supposed to control, and the government officially insists on their leadership role while publicly ignoring the real representatives. This distance, however, only enhances the credibility of the rejected. Any consultation on the part of blacks with the government amounts now almost to a kiss of death. Even if the exiled ANC president were to fly to Pretoria tomorrow, he would be immediately suspected of selling out a militant internal leadership. Hence, both sides have a vital interest in keeping contacts secret and confidential for different reasons. Black activists cannot afford to be compromised, and Pretoria, in turn, takes propagandistic risks by negotiating with an official enemy. What, therefore, are the prospects for serious talks beyond the informal individual contacts and proxy dialogues already taking place?

The victory of Pretoria's aggressive destabilization strategy and the general militarization in the country have encouraged the voices that advocate resorting to traditional coercion. On the other side, there is a growing realization that township unrest may be contained militarily but can only be solved politically. Individual business leaders have urged the government to realize the "historic inevitability" of talks with the ANC and have themselves set a much noticed example. Under the impact of successful strike action, organized business for the first time has spoken out forcefully against traditional repression of union leadership on whom it increasingly depends for industrial peace. Although the Afrikaner business segment soon retracted its criticism of government incarceration of trade union leaders after a meeting with President P. W. Botha, the influence of business on government is likely to increase in a severe recession. With a worsening economic crisis, massive costs for ideological projects will become the obvious target for savings. It is not true, as Basil Davidson asserts, "that nothing has been officially proposed, or even discussed, that could in any way improve the social and political situation of the Africans."[22] On the contrary, from a cabinet secretariat to the Urban Foundation of big business and the Human Science Research Council of academia range dozens of eager attempts to find "solutions to intergroup relations." Their common thread lies in a "management approach" that implies a priori continued white control, albeit with sufficient modifications to appease, contain, manipulate, and coopt black militancy. Only a minority seeks an open-ended dialogue, and even a smaller one advocates serious negotiations about formulas of power sharing that would be mutually agreed upon instead of imposed.

The flurry of statements regarding Pretoria-ANC negotiations are part of a Western-supported campaign to parallel the Mozambican reorientation by also drawing the ANC closer into the Western orbit. A success in this drive would signal a far greater danger for Pretoria's hardliners than having the ANC safely labelled "communist." Nonetheless, it would obviously suit South Africa if the ANC were to suspend its military activity as part of a formal agreement. Although such an accord is a distant possibility, a truce is not. The government has no intention whatsoever of offering the ANC a share in political decisionmaking. By showing a willingness to talk, Pretoria hopes to exploit differences within the ANC and eventually split the organization into so-called radical communists and compromising "Nationalists." Pretoria's goal remains to crush the opposition rather than incorporate it as a partner in power.

On the other hand, the level of politicization restricts Nationalist party maneuverability. If only a semblance of stability is to be restored in the country and international credibility regained, the government will have to recognize the vital ANC role. With fading control in township streets and schools—the result of rent strikes, consumer boycotts, and self-devised curricula—Pretoria can no longer "normalize" a situation without legitimate black cooperation. An already divided ruling group is most likely to split further about the appropriate strategies of its survival. Pragmatic interest calculations rather than ideological dreams will exert themselves in future negotiations. In the interim, it is much easier to reach an external accord between sovereign hostile governments than between internal, heterogeneous factions, even if they share a much more obvious common interest.

Notes

This chapter results from a close collaborative effort in which Stanley Uys contributed substantive data and critiqued several drafts by the principal authors, Heribert Adam and Kogila Moodley. Supported by a grant from the Canadian Social Science Research Council, the analysis is based on numerous interviews in Southern Africa during two research visits in 1984 and 1985, in addition to discussions with officials in the U.S. State Department, various academics, journalists, and ANC representatives in North America and Europe. An initial shorter version of the paper was presented to the Durban branch of the Institute of International Affairs, 7 August 1984, and to a Conference on Economic Development and Racial Domination at the University of the Western Cape, Bellville, South Africa, 8–10 October 1984. The latter part of this analysis, concerning ANC-Pretoria relations, is further elaborated in Heribert Adam and Kogila Moodley, *South Africa Without Apartheid* (Berkeley: University of California Press, 1986).

1. Simon Jenkins, "Destabilization in Southern Africa," *The Economist* (16–22 July 1983):19–28.
2. *Sunday Times,* 26 August 1984.
3. For the history and operation of the MNR see the work of Colin Legum and Gillian Gunn.
4. Edwardo de Silva, "Mozambiquan Socialism and the Nkomati Accord," *Work in Progress* 32 (1984):16–29.
5. Basil Davidson, "Apartheid: A System Beyond Reform," *Socialist Affairs* (March 1984):12–17.
6. SABC Commentary, 19 October 1984.
7. *Financial Mail,* 26 October 1984.
8. Gillian Gunn, "Post Nkomati Mozambique," *CSIS Africa Notes* 38 (8 January 1985).
9. Ibid., 2.
10. See, for example, *The Washington Times,* which campaigned for a similar support of Renamo as given to UNITA in Angola. The Washington administration is itself split on these issues. The State Department takes the White House to task for not actively supporting insurgent movements against "Marxist" governments in power.
11. *Leadership SA,* 3 February 1984, 13.
12. *Washington Post,* 14 October 1984.
13. *Africa* 161 (January 1985):11.
14. Simon Jenkins, "Destabilization in Southern Africa," *The Economist* (16–22 July 1983):27.
15. John A. Marcum, "Angola: A Quarter Century of War," *CSIS Africa Notes* 37 (21 December 1984):7.
16. Ironically, the same P. W. Botha, as minister of defense, supported the 1975 aborted invasion of Angola that led to the collapse of detente. Together with covert U.S. intervention against a Marxist government in Luanda, this action gave the Soviet Union and Cuba a pretense to establish themselves in the region. The same forces that facilitated this internationalization of the conflict now aim at a regionalization of the issue.

17. It is not argued here that foreign investment in the republic itself makes South Africa more vulnerable and sensitive to outside pressures. This vision amounts to a fiction in practice. Hypothetical repatriation of fixed assets, if possible at all, would mean local sales that would depreciate the investment in the case of wholesale withdrawal. Far from increasing outside influence, larger foreign investments tie the outsider more closely to South African developments. The point stressed here is that South Africa will have to reciprocate and make its open ties less vulnerable to liberal critics if it wishes to involve foreign public bodies in southern African affairs under South African dominance.

18. SABC Commentary, 4 April 1984.

19. After the massive bomb blast in the center of Pretoria in May 1983, for example, there was an immediate upsurge of feelings of retaliation. Ordinary whites came close to assaulting any blacks in Pretoria streets that night. Newspapers published special editorials imploring readers not to take the law into their own hands. The subsequent military raid against targets in Maputo aimed as much at pacifying potential vigilante sentiments at home as it was directed at deterring support for the ANC in host countries. An upsurge in extreme right-wing activities expressed itself in the active persecution of members of the Afrikaner Weerstandsbeweging (Afrikaner Resistance Movement), including its leader, Eugene Terreblanche, several weeks afterward. The state prosecutor changed his charge from illegal possession of firearms to terrorism, and several "*ware* Afrikaners" (real Afrikaners—those who resist any changes in apartheid) for the first time were sentenced to suspended jail terms.

20. Helen Kitchen and Michael Clough, *The United States and South Africa: Realities and Red Herrings* (Washington, D.C.: CSIS, 1984), 27–31.

21. Frank Wisner, "Southern Africa: An American Perspective Today," *South Africa International* (January 1984).

22. Davidson, "Apartheid."

10

WILMOT G. JAMES

Concluding Remarks

Mﾠore than one hundred years of racial segregation and forty years of apartheid sired a state with a deeply entrenched racial architecture. State institutions were expressly created to control and regulate the private and public lives of black people, and a battery of laws underwrote and conferred a jurisprudential legitimacy to authoritarianism and to the most flagrant violations of democratic principles. As the state developed, more and more controls were added, loopholes in the system were closed, and inconsistencies were ironed out, so as to create a political order with the most extensive and elaborate set of racial institutions in the world whose purpose was to control the lives of blacks, down to the minutiae of intimacy. This is the modern racial machine of apartheid, which derives its logic from the desire to oppress the majority of the populace. This book has sought to comprehend the structure of the machine and peer into its internal configuration.

Black people are identified, treated, and abused, we noted, as mere objects of state policy. They are things shunted around, told where to live, instructed where to school their children, discriminated against, and when they do not behave as told, they are faced with the cold racism of a police and an army whose central purpose is to keep blacks in line. Worse, the army and police now have learned how to kill civilians regularly and get away with it. Recently, as we documented, the state has sought to change its customary ways. It admits freely that racial discrimination is indefensible, that blacks ought to have the same rights as whites, and that "apartheid is dead." The outcome of the state's deracialization strategy is limited. We demonstrated that deracialization means a reordering of racial relations in state and society, not the genuine transformation of these relations; we documented that the granting of voting rights to minorities does not result in the desegregation of their social environment, nor does it result in their being sufficiently endowed with the power to change their social environment. We argued that whites still retain their group rights, and Africans are still left out of the state. The effect of deracialization policies is to maintain, in other words, the fundamental parameters of apartheid. This is true for all layers of social organization, including unlikely aspects such as sports.

We also wrote that state attempts to create institutions of African self-governance in townships had consequences hardly intended by policymakers, the most serious of which is a loss of control of the political process, which has led to a breakdown. This book has established the breakdown of state collaborative strategies, a breakdown that reflects a larger inability on the part of regime institutions to effectively procure regime goals. This is true on the level of governance—African self-governance has been dismantled, and the tricameral Parliament, a sideshow compared to what really matters, lacks legitimacy—and it is true on the level of control—labor regulation is in shambles, and township control is nearly impossible. The result is direct control by the police and army of the African population, but that, too, is tenuous and problematic for direct control drains the resources, morale, and capacities of state repressive institutions, creates war in the townships, and gives the antiapartheid opposition the opportunity to control township life. Indeed, direct control brings the struggle about state power within reach of ordinary blacks.

This is underscored by the regime's attempt to subjugate the southern African region to its hegemony and its provocative routing of the African National Congress (ANC), the premier liberation movement, from the region. Given this, blacks are forced to focus on internal means of making changes in the political economy. The last two years of civil protest demonstrate that such a shift has occurred and that blacks have come to believe in their ability to challenge the state. In their attempt to smash the ANC and keep the lid on domestic protest, the state and military become more and more deeply committed to regional destabilization and domestic pacification. The result is that the regime's ultimate strength—its military capacities—is being put to its severest test ever, perhaps to the point where it becomes overtaxed, weary, and eventually breaks down. As other fallen regimes have regretfully discovered, wars on multiple fronts are the beginning of the end.

Approximate Exchange Rates:
The South African Rand and the U.S. Dollar

Approximate Exchange Rates:
The South African Rand and the U.S. Dollar

	S.A. Rand	U.S. Dollar
1977	1	1.12
1980	1	1.00
1982	1	.90
1984	1	.90
1985	1	.65
1986	1	.40

The Contributors

Heribert Adam is professor of sociology and anthropology at Simon Fraser University, British Columbia, Canada. He is author of *Modernizing Racial Domination* (Berkeley: University of California Press, 1972), co-author with Hermann Giliomee of *Ethnic Power Mobilized: Can South Africa Change?* (New Haven, Conn.: Yale University Press, 1978), and co-author with Kogila Moodley of the recently released *South Africa Without Apartheid* (Berkeley: University of California Press, 1986).

Simon Bekker has studied at universities in South Africa, the United States, and England. He lectured in sociology at the University of Stellenbosch, South Africa, and was chair of development studies at the Institute of Social and Economic Research at Rhodes University. He is co-author with Richard Humphries of *From Control to Confusion* (Johannesburg: Shuter and Shooter, 1985). At present he is attached to the Urban Foundation, Johannesburg.

Craig Charney is a graduate student in the Department of Political Science, Yale University. He holds a M.Phil. from Oxford and a D.E.A. from Institut d'Etude du Developpement Economique et Social, Sorbonne, Paris. Charney is the author of numerous journal articles on South African politics.

Hugh Corder is senior lecturer in the Department of Public Law, University of Stellenbosch, South Africa. A Rhodes scholar, he holds a D.Phil. from Oxford and an LL.B. from Cambridge. He is the author of *Judges at Work* (Cape Town: Juta, 1984).

André du Pisanie is senior lecturer in the Department of Political Sciences at the University of South Africa, Pretoria. He is author of *SWA/ Namibia: The Politics of Continuity and Change* (Johannesburg: Jonathan Ball, 1986).

Stanley B. Greenberg is an associate director of the Southern African Research Program, Yale University. He is author of *Race and State in Capitalist Development: Comparative Perspectives* (New Haven, Conn.: Yale University Press, 1980) and *Legitimating the Illegitimate: State, Markets and the African Working Class in South Africa* (Berkeley: University of California Press, forthcoming).

Richard Humphries was educated at Rhodes University, where he studied political science and journalism. After a short spell in journalism, he returned to Rhodes where he was attached to the Institute of Social and Economic Research. He currently teaches African politics at the University of South Africa. He is co-author with Simon Bekker of *From Control to Confusion* (Johannesburg: Shuter and Shooter, 1985).

Wilmot G. James is lecturer in the Department of Sociology, University of Cape Town, South Africa. He holds a Ph.D. from the University of Wisconsin and has published in the areas of income determination, ethnic relations, and class analysis. In 1985, he held a visiting fellowship at the Southern African Research Program, Yale University.

Kogila Moodley teaches at the University of British Columbia, Vancouver, Canada. She is co-author with Heribert Adam of *South Africa Without Apartheid* (Berkeley: University of California Press, 1986).

William A. Munro is a graduate student at Yale University. He studied history at Natal University and politics at Cambridge University and has taught in the Department of Political Studies at Rhodes University. His current research is on the state and state-peasant relations in colonial Zimbabwe.

Annette Seegers is lecturer in the Department of Political Studies at the University of Cape Town. She holds a Ph.D. from Loyola University, Chicago, and has published in the area of civil-military relations and southern African politics.

Index